ABOVE ALL ELSE

ABOVE ALL ELSE

A World Champion Skydiver's Story of Survival and What It Taught Him About Fear, Adversity, and Success

Dan Brodsky-Chenfeld

SKYHORSE PUBLISHING

Skyhorse Publishing books may be purchased in bulk at special discounts for sales promotion, corporate gifts, fund-raising, or educational purposes. Special editions can also be created to specifications. For details, contact the Special Sales Department, Skyhorse Publishing, 307 West 36th Street, 11th Floor, New York, NY 10018 or info@skyhorsepublishing.com

Skyhorse® and Skyhorse Publishing® are registered trademarks of Skyhorse Publishing, Inc.®, a Delaware corporation.

www.skyhorsepublishing.com

10 9

Library of Congress Cataloging-in-Publication Data is available on file.

ISBN: 978-1-61608-446-2

Printed in the United States of America

For Kristi, Chloe, and Landen

Special thanks to Mary Pat Avery, Chris Shaw, and Igor Sitnikov

Contents

CONTENTS

PART I

ABOVE ALL ELSE

1
Waking Up

SOMETHING WAS WRONG. I was groggy, fading in and out. My body felt tired, weighted down. What was going on?

I tried to see but my eyelids were too heavy to lift. I summoned all the strength I could but still didn't have the power to peel them open.

The last thing I could recall was training with my new skydiving team, Airmoves. After nine years of competition, much of which was spent living in my van and eating out of a cooler so that I could afford team training, the owners of the Perris Valley Skydiving Center in California had presented me with a team sponsorship opportunity. I would get to pick and run the team. They would cover the training costs.

This was it, the opportunity I had always hoped for. Since money wasn't an issue, I was able to pick the teammates I most wanted. The first person I called was James Layne. I had known James since he was eleven and had taught him to jump when he was only fourteen. His whole family had worked at my drop zone in Ohio.

James was like a little brother to me. Even before his very first jump seven years earlier, we had decided that someday we were going to win the national and world championships together. This was our chance, a dream come true.

Troy Widgery was next on my list. Troy was a young entrepreneur and good friend whom I had coached when he was on the University of Colorado Skydiving Team. At the collegiate national championships a year earlier, I had told James and Troy that somehow, someday, I was going to get them both on my team.

Richard Stuart had been the camera flyer on my previous team, the Fource. But like me, Richard still just hadn't had enough of team training and competition.

To fill the one remaining position, I held tryouts. Tom Falzone outperformed the rest and completed the team lineup. Perris Airmoves was born.

We were five months into our training and had made about 350 practice jumps. Everything was going better than I had ever imagined, and I have quite an imagination. We were improving at an unheard-of pace and had already gone head-to-head with some of the top teams in the country. The U.S. Nationals gold medal was in our sights.

And then . . .

The crust on my eyelashes glued them shut. Using the muscles in my forehead, I finally pried them open a crack. A faint white light was all I could see, like I was inside of a cloud. It was silent. Where was I waking up? Was I waking up? Was I dead?

I had no idea what was happening, how I got here, or what was going on. But I did have one absolutely vivid image in my head, a crystal clear picture of something that seemed to have happened just moments before waking up. It wasn't a dream. It was as real as any real-world experience I had ever had. I could remember the entire thing, every action, every word, and every thought.

It went like this: I was in free fall. Almost as if I had just appeared there. I love free fall, and finding myself there at that moment seemed natural. I was at home, at peace, part of the infinite sky.

But after a few seconds I noticed that this wasn't normal free fall. It was quieter. The wind wasn't blowing as fast. I wasn't descending. A gentle breeze was suspending me. It was okay, it was fine. I was floating, flying, but it wasn't right. What was I doing there? I wasn't afraid. I felt safe, but confused.

I looked up and saw James flying down to me just as if we were on a skydive together and he was "swooping" me. His expression was that silly, playful smile he so often had in free fall. He was obviously not confused at all. He knew exactly where he was and what he was doing there.

He flew down and stopped in front of me. Still with a smile on his face, he asked, "Danny, what are you doing here?"

I answered, "I don't know."

James said, "You're not supposed to be here, you have to get back down there." I began to get a grasp of the situation.

I asked him, "Are you coming with me?"

His expression changed to one with a hint of sadness. He said, "No, I can't."

I tried to persuade him to change his mind, "C'mon, James, we were just getting started. You gotta come with me."

James raised his voice, interrupting me. "I can't!" It was obvious that the decision was final. It seemed as if it wasn't his decision. He continued with a gentle smile. "I can't, but it's okay. There are more places to go, more things to do, more fun to have. Tell my mom it's okay. Tell her I'm okay."

For a few seconds we just looked at each other as I accepted this for the reality it was. He changed his tone and spoke with some authority as he gave me an order. "Now," he said, "you need to get back down there. You need to go get control of the situation." I unquestioningly accepted this as well, still not knowing what the situation was that he was referring to.

James stuck out his hand palm down, the way we always did when practicing our "team count," our "ready, set, go" cadence we would use to synchronize our exit timing. A couple of minutes before exiting the plane on a training jump, we would always huddle up and practice this count. The purpose was as much to get psyched up for the jump as to rehearse the cadence. I put my hand on top of his.

He put his other hand on top of mine. I put my other hand on top of his. We looked each other in the eyes. Both of us with gentle smiles of love and confidence and sadness. James started the count. "Ready." I joined in as we finished it together. "Set. Go." As was our routine, we clapped and then popped our hands together, locking them in a long, strong, brotherly grasp.

James had one more thing to say, and he said it with absolute certainty, "I'll see you later." It was clearly not a "good-bye." I had no doubt that we would see each other again. Before I had even thought about an answer, the words "I know" came out of my mouth.

Slowly I started to descend. As I did, James began to fade from my grip. The wind picked up as I was now falling through it, no longer suspended by it. Everything went black.

As I woke, James's words, "Get control of the situation," still rang clearly in my mind. If only I knew what the situation was.

I knew I wasn't dead. I squinted, trying to see more clearly. The white light slowly brightened. A few small red and green lights came into view. As if coming from a distance, faint electrical beeping sounds began to reverberate from the silence.

My vision started to sharpen. I could see I was surrounded with lights, gauges, hoses, and wires running in every direction. The glowing white light wasn't the heavens. It was the bedsheets and ceiling paint of an ICU hospital room.

I stared straight up from flat on my back, the position I found myself in. What's the situation? I thought that James and I must have been in some kind of accident together. James was gone and I wasn't.

I tried to pick my head up to look around the room. My head wouldn't move. I tried to turn my head to look to the side; it wouldn't move. *Oh my God,* I thought. *I can't move my head. I'm paralyzed. It can't be true. Don't let it be true. This can't be the situation.*

I was filled with a sense of fear far greater than anything I had ever experienced before. I felt myself starting to give up and caught myself. *Don't panic, don't panic.* I closed my eyes, took a breath, and tried to calm down. *It's got to be something else, there has to be more.* I told myself not to come to any conclusions too soon, to pause and reevaluate the situation. I started again.

I opened my eyes. I could see a little more clearly now, and there was no doubt I was definitely in a hospital bed complete with all the bells, whistles, buzzers, and instruments. I tried to move my head again. It wouldn't budge. "Stay cool, stay cool. Try something else," I told myself.

I tried to move my toes. I thought I felt something, but I couldn't lift my head to see them to confirm. I remembered hearing about people who were paralyzed but had ghost movements when it felt as though they could move even though they couldn't. "Stay cool, Dan, stay cool. Look for options. Try something else." I had to talk myself through it every step of the way.

I tried to wiggle my fingers. It felt like they moved. I tried to move my hands. I could swear they worked. Did they move? I couldn't turn my head to see my hands but nearly stretched my eyes out of their sockets trying to look down to verify that my hands were actually moving.

Peering past the horizon of the bedsheet, there were no hands in sight. I tried to lift my hands higher. They felt so heavy. Were they moving, or was it my imagination wishing them to move? Slowly, I saw the bedsheet rise. Like the sun rising in the morning, slow but certain. I brought my hands all the way up right in front of my face, trying to prove to myself that it wasn't a hallucination. I stretched out my fingers, clenched my fists, and then stretched them out again. I put my hands together to see if my right hand could feel my left and my left hand feel my right. They worked. Yes! What an incredible relief. My arms and hands weren't paralyzed. Okay, so far so good, back to my legs.

I tried again to move my toes and lift my feet. They were too far away to see and too heavy to lift. I gathered all the strength I had, as if I was trying to bench-press four hundred pounds, and focused it on my knees. Ever so slowly, the bedsheet started to lift. Slowly my knees came up high enough that I could see they were moving. I wasn't paralyzed, not at all.

I still didn't know what the situation was, but no matter what, it wasn't as bad as I had feared. I felt a sudden relief, and though I had never been a person who prayed very often, without even thinking I found myself thanking God for lessening my burden.

Why couldn't I move my head, though? I reached up with both my newly working hands to feel my head. As I did, I came in contact with two metal rods. As I explored further I realized my head was in a cage. I couldn't move my head not because I wasn't capable but because it was being held still by a halo brace.

My neck must be broken. But for a person who moments earlier thought he was completely paralyzed, a broken neck seemed like the common cold. The experience of thinking I was paralyzed from head to toe was truly a gift. It would forever put things in perspective for me. I decided at that moment that I would never complain about my injuries, no matter what they were.

But what had happened? I asked the doctor, but he skirted the question and instead filled me in on my condition. In addition to breaking my neck, I had a collapsed lung, cracked skull, a severe concussion, and crushed insides causing other internal injuries. It's hard to believe, but none of this really fazed me. It was still much better news than I had feared. I asked him again, "What happened?" He acted like he didn't hear me.

The doctor was concerned about the nerve and brain damage but seemed confident that I would ultimately be able to walk out of the hospital and lead a relatively normal life, as long as my normal life didn't include any contact sports or rigorous activity at all. I would certainly never skydive again.

A little while later, Kristi, my girlfriend, came in. I asked her what had happened, but she dodged the question. I kept asking her, pushing her; I had to know. Finally she said, "It's bad, Dan, it's so bad."

That was the first time it occurred to me that if James and I were in an accident of some kind, it was likely that the other members of Airmoves were in the same accident. I asked her again what had happened. "It's so bad" was all she could say. I pushed her relentlessly.

Finally, she told me. There was a plane crash. A plane crash? I hadn't even considered a plane crash. I realized what that could mean and tried to prepare for the worst, that my entire team may be gone. The sudden emotional barrage that hit me was overwhelming. I was starting to lose control and caught myself. I closed my eyes, took a breath, and calmed myself down.

I later learned that Kristi had been by my side since the crash. She and my friends and family did not know how, if and when I woke up, they would tell me that James was gone.

I asked her, "How's my team?" She tried to speak, but still, the only words she could muster were, "It's bad, Dan, it's so bad."

I needed an answer. I said, "I know James is gone. How is the rest of the team?" She froze in disbelief. She looked at me, staring deeply into my eyes, and asked, "How do you know that?"

I answered directly, "He told me."

She continued to stare at me, wondering how that was possible. Almost relieved that I already knew about James, Kristi told me that, compared to me, my other teammates were fine. Troy and Tom were banged up and had broken a few bones. Troy had to have surgery on his hip. But all things considered, they were basically okay.

Richard had missed the plane. His camera helmet broke just minutes before we boarded, and he had asked another cameraman to take his place while he went to fix it. In the thousands of training jumps Richard and I had together, I could never remember him missing a jump. Kristi was quiet. There was more.

We were flying in the Twin Otter, which carries twenty-two people. It was worse than I thought, way worse. For some reason, I had assumed that Airmoves had been alone in a single-engine Cessna. Of the twenty-two people on board, sixteen had died in the crash. Most of them my friends, including Dave Clarke, the cameraman who took Richard's place.

The emotional bombardment continued as Kristi told me who we lost. The names included members of Tomscat, a team from Holland that I was coaching, the pilots, instructors, and camera flyers who worked at the skydiving school, and students who were there for their first jump, in what was supposed to have been an experience of a lifetime for them. Kristi was right: It was bad. So, so bad.

Because I was just learning about this, I had assumed that it had all just happened. As I was absorbing this information, I was hit with another shocker. The crash had occurred over a month ago. I had been in a coma for nearly six weeks. How could that be? I picked up my arms and held them in front of my face. They looked skeletal. I had lost forty pounds. I touched my face and discovered a beard. It was true.

What hell the families and friends must have been going through over the last month while I had the luxury of being unconscious. What sorrow and grief they must have been experiencing. I felt so badly for them, and guilty that I wasn't there to be with them through this difficult time.

It immediately occurred to me that I had to be strong. It may have been new to me, but they had been dealing with it for over a month. I was experiencing this grief for the first time, but I would have to do so on my own. I didn't want to drag my friends and family back through it all again.

If only they knew what I knew. If only James had been able to share with each of them what he shared with me. I knew that our friends were gone, but that they were okay. I knew they had more places to go, more things to do, and more fun to have. I knew we hadn't said good-bye, only, "See you later." I wanted to share this with everyone, but I also knew that they would think I was nuts and that the brain damage I had suffered was more severe than they thought. I kept it to myself, except for telling one person. As James had requested, I called his mother, my dear friend Rita, from my hospital bed and passed his message on to her.

"*You need to go get control of the situation.*" What exactly did James mean? I thought about that a lot. I believe he was alerting me to the fact that I was about to wake up in a different world than the one before the crash. I would be arriving in the middle of a situation that was overrun by sadness, fear, helplessness, and defeat. I believe he was warning me that many people were going to try to define the situation for me and tell me what my limitations were. He was telling me not to be a victim, not to let anyone but me decide my fate and that I didn't have to let go of my dreams. There was more to "life" than what we experience in this physical world. He was telling me it was all okay.

James was reminding me that prior to the crash, I had taken control of my life. I had found an activity that I loved, pushed myself to be the best I could possibly be at it, and set my sights on becoming the best in the world. I had shown the courage to follow my dreams and the faith in the world to believe that the few things that were out of my control would work out as they should. This attitude toward life had never steered me wrong in the past. And it wouldn't then.

I believed him. I trusted him. And I decided.

2

Following Your Dreams

HUMAN BEINGS ARE born dreamers. Through dreams we explore our limitless imaginations and consider the true possibilities of things we perceive to be impossible. Most great human achievements began as someone's impossible dream, a crazy fantasy. It was the dreamers of their day who imagined electricity, flying machines, walking on the moon, running a four-minute mile, or instantly communicating on a cell phone or the Internet. All of these were considered impossible right up until the moment they actually happened. Soon after, they were thought of as everyday occurrences.

Our dreams provide us a stage from which we can fantasize about things that don't seem feasible within the constraints of our physical realities. They encourage us to question our often false perceptions of the limits of those realities. Through our dreams we are open to exploring all possibilities. Without our dreams, we too often surrender to our established limitations and underestimate our true potential.

Dreaming is an essential part of what it means to be human. The same way we are born hungry and need to eat to grow, our minds and souls crave inspiration and need our imaginations to show us all what we are truly capable of being and doing.

It is human nature to want to expand our capabilities. As long as we can imagine reaching the next level in our chosen field, most of us will instinctively want, and choose, to do so. Once babies have crawled, they want to walk. As soon as they walk, they want to run. Once they can run, they want to jump. *We are rarely satisfied with where we are while we can still imagine, and believe, that we can do more.*

Few things have the power to motivate and inspire us to reach for our full potential the way our dreams do. Successful people from every walk of life—be they athletes, musicians, soldiers, doctors, policemen, firefighters, entrepreneurs, or entertainers (just to name a few)—usually agree on one thing. As children, long before they ever achieved success in their field, they dreamt and fantasized about becoming great at what they did. It wasn't money or fame that inspired them as children. *It was the pure love and purpose for the activity itself.* Most of them can hardly remember a time when they weren't insanely passionate about it. *Every dreamer is not successful. But every successful person is a dreamer.*

As children, we all had dreams like these. But in our early years, most of us were discouraged from believing that we could actually live our dreams and achieve our highest ambitions. We were more often pushed by family, friends, and society in general to take a more secure route, keep our expectations low, and avoid failure and disappointment. We were guided by advisors to go after goals they thought we had the best chance of accomplishing, ones that didn't demand too much effort from us.

As opposed to looking at things from a perspective of abundance, we chose to see things from a minimalist perspective. Minimal desire leads to minimal goals, requiring minimal effort. Since we would be aiming so low, the likelihood for success was high so there was minimal chance for disappointment. But is the definition of success aiming to be half of what we are capable of being in a field that we tolerate but certainly aren't passionate about? I don't think so. And fortunately for me, my family didn't think so either.

3

It All Starts at the Beginning

I WAS BORN DANIEL Lee Brodsky on February 5, 1962, in Albany, New York, the second child of Len and Mimi Brodsky. My brother Cliff was born twenty-three months earlier. I have amazingly clear memories of my parents from when I was as young as three years old, snapshots of the treasured moments that occurred most often. I remember running up and jumping in my dad's arms when he came home from work, being held between him and my mom while they were dancing and listening to music, and sitting on the couch together while they read to me.

Most vividly, I remember learning to swim. My dad would put a hand under my belly to hold me up while I practiced kicking and swimming strokes. I was terrified, but I knew as long as I could feel his hand, I was safe and would never sink.

Before I could swim on my own, that hand was gone. My father died in a car accident just before my fourth birthday.

There may be some cosmic design determining the mother who gives birth to us, or it may simply be a matter of pure luck. But if it's luck, I hit the jackpot with Mimi Brodsky.

I realize I am somewhat biased, but I believe my mother to be the sweetest, kindest, most loving, giving, unselfish, compassionate person the world has ever seen. And as long as I'm bragging, I will back that up by saying I have no doubt that I could send out an e-mail requesting references for her and would receive literally thousands of responses before the day was over.

I am in awe of how my mother handled being a thirty-year-old single parent of two young boys whose father had just died. It was her desire to be the best mom she could possibly be and to raise her boys to believe that pure unconditional love was their birthright. *Achieving this goal was her definition of winning, and nothing was going to stop her.*

My mother is a world-renowned early-childhood educator. She has written several books, including textbooks for college students majoring in education. In the early 1960s she wrote a book, *The House at 12 Rose Street*, about a black family moving into a white neighborhood and the difficulties they faced. She wrote this in the early years of the civil rights movement, always way ahead of her time.

Her capacity for love is endless. She sees the potential for greatness and genius in everyone she meets and, given the chance, will discover that potential in them.

She believes that at the core of every person is an imaginative, optimistic young child. Like that child, my mother has an uninhibited love of life, games, and fun. *She understands that it is through this pure joy that children recognize and live their dreams, no matter how silly those dreams may be. It is through those dreams that children and adults are genuinely motivated, inspired, and in a place where they are most capable of learning and excelling.*

Mom always encouraged me and my brother to be the best we could be at whatever we chose to do, but didn't care if we were better than anyone else. She sees a person's level of enjoyment, fun, learning, sharing, and giving as measures of success as opposed to the standard judging tools of scores, results, and placements.

But she also made it clear that the bigger our dreams, the more work would be required of us. The work should be fun, but hard work it would be nonetheless. She was a living example of this. Every free second she had, and most of them were in the middle of the night, we could hear her typing away on whatever writing project she had going at that time.

Mom's parents, Joe and Iris Kaplan, were her examples.

My grandfather Joe was the son of Russian immigrants who had escaped to America in the early 1900s. Iris was born in Romania, one of seven children, walked across Europe, got on a boat, and finally made it to New York when she was about fourteen.

Despite having only an eighth-grade education and three children born between the Great Depression and the start of World War II, my grandfather still managed to take care of his family. He made it possible for them to have opportunities and freedoms beyond anything his parents could possibly have imagined when they boarded the boat to come to America. *This was his definition of winning, and nothing was going to stand in his way.* He accomplished this through hard work, a fantastic sense of humor, and a persona that made everyone want to be his friend, his partner, and his colleague. Or if possible, just more like him themselves.

Joe Kaplan was a huge person in my life. He was the pillar of strength, both physically and emotionally. He was strong, confident, and not to be messed with. But he was also every bit as warm and loving as he was tough. He sang to us, played with us, and constantly made us laugh. He was whatever any of us needed him to be, the perfect teammate.

After my father died, my grandfather was in many ways like a father to me. Over time our relationship evolved and grew. He never stopped being "Gramps," but he also became my best friend.

We never lived in the same town and only the same state for a few years, but I traveled to see my grandparents as often as I could. Sometimes it was with the family, but I also did many trips on my own.

They had a quote on their kitchen wall:

> God, grant me the serenity to accept the things I cannot change, the courage to change the things I can, and the wisdom to know the difference.

I didn't really understand what it meant, but thought it must be important.

My brother Cliff and I were the classic middle-class American brothers: rough-and-tumble, playful boys. Being the older, bigger, stronger brother, Cliff would always beat up on me a bit, but just enough to keep me in line and to be sure I knew he was the boss, never enough to hurt me—much.

Cliff was always a great role model. Besides being tall, handsome, funny, and brilliant (every bit that obnoxious), he also had the confidence and drive to pursue the things he loved with utter conviction. He had many interests and excelled at everything he did. If he did it, he was the best at it, and there was nothing he couldn't do—sports, music, writing, school. I remember thinking how cool it must be to be so good at everything. And wishing I was that good at anything.

As Cliff's little brother, it was hard to follow in his footsteps. Not that anyone in my family had asked me to follow anyone. No one in my family asked me to be as good as Cliff at anything or to even pursue the same things he did. But little boys recognize the admiration that "winners" receive, and they dream about being good or even the best at something. If only I knew what I wanted to be the best at.

Despite being surrounded by great influences, I was a very average kid, and that's putting it generously. If you ask my mom, she'll tell you that for the most part I was a sweet, kind, fun child. I usually made a positive contribution to whatever I took part in, just not that much of one.

I was by far the shortest kid in school, camp, and in my family. Being so tiny, I couldn't help but be cute, but had no chance of being handsome. I may have been funny in that I provided some degree of entertainment for people, but definitely not because of my quick wit or sharp sense of humor. I wasn't stupid, but was certainly never accused of being a genius. I liked music and enjoyed singing, but was always in the background, never the lead vocalist. I liked sports and took to most of them pretty easily, but didn't excel at any. I was a good teammate but never the all-star or team captain.

In school when the other kids had learned their times tables, I was still counting on my fingers. When they were reading chapter books, I was still trying to grasp *Run, Spot, Run*. Mom couldn't figure out my resistance to opening a book. Cliff had been reading sports books and memorizing hundreds of facts at the same age.

Mom took me to an optometrist. I was thrilled at the potential excuse of bad eyesight. I eagerly walked into the doctor's office and sat down to have my eyes examined. I looked through the test glasses at the rows of letters, each one smaller than the one above it. I was disappointed to discover that I could see them all just fine, crystal clear, even the tiniest ones. I guess it really was my fault I was doing poorly at school.

But I didn't want to take the blame, or be without the comfort of an excuse, so I faked it—I lied. I told the doctor the wrong letters on the lower rows. I chose to create a false reality that gave me the convenient excuse of having a problem that didn't actually exist. But once I had glasses, I still couldn't read. *This would be my first (unfortunately not my last) lesson: that my excuses, no matter how convenient, were rarely my real reason for not excelling.*

I put very little effort into practicing sports and trying to become better because I didn't believe I could ever be really good. "Why should I try to be better at basketball when everyone towers over me?" "It's not my fault I'm so short." "I'd make the football team if I wanted to try out." "I'm as smart as those honor roll students. They couldn't get Cs like me if they cut class as often as I did." I had such a huge selection of excuses I didn't know which one to pick first.

I mostly got involved in activities that boys were expected to do. These were the things the kids in the neighborhood did, or Cliff did, not necessarily the things I loved and was drawn to.

As a child, the thing I enjoyed most was to play with my action figures. I could play for hours and just live in fantasyland. Very often I would even act out the game without the toys. In my pretend world, I could be as good as I wanted to be at anything. I could fly around as Superboy (rarely Superman) or fight the bad guys as Robin (never Batman though). I liked to play these games with friends, but they only pretended to pretend; to me it was real. I was the best pretender around.

Most of my friends grew out of these childish pastimes long before I did, and Cliff was never into this sort of thing. Playing these baby games was looked down upon. So I became a closet pretender and would play by myself where my fantasy and my dream could be undisturbed by anyone else's limited imaginations.

It was difficult to excel at something if I didn't love it enough to put the work into it. But the things I loved weren't things that others saw as worthwhile, and were certainly not praiseworthy. There was nothing to be gained and no victory to be won from them other than the love and joy of the activity itself.

4
Finding My Passion

AFTER MY FATHER died, Mom felt the urge to move away and have a fresh start. In 1967, she loaded up her boys and moved from Albany to Honolulu. Hawaii was still a young state then, a secret-paradise location that had hardly been discovered.

It was in Hawaii that I first remember falling in love with the idea of flying. The Hawaiian sky was such a dynamic, incredible sight. It was bluer than blue and the clouds were alive. I'd watch them build high into the sky as they reached the mountains and just as quickly fade away when they came over the water again. They were constantly changing, evolving, growing, and disappearing.

There were many species of beautiful birds that called the Hawaiian sky their home. I couldn't take my eyes off of them as they soared in the sky or cruised just inches above the ocean water. Sometimes they would circle quietly overhead then suddenly dive straight down like missiles, hit the water, and launch right back in the air, carrying fish they caught. As they flew in to land on the beach, they would "flare" their wings to sit up and stop as they gently stepped onto the sand.

I remember not only watching the birds fly, but also watching *how* they flew. Analyzing how they would use their wings, their angle of attack, when they would flap their wings, and when they could glide without flapping. They were even better flyers than Superman.

I couldn't understand how we could call ourselves the dominant species when we required elaborate machines to carry us in the sky while baby birds just had to have the courage to take that first step out of their nests. I would chase after the birds leaping into the air with my arms outstretched like wings, trying to launch into flight. Flying in planes was great also, but I wasn't flying, the plane was. I didn't want to fly in a flying machine. I wanted to be the flying machine. And I wanted it more than I'd ever wanted anything.

Flying became the most frequent theme in my pretend games. It was always the greatest superpower of all. X-ray vision and a body so hard that bullets bounced right off it were nothing compared to being able to fly. Flying was the full-purpose power; I could fly to the rescue or fly away to escape, whichever the situation called for.

By six I was searching for ways to be airborne. I would jump on trampolines or leap from the highest diving board I could find just to hang in the air and enjoy those few seconds of flight. I would swim underwater by pushing off the wall and gliding like a bird on the air. Even flaring to land like the birds I watched had taught me.

In my fantasy world, I was flying and I loved it. But even with the imagination of a six-year-old, I knew there was no chance of ever really achieving my dream. My dream would never be more than a fantasy. Human beings can't fly.

Watching TV one day, I came across a show about skydiving (commonly called "sport parachuting" at that time). There were people flying through the air, miles above the earth, unattached to any man-made flying machine. They looked like human birds, maneuvering in every direction with total freedom. They were flying! It wasn't a fantasy; my dream was possible.

I yelled, "Mom, look at this! They're flying, without a plane or anything! I want to do that. Can I do that?" Nothing made Mom happier than seeing the glow on her boys' faces when we were excited about something. But this was the last thing she would ever want me to be excited about. "Oy vey. Promise me you'll never jump out of an airplane," was her only response.

I put strings on a blanket, tied them to myself, and jumped off my bunk bed with my homemade parachute. I thought it could work, and even wondered whether I could jump out the window of our eighth-floor apartment. Walking home from school one day, I saw several ambulances parked at the sidewalk next to our building. Apparently, someone had jumped out of a window and died. I remember thinking, "That wasn't too smart. They should have tied my blanket on." But just the same, I gave up on the idea of trying that myself.

Even with all of this convincing discouragement, I still thought skydiving was the closest thing to true human flight and knew someday I was going to fly like that. But I had to be eighteen before I could make my first jump. I wasn't sure my dream could survive the years of growing up.

5
Growing Up

AFTER A YEAR in Hawaii, Mom's brother, my uncle Mike, was drafted into the army and would be leaving for Vietnam. Anticipating his departure, Mom moved us back to Albany so that we would be closer to Grandma and Grandpa in Yonkers, New York.

About that time she met Howard Chenfeld. Howard's wife had died before their daughter, Cara, was one year old. Howard was eight years older than my mom and a sophisticated intellectual; a lover of art, history, culture, fine food, fine wine; and a complete gentleman. He and my mom were perfect for each other. We started to spend more and more time with Howard and Cara.

Cliff and I were catching on to what was going to happen. I was hiding behind the couch in anticipation when Howard proposed to Mom. I heard her say that she had to ask the kids, but before she had the chance, I answered by cheering and dancing around the room in celebration.

On February 22, 1970, Howard and Mom were married. Cliff was ten, Cara was nine, and I was eight. From that moment on, Howard became Dad. By definition, he was my stepfather, but that was never how I saw him. Many kids don't even get to have one great father. I had the privilege of having two.

Cara quickly became a wonderful big sister. When Cliff's love was tough, Cara's was accepting. When he thought I was a dork, she thought I was cute. If he thought I was stupid, she thought I was funny. She loved me just the way I was with all my quirks and weaknesses.

Dad was not the athletic type. When Cliff and I would wrestle down the stairs, he would be more likely to get out of the way and tell us to "stop that stupidity!" than he was to jump in.

My father had many qualities, but the one that stood out more than any other was his absolutely clear definition of the difference between right and wrong. To Dad, there was never a gray area, never a doubt. He knew what he thought was right, and he consistently chose to do it.

Dad had rules he lived by, and he expected and demanded the same from us:

1. Treat *every* person you meet with respect. No matter who they are, what they do, or how they look, they deserve to be treated kindly, courteously, and respectfully.
2. If later it is proven to you that they are not worthy of this respect, then ignore them.
3. If you can't ignore them, treat them as they deserve to be treated.
4. If you are capable of doing a good deed for another person, then do it.
5. Always tell the truth.
6. If you say you're going to do something, do it.
7. Always do the best you can do even if you have to do something you didn't choose or don't like.
8. Always remember that you are no better a person than anyone else.
9. Never forget that there is no one who is any better of a person than you.

Simple enough, it all made sense to me.

My father wasn't particularly competitive—he always encouraged us to do our best, but we weren't pushed to be *the* best.

My father knew I was capable of doing better at everything I did, and it frustrated him that I wouldn't. If I didn't do well on a test or school project, he would say to me, "It doesn't matter what your grade was or where you finished, as long as you did the best you could." And follow it with, "Danny, did you do your best?" I would usually say yes even though I knew it wasn't true. Because he had taught us not to lie, he would demonstrate that he trusted my word and accepted my answer as the truth. But I'm pretty sure he knew it wasn't. That he said he believed me and trusted I had told him the truth made me feel terrible for lying.

I felt so bad for lying that I remember considering it might really have been the truth. Being a failure was preferable to being a liar. I created thoughts in my head like "Maybe that really is my best. Maybe I can't do any better. I'm not really good at anything." It was good justification for underachieving, and I was the classic underachiever. I had the brains to do well at school but was satisfied with Cs and the natural athletic ability to excel at sports but was okay with being mediocre.

At the root of this problem was that I hadn't discovered anything I enjoyed so much that I eagerly embraced doing the work it would take to excel at it. All I wanted to do was fly. My head was in the clouds.

6
Another Passion

MY PARENTS SEARCHED for something I could apply myself to. I was eight when our new family moved to Columbus, Ohio. The Jewish Community Center there had a theater group called Gallery Players. In the upcoming play there was a part for a kid. Mom and Dad asked me if I'd like to try out for it. Unfortunately, it wasn't a part for a superhero kid, but the idea of being encouraged to pretend sounded like fun.

The play was *Camino Real*, and the part was the frequently onstage but nonspeaking role of a jester. I had a blast. It wasn't much different than the games I had played by myself.

Acting became the first thing that I really loved, and I willingly poured myself into it. My progression in acting went far beyond childish play. I took classes, listened carefully to the directors and coaches, and practiced a lot. Nearly every free second I was rehearsing on my own. It was much more than a game. It became a skill, a challenge to not "act" like the character but to "become" that character. I loved it so much that I tried out for every play I could get a part in at the community theater, junior high school, and high school.

The best part of acting is the moment before walking onstage. I remember at first being terribly nervous and trying desperately to calm down. I didn't want to screw up, not in front of all those people.

I had started getting anxious weeks in advance of the show, and the tension continued to build as opening night drew closer.

As I waited offstage for my cue, my heart pounded like I'd just run a three-minute mile. A little voice in my head said, "S——t, Danny. What have you gotten yourself into this time?" The voice wasn't all that little. I had to drown it out I reminded myself I could do it, that I had practiced it hundreds, even thousands, of times by myself and rehearsed over and over again with the entire cast. I told myself, "Just relax. When you hear your cue, walk out onstage. You've practiced enough. It will be fine. Just walk onstage."

The voice came back. "Is running away an option? Why don't you run? Run!" The fear got bigger, the voice louder, as I knew my cue was coming up. I kept talking. "If a baby bird can take that first step out of their nest and fly, then you can walk onstage and act. Take the first step. Just walk onstage, walk onstage." My cue came and I went.

As my feet came out from behind the curtain and the stage lights hit my eyes, the fear was instantly gone. It was like some kind of magic spell came over me as I immediately transformed into the character I had practiced being. It seemed to happen automatically, instinctively. *Almost as if I was just along for the ride as I watched my body, mind, and soul do what they had rehearsed and play the part. If I started thinking too much about it, I got in their way, so I just let it happen.*

The first time this happened, I was completely surprised. But after doing several plays and experiencing much the same scenario each time, I realized this is how it's done.

You work your butt off practicing for hours and hours. Then when it's actually performance time, you relax and let it happen. I started to expect it and plan for it. *I never completely stopped being nervous, but I stopped being scared of being nervous.* I knew it was part of the plan, and as long as I calmed down, trusted myself, and let it happen, I would perform the best I was capable of. Little did I know that it would become one of the most valuable lessons of my life.

Since there weren't many boys involved in theater, it wasn't particularly competitive. It wasn't about being better than anyone else, but it was absolutely about being the best I could be and being good enough to stand up on a stage in front of hundreds of people and make them laugh, cry, and hopefully cheer because it was a good show.

The only thing that motivated me to do this work was the pure love of it. It certainly wasn't the goal of impressing my friends and schoolmates. In junior high school and high school, boys who were in theater and choir were looked at as gay or nerds or both. But it was theater that I loved, and I was determined to put 150 percent into it.

Finally, by my senior year of high school, I reached the towering height of 5'8" (if I stood up really straight). We were advised by counselors and teachers to select our chosen career directions based on what they felt were our strengths. I wanted to be an actor. No responsible counselor would advise a student to pursue acting. I was told that acting wasn't a real career. That the vast majority of the most talented actors in the world are waiting tables. I would pour my heart and soul into it and probably come out with nothing.

There was no guarantee of success. The likelihood of becoming a successful professional actor was slim at best. But if my family had taught me one thing, it was to find my passion and go for it with conviction. There was only one thing I loved and believed I was good at. One thing I had become so passionate about that *the enjoyment alone made the challenge to improve worth the effort even if there was no guarantee or even clear definition of success.* I couldn't imagine doing anything else. Despite the odds and naysayers, I believed I could make it happen. At seventeen, I started my freshman year at Ohio State University as a theater major.

7
Defining Spirituality

I HAVE NO MEMORY of the day of my father's death or his funeral. But I do remember wondering where he went. Is he okay? When will I see him again?

My Christian friends would tell me Daddy was in heaven. Couldn't tell me exactly what or where heaven was, but it was definitely the place to be. That sounded pretty good, but then from other Christian friends, I learned that the prerequisites for admission into heaven were very strict, and a belief that Jesus was the son of God was the most important one. That would exclude Jews from getting into heaven and would leave us having to go to the only other alternative, hell. That meant my father was in hell? What god would send my mother to hell? No, that didn't make sense to me.

I asked our rabbi, "What happened to my dad? Where did he go?" The rabbi walked me outside and showed me the leaves changing colors and falling off the trees and explained how there would be new buds growing from the same trees in the spring. The grass was dying, but new grass would grow in its place. It is nature's way. Life works in cycles. No one and nothing lives forever. He assured me that everything my dad was lives on in me, Cliff, and other people who loved him and whom he loved. *Hmm, that sounds good*, I thought. "Okay, but what happened to my dad, where did he go?

Is he okay? When will I see him again?" The rabbi couldn't give me a definite answer.

What a waste it would be if we could put so much into our lives only for those lives to be so fragile that they could end in a second. That we could be walking around one moment a loving, positive, person bringing joy, comfort, and happiness to people around us and the next second be dead from a car accident, a heart attack, or a random bolt of lightning. Completely gone, finished. I really wanted to believe there was more, but I needed more evidence than just my gut telling me so.

I did believe in God, or at least I wanted to believe in God. At the very least, I really hoped there was a God. But I still hadn't yet found an explanation of who or what God was that made sense to me. If God is all-powerful, how could he allow for such cruel and terrible acts to occur on earth?

Like many other people, my teenage years were the height of my questioning and wondering about how the world worked. Without having gotten any solid answers up until that point, I was beginning to feel a bit pessimistic about it all. Maybe there really wasn't anything but this. If that's the case, we may as well just party and have a good time. Why not? It could all be over any second anyway.

The first *Star Wars* movie was released in 1977 when I was fifteen. I loved it. And it wasn't the special effects or the story I was so crazy about. It was the idea of "the Force." The Force was described as a power that connects everything in the entire universe. It is a power that is both within and surrounding all living things. It is the natural force that organizes our DNA, keeps our hearts beating, and coordinates the stars, planets, and galaxies. It is a power that we can all tap into when we need physical, emotional, or psychic strength. It is something that works best for us when we truly have an unending faith in it. It is part of us, and we are part of it. It doesn't control us or us it. It can be used for evil by evil people. But it is good by nature, and ultimately, through the Force, good will prevail over evil.

These were ideas that worked for me. In the final scene of *Star Wars*, Luke flies down into the channel of the Death Star. He has one chance, one shot, to blow it up. He's nervous. He carefully aims his sights, trying to use all the tools and technical expertise he has. He has a hard time lining up his scope. Obi-Wan Kenobi's voice comes on: "Let your feelings go. Use the Force, Luke."

Luke turns off the computer and pushes the scope away. He stops trying to aim. He takes a deep breath, relaxes, and trusts that he knows what he's doing, and has faith that it will work out as it should. He takes the shot, it's a bull's-eye. The Death Star blows up.

As I watched this scene, I realized that was exactly what I did when preparing to walk onstage in a play. For me, becoming the character and playing the part was hitting the target. I was nervous that I would "miss," but I knew as long as I calmed down, trusted myself, and let it happen, I would perform the best I was capable of. I was feeling the Force, using the Force, and trusting it to work for me and with me. And it did. Maybe there was something to the *Star Wars* philosophy.

As to an afterlife, maybe I would never know. Maybe I would someday find out. Maybe the answers had to wait until I myself left this world. But for now, I was intrigued with the concept that a greater force existed in the universe that could be tapped into to achieve great things, to rise to any occasion, to save the planet.

> "You are quoting Snoopy the Dog, I believe?"
> "I'll quote the truth wherever I find it, thank you."
>
> —From *Illusions* by Richard Bach

8
The Process of Pursuing a Dream

FANTASY—————-DREAM——————GOAL

These three words are often interchanged as if they were synonymous. But I see them defined quite differently.

In my thinking, a fantasy is something we want to do but believe is impossible. We think about it but don't really consider that we could or would actually ever do it.

A dream is something we want to do and believe is possible for us to achieve. It's on our radar; we plan to do it someday when we have the time or money or courage. But the excuses are too many, and that time rarely comes.

A goal is a dream we decide we must achieve and we will do whatever necessary to achieve it. A goal is the specific target, or series of targets, we aim for when we decide to pursue our dreams.

As much as I loved pretending I could fly like the birds in Hawaii or at the speed of light like Superman, I knew it wasn't possible. It was only a fantasy.

When I saw people skydiving, I knew that was as close as I was going to come to experiencing true human flight. But in order to learn to skydive prior to turning eighteen, I had to get permission from my parents. As free-spirited as my parents were, there was no chance they were going to sign off on that. So until I turned eighteen, flying in free fall was no more than a dream.

During my freshman year at Ohio State University, about a dozen of us living in the Taylor Tower dormitory started talking about making a jump. Everyone said, "I've always wanted to do that!" But it was January and the parachute club we had found didn't open until the spring, so talk was cheap. It was easy to be fearless while we were only dreaming about it.

On my eighteenth birthday, everything changed. My excuse for not having made my first jump was removed. Finally, it was possible. The Columbus Sport Parachute Club, located an hour north of Columbus in Centerburg, was scheduled to open back up on May 1. The day was set and the goal was clear. It wasn't a dream anymore; now it was real. And now I was scared.

A fantasy is low risk and low investment. We live the desire in our heads and imaginations. Actually pursuing a dream is different. To truly "reach for our dreams" and achieve a specific goal, certain steps need to be followed, information researched, decisions made, and action taken. If I wanted to pursue my dream, I had to stop dreaming and get down to business.

I discovered that the general process of pursuing a dream usually involved six steps that looked something like this:

1. FANTASIZE – Something grabs us. We fantasize about it, imagine it, visualize it. We think about how incredible it would be to do it and to have done it. But we don't believe it's possible for us to achieve.
2. DREAM – We begin to believe that we may actually be able to do the thing we only imagined.
3. INVESTIGATE – We examine what it would take to make the dream happen.

4. DELIBERATE – Now that we know the risks, sacrifices, commitments, and costs involved, we ask ourselves two questions: Is it possible for us to achieve? Do we want it badly enough to do what it is going to take to make it happen?
5. TAKE ACTION – If we decide it might be worth the effort, we then begin to take a series of steps that opens the possibility of our dream becoming a reality. One by one, the steps take us closer to our goal. With each step, even the smallest ones, we build momentum and become more committed. But we're not there yet. The final decision hasn't been made. We can still change our mind and turn back around.
6. DECISION TIME – We have thought it through completely. We have taken step-by-step action and have now finally reached that moment. We can still go back, it's not too late. But it is now decision time. Once the decision has been made, there is no turning back. It is this next step forward that will turn our dream into reality. Will we take the step?

My dream was to fly like the birds, to come as close as I could to experiencing true human flight. Once I discovered skydiving, this was no longer a fantasy. I believed I could do it and had been dreaming about it for years. The first steps were complete.

But I didn't want to simply plummet out of an airplane one time. I wanted to fly, to be flying in free fall with other jumpers. What was it going to take to make it happen? For starters, before I could fly, I had to make my first jump.

The club in Centerburg ran a first-jump course every Saturday at nine o'clock. The course took three hours and cost $35. If I signed up for the class, showed up on a sunny day, and paid the money, then I could jump. Simple enough.

I would be doing a static line jump from 2,800 feet. A static line is a cord that is attached to the plane and automatically deploys the parachute immediately after exiting. This meant that the parachute would be open within three seconds out the door so there would be very little, actually no, free-fall time. Static line was the only way to make a first jump back then.

Here is where it started to get complicated. Before being allowed to fly with other skydivers, I would need to demonstrate I could free fall safely by myself. To do this, I would have to earn my A license. This would require a minimum of twenty-five solo jumps, progressing from static line to thirty-second free falls. The jump progression involved making the following:

- 5 static lines
- 3 clear and pulls. On these jumps I was no longer hooked to the static line. I would have to pull the rip cord myself but would do so immediately after exiting. Basically "clear" the plane and "pull" right away.
- 3 five-second delays. Count to five then pull.
- 3 ten-second delays.
- 3 fifteen-second delays.
- 3 twenty-second delays.
- 3 thirty-second delays.

At this point, I could take a test and become a licensed skydiver. Only then would I be allowed to jump with other people.

I would be jumping with an old, twenty-eight-foot-in-diameter, round parachute that crawled at a maximum forward speed of 3 mph. These old parachutes didn't really fly, they just slowed your descent. For all practical purposes, I would be drifting downwind until impact.

There was no chance that I would land softly enough to "stand up" the landing. If I wanted to walk away from it, I would need to do a PLF, a "parachute landing fall." On a PLF you put your feet and knees together, bend your knees slightly, and bring your elbows close in to your torso. As your feet hit the ground, you twist your body to present your side to the dirt with your points of contact being feet, side of your calves, side of your knees, side of your hips, side of your torso, then twist and continue rolling to the other side. This way you spread the impact of landing over your entire body and bruise everything rather than taking it all in a single area and breaking one thing.

All this was much more involved and would require way more time, effort, and money than I had anticipated. Did I want it badly enough to do what it would take to make it happen?

My dream wasn't to fall like a ton of bricks under an old military parachute, which if done correctly, wouldn't involve any free fall at all, but would almost certainly result in me bruising half my body on landing. And, if not done correctly, could result in dying.

My dream was to free fall, to fly through the sky using my arms and legs as wings, and to fly together with other people.

Considering the weather in Ohio, getting through twenty-five jumps would require me to dedicate every weekend for the entire summer and spend about $750 just on the jumps. At the time I was working as a cook and delivering pizzas. Both these jobs I did in the evening so I could be back from the drop zone in time to work.

Would it be possible to reach my goal? Sure, thousands of people before me had accomplished it.

Would I be willing to do whatever it was going to take to make it happen? The commitment required was doable. It wasn't really going to take all that much. I wouldn't have to leave school, quit my job, or make any monumental life changes to make it happen.

I'm not a person who generally hides from his fear, but on the other hand, I'm not an adrenaline junkie who thrives on the rush you get when putting your life on the line. *For me, the anticipated fun factor has to warrant the anticipated fear factor.* The idea of flying in the sky, unattached to any man-made flying machine, was the most fantastic thing I could imagine. The chance to do that would be worth the fear. I decided to at least make the first jump and take it from there.

I started taking action, specific steps. Each individual step, no matter how small, brought me closer to achieving my goal. The closer I got, the more real it became and the more the fear grew. But each step also presented the opportunity for me to change my mind. I had to make a conscious decision to keep moving forward. I knew that if I didn't, I would retreat.

I called the club and scheduled me and my friends for the first-jump course for the following Saturday. Now my dream, my goal, had a date, and it was only a few days away.

I woke up Saturday morning and peeked out the window to check the weather, half wanting to see beautiful blue skies and half praying for rain so that I had an excuse not to go. Beautiful blue skies it was. My friends that were supposed to go with me must have looked out a different window. Most of them changed their minds and decided to stay home. Of the dozen of us who under the safety of the cold winter months were talking about jumping, only three made it to the car.

I got in the car and turned the key. Damn it, it started. The fear was building and my heart was beating faster with each mile.

We actually made it to the club without finding a good enough excuse to turn around. The facility consisted of a picnic table surrounded by farm fields with a grass strip for a runway. There was a stack of old worn-out military parachutes piled into a dirty, smelly, old shed. At the picnic table in front of the shed sat the club president, ready to welcome the day's new jumpers. It looked like he had been there all night and just switched from beer to coffee. He handed me a release form that basically said I was likely to die or get seriously injured, and if I did, I couldn't blame (or sue) anyone but myself.

It wasn't quite what I expected, but I really didn't know what to expect anyway. I paid the money, signed the release, and started the course.

The instructor wasn't a confidence-building character. He had barely over one hundred jumps and was terrified just talking about skydiving. He was sweating profusely when he demonstrated emergency procedures and twisted his ankle when he showed us a PLF. The only thing that reassured me was the thought that if this guy could skydive, anybody could.

He explained that at 2,800 feet, the jumpmaster would tell us to climb out one at a time, about two minutes apart. When instructed,

I would climb out under the wing, facing forward, holding on to the wing strut while standing on the landing gear wheel. The pilot would hold the brakes tightly so that the wheel didn't start spinning under my feet. The jumpmaster would then yell, "Go!" On "go," I would jump off the wheel, let go of the strut, and arch my body like my life depended on it because it did.

Either way I should have a good parachute over my head a few seconds later. If I didn't have a good parachute, then I needed to put my left arm around the reserve parachute container on my chest and pull the reserve rip cord with my right hand. With the reserve parachute container now open, I would have to reach into it, grab the fabric of the reserve canopy, and manually throw it out into the wind. I thought, "You gotta be kidding. I'll be dead by then."

I got geared up in an old piece-of-crap parachute system and boarded a four-place, single-engine Cessna 172XP that appeared to be held together with lots of duct tape. All but the pilot's seat had been removed, so we sat on the floor to the right side of the pilot, facing the rear of the plane. I squeezed up as close to the pilot as I could because on my left side was a big hole in the plane where the door had been removed. To my amazement, the plane successfully took off and very slowly climbed to altitude.

Most people do better when something frightening happens suddenly and requires them to instinctively respond. They don't have time to think about it, analyze it, or worry about it. Something happens that shocks them and they respond, and it's over before they even realize how scared they are.

But first-time skydivers have a fifteen-minute plane ride that allows time for the fear to boil over in anticipation of the jump. My fear was growing by the second, my heart beating faster and faster. I felt like I had two "Dans" fighting against each other. The fun-loving, enthusiastic, Lover of Life Dan was wrestling with the Doomsday Dan.

"Don't go!"

"Do it, it's going to be fantastic."

"It's not too late. You can still change your mind!"

"What will people think of you if you chicken out?"

"C'mon, you've been dreaming about this your entire life. You'll never forgive yourself if you back out."

"But you're going to die!"

At that moment, I still hadn't decided for sure if I was going to jump or not.

The jumpmaster hooked up my static line and told me I was two minutes from jumping. One second later, he yelled to the pilot, "Cut!" The pilot pulled back the power so that when I climbed out, the "prop blast" wouldn't blow me right off the plane. The jumpmaster pointed out the door and yelled, "Climb out!"

I started yelling too. "Son of a b——! What the h—— am I doing here!" The voices in my head were also screaming, "Don't do it, Danny, think about your poor mother!" "Go for it! One more step. You're almost there!" I turned, put my feet out the door onto the wheel, and reached for the wing strut. The Cessna was flying at about 70 mph when I climbed out. I had to lock my hands onto the wing strut to pull myself out in the wind and keep my head down so that it didn't just blow me off. I stood on the wheel, facing forward.

Doomsday Dan still yelled, "Climb back in, it's not too late!" I turned and looked back at my jumpmaster. He yelled, "Go!"

This was it—decision time. All the fantasizing, dreaming, investigating, deliberating, and action taken came down to this moment. I didn't have to go. I could've still changed my mind, said no, and climbed back in the plane. This was the moment. Would I face my fears in pursuit of my dream, or would I give up, not follow through, and forever regret it?

The jumpmaster yelled again, "Go! Go!" Holy crap! I've never been so scared in my entire life. What was going to happen if I let go? Was it going to be everything I'd dreamt about or was I going to die?

I'd been holding on for so long now that we'd flown past the exit point. He yelled again, "Go! Go!" Even with all the preparation, I still had no idea what to expect. I had never seen or felt anything like this before. I was in way over my head and more terrified than I'd ever been in my life. There was nothing but faith guiding me. I found out which Dan was the real Dan at that moment. "Just do it, just jump. Just jump. Just jump."

It wasn't until I actually made the decision to *let go* of the plane and started falling away that I realized there was no turning back. At that instant, the fear was gone, vanished, defeated by pure excitement and exhilaration. I was stepping into the unknown. I had never felt as wonderful and alive as I did at that moment.

Making the final decision to jump was literally "taking a leap of faith." I didn't know exactly what was going to happen next, but had decided to have a little *faith and trust* in the equipment, myself, and the world I had just leaped into.

As soon as my parachute opened, I was just hung under it in silence. I wasn't swaying, swinging, or flying. From these old round parachutes a jumper would just hang. Once I caught my breath and my heart rate slowed down to less than 120 bpm, I became totally aware of my surroundings—or, more accurately, the lack of surroundings. It was like being a speck in the sky, an eternity away from the ground, the horizon, and the plane I had just jumped from.

The landing was like jumping off a five-foot-tall pickup truck as it was backing up at about 8 mph. I hit the ground hard and had to roll to spread the impact over my body.

My first jump and the entire process leading up to it was a great lesson in learning how to pursue my dreams, face my fears, and to have faith in the world around me. But it wasn't free fall, it wasn't flying. It was only the first step toward my dream. If I really wanted to fly, I would have to commit further.

If it wasn't for the goal of ultimately learning to fly in free fall, I never would have continued. The static line jumps themselves weren't enough fun to justify being that terrified. I had to force myself to go every time. It wasn't about flying then. It was all about overcoming the fear and getting myself out the door of the plane. After my second static line jump, I had a clearer idea of what to expect, so the fear and sensory overload started to become less intense. But with each "first" jump of a new level, the fear was back.

My first free fall, a "clear and pull," was horrifying. I had to "clear" the plane and "pull" the rip cord myself to start the parachute deployment. It was now entirely up to me if I was going to live or die. After a couple of clear and pulls, I became more confident that I could save myself. But the free fall was still very short, only a couple of seconds.

After three successful clear and pulls, I progressed to five-second delays. And they had to be a true five seconds. You know the kind, a slow, "One, thousand, two, thousand, three, thousand, four, thousand, five, thousand." These were without question the longest five seconds of my life. While doing this slow count, I could see the plane shrinking as I accelerated away from it. I could hear the wind pick up as I went from the exit speed of the Cessna toward terminal velocity.

On my first five-second delay, it was all I could do to keep my hand away from the rip cord. Every instinct told me to pull the rip cord as soon as I left the plane. After yelling "five, thousand," my hand came in like lightning and ripped the rip cord out of its pocket to start the deployment. But after a couple of successful five-second delays, I was starting to feel more comfortable.

Free fall is fast and loud. But as the parachute opens, everything slows down. It becomes quiet and serene as you gently float.

On to ten-second delays. After ten seconds you are reaching terminal velocity, a speed for most skydivers of about 120 mph. At this speed, even a small imbalance in your body position can deflect the wind, causing you to spin like a propeller. New skydivers today have instructors with them in free fall who will stop them if they start to spin and give them hand signals to correct their body position and fix the misalignment. But in 1980, when I was learning to skydive, if I started spinning, there was no one there to stop me. I had to figure it out myself. And spin I did.

I spun so fast I thought my helmet was going to fly off with my head in it. At the same time as trying to stop the spin, I had to keep counting the seconds for the particular delay time. When I hit ten seconds and was still spinning, I had to pull the rip cord.

A parachute works much better when the skydiver it is attached to is falling in a stable, steady position. The old round parachutes we used then had very long lines. Sometimes when I was spinning as I pulled my rip cord, I would end up with line twists that started just above my shoulders and went nearly all the way up to the canopy itself. I'd have to kick and kick and kick to try and undo the line so I could see where I was going.

It was no fun to be unstable and unable to control myself in free fall. But my dream of flying like a bird was still powerful enough to push me along, hoping the next jump would be the one I'd get it figured out on.

Despite my unstable ten-second delays I still managed to pull the rip cord and survive, so my instructor advanced me to fifteen seconds, figuring I just needed more time to learn to control the free fall.

Finally it happened. I exited the plane, arched like hell, and started counting. I started turning again and the spin started to accelerate. But before it gained too much speed, I banked my arms over like a wing and stopped the turn. I had control! As I continued my count, I did a slow 360-degree turn to the left and gazed out at sky, the bubbling white clouds, and the horizon so far away. I stopped and slowly turned back to the right, enjoying the incredible view. For the first time I realized I wasn't looking *at* the sky. I was a part of the sky, sharing it with the clouds and the birds and the angels.

The rest of my solo student jumps were wonderful. Now that I was able to control my free fall much more, the fear was almost gone. Free fall seemed to last forever, and I truly felt like I belonged in the sky. I could feel and hear the speed, but there was no sensation of falling unless I was falling down the side of a cloud and could watch it as I fell past.

Within a couple of months I had done over forty jumps. The fear was mostly gone by then. I was really starting to fly, and it was more incredible than I had ever imagined. With each jump, I was learning new skills and ways to maneuver in free fall. I couldn't get enough. The better a flier I became, the more fun it was and the more I wanted to keep jumping. I bought my own parachute system with a square canopy that I could actually control and that I could land where I wanted to without smashing into the ground. There was no doubt in my mind that in some way or another, skydiving was going to become a big part of my life.

If my friends thought I was nuts, there was no telling what my parents might think. Dad was the most cautious person I have ever met. In his eyes, life and health were much too precious to risk unless behind that risk was a bigger, more honorable purpose, a purpose so important that it had to be done. Risk your life running into a burning house or diving into the rapids to save a child, yes. Was there a certain level of acceptable risk in following a passion? Yes. But if that passion is something that offers nothing but an adrenaline rush, and is likely to kill or severely injure you, forget it, it's just plain stupid.

So, when I decided to make my first skydive, I chose not to tell my parents about it. I knew that they would worry too much and that Dad would think I was an absolute idiot for even considering it.

But I knew I couldn't keep it a secret forever and decided it was time to tell them. I was a bit nervous, so I laid it out a little at a time. "Mom and Dad, I have to tell you something. I went skydiving." Their reaction wasn't as bad as I had feared. They were almost excited about it.

"Wow. We knew that someday you were going to do it. We're glad you didn't tell us before you went. Better we didn't know. We would have been terrified waiting for you to call. When did you go?"

I guess I was going to have to tell them a little more of the story. "I did my first jump back in May."

Uh-oh, here we go. "May? Why did you wait so long to tell us? Did you say 'first' jump? What do you mean 'first jump'? You didn't do it again, did you? How many times have you done it?" I told them everything; I had to.

Boy, was my Dad pissed. He called me every name in the book. "What kind of person risks their life for a thrill? And not just once, but does it again and again? How could you think so little of yourself that you'd be willing to throw your life away for nothing? Do you love your mother so little that you would put her through this?" He finished it with, "You're a f——ing idiot!"

My folks had always pushed me to find my passion and pursue it. They were okay when I chose theater and poured all my time and energy toward developing my acting skills. They had even encouraged me to pursue acting as a career. But this was different.

I tried to explain to him that this wasn't just a thrill for me, it was a dream come true. It wasn't as dangerous as he thought; it just required that I play by the rules, follow the safety guidelines, and use good common sense. I told him how much I loved it. How incredible it made me feel.

He didn't understand how skydiving could be anything more than a life-threatening adrenaline rush, and he certainly didn't see it as a sport. But he clearly understood being passionate about something and living your dreams. He knew from looking in my eyes that I was serious, I really did love skydiving. I was finally able to enjoy true human flight as he had seen me pretend for so many years. He knew this was my dream, and though he wished I had dreamt about something else, he never asked me to quit again.

9
It's a Sport?

DISCOVERING THE COMPETITION Sport of 4-Way Formation Skydiving

The feeling of *flying* as opposed to *falling* really comes when you are jumping with other people. Relative to other jumpers, you can fly in any direction, even slow your descent rate and "fly up" at them. I still remember the first time I exited the plane after the people I was jumping with. I hit the air, arched hard, and got stable. I looked down to find the other jumpers and they were hundreds of feet below me. My instructor had told me how to "dive" down to get to other jumpers, but I had never actually tried it. This was my chance.

I slowly brought my arms back along my sides like the wings of a fighter jet. As I did my head lowered down to the correct approach angle. I put my legs out and pointed my toes, the free fall equivalent of "flooring it." I was headed right at the other jumpers and approaching them at high speed. As I got to them I pulled my legs in tight, my knees toward my belly, and threw my arms up and out like a bird flaring to land at the beach. This was like slamming on the brakes, and I stopped just as I grabbed on to their arms and entered the free-fall formation. I DID IT! For the first time I really felt like I was flying. At that moment, there was no turning back. I wanted to fly more, to fly faster and better.

I was at the club every weekend and doing as many skydives as I could. Most of the time we jumped from 9,500 feet, and on every jump, we attempted the same thing in the forty seconds of free-fall time we had from that altitude. Two of us would climb out holding on to the strut and standing on the wheel. The other two (four was the most jumpers the Cessna could carry) would launch from the door. One jumper outside the plane would be designated the "base" for each jump. The base would give the "ready, set, go" count, exit first so they were the lowest in the sky, and then try to fall straight down.

The other three jumpers chased the base through the sky, flying like unguided missiles, zinging around in every direction in an attempt, usually futile, to try to "dock" on the base and build a "star" or circle formation. The base was the target (and I do mean target). If one of us went low by sailing past the base, that lower person then became the new base. The complete plan for a jump amounted to "low man is base." Sometimes, even after following the most inefficient flight paths possible, and each of us taking a different one, we all managed to get together by running into the base, grabbing any part of them we could, and climbing our way across each other into a star.

The few times we actually did, we were so excited that we would just hold on tight and scream for whatever free-fall time was left before we had to break apart and deploy our parachutes. At the Columbus Sport Parachute Club in Centerburg, Ohio, that was skydiving, that was all I knew, and I thought it was awesome.

One day strangers rode into town. Our club was small, and any unfamiliar faces stood out. These four skydivers were driving by and had stopped to make a jump. I watched them as they practiced on the ground climbing out of the airplane for exit. They were "dirt diving," practicing a sequence of five formations on the ground. It looked like they were planning to exit the plane holding onto each other with the grips of a star formation already intact.

I couldn't believe it. They were actually planning to "launch" a complete star formation right off the plane. And that wasn't all. After they left the plane with the formation stable and under control, they were going to let go of each other and then reform in a different formation. After building that formation they were going to break apart again before reforming into yet another formation and then another formation.

I was blown away, hadn't known that it was even possible. Why would they ever let go of each other? On all the jumps I had done, I worked so hard just to get close to someone. If I managed to get a hold of them, I was definitely not letting go.

I asked them if what they were practicing was really possible. They laughed and told me they were doing 4-way RW, "relative work" (now called formation skydiving). RW was the name for the type of free-fall skydiving that involved jumping with other people and trying to fly "relative to them" as opposed to flying on your own. The 4-way RW was the biggest competition event at the U.S. National Skydiving Championships.

Hold on! There were national skydiving competitions? Skydiving was a competitive sport? They went on to tell me how the sport worked.

In a nutshell, on every 4-way jump, a team of four people would fly through a sequence of five formations and had thirty-five seconds from the moment they exited the plane to complete as many of these formations as possible. Each formation was defined by the grips the team members had on each other. Each correctly built formation within the thirty-five seconds of working time was worth one point. Some of the "transitions" from one "point" to the next required specific moves like separating into two pairs and the pairs each doing 360-degree turns before rebuilding the same or possibly different formation. These were called "block" moves, and there were over twenty of them.

On other transitions, with individual "random" formations, everyone would have to let go of all the grips at the same time and could fly back together in whatever way the team decided would be the

4-Way IPC Dive Pool—Blocks 1-4

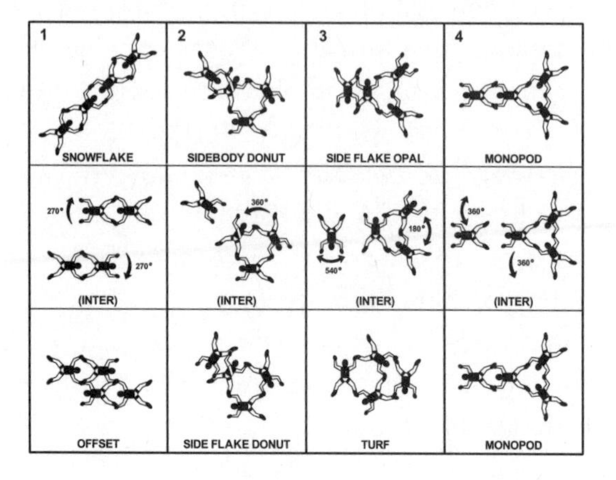

Formation Skydiving competition jumpsuits are skintight through the torso, arms, and upper legs. This sleek design is more aerodynamic than the old-fashioned baggy suits skydivers used to use. Because of the tight design, there are long tubular "grippers" sewn to the arms and legs of the jumpsuits. This gives the competitors a strong handhold when flying in pairs and aggressively spinning the "piece" together.

4-Way IPC Dive Pool—Randoms

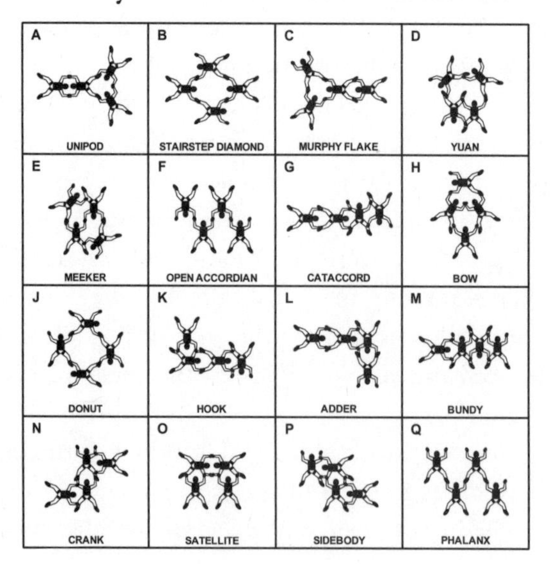

fastest way possible. There were another sixteen different random formations.

At the national championships, teams would do ten rounds or ten jumps each. In the months leading up to the competition, they would practice all the different blocks and randoms, but they wouldn't know the actual sequences of these formations they would be assigned until the day of the meet when the judges would do a "draw" and pick them out of a hat. Judges would then score the jumps from the ground using telemeters.

I wanted to try it as soon as possible. But no one at Centerburg did 4-way, and just as I was finding out about it, the club closed down for the winter.

10

The Greene County Sport Parachute Club

BACK ON CAMPUS it had been weeks since I had last jumped. It was pouring rain one day, but I needed my free fall fix, so I headed down to the Greene County Sport Parachute Center, a state-of-the-art skydiving facility in comparison to Centerburg, and the only one that was open all year round.

I drove onto the grass airport in my 1966 Barracuda that I paid $125 for. As I parked the car in the near-empty lot, my jaw dropped in amazement. Tied down in the grass field was not one, not two, but five jump planes. Five! Three single-engine and two twin-engine planes, most with in-flight doors. At the end of the parking lot was a real clubhouse.

About a dozen of the local experienced jumpers were hanging out inside the clubhouse, mostly huddled around the wood-burning stove. As I walked in, I did my best to look like a real skydiver, proudly carrying my newly purchased, but outdated, parachute system over my shoulder.

They appeared to be both entertained and curious by my appearance. Their expressions seemed to say, "Who is this long-haired eighteen-year-old punk, driving down in the rain in his piece-of-crap car, strutting in with his gear on his back when there is no chance of jumping today?" All I could do was smile. I was just so excited to be there.

Two of the most experienced skydivers saw something else in me. John Woody and Jim Fangmeyer were members of the local 4-way team, and both had well over a thousand jumps. Woody and Fang always had their net out looking for any possible future teammates. They didn't want to let any potentially good players escape unnoticed. They knew that potential was a common quality to come by so they kept a closer eye out for people with the more rare qualities of passion, drive, and desire that define the best teammates.

They saw more in me than a long-haired eighteen-year-old punk with a piece-of-crap car. They saw a very enthusiastic long-haired eighteen-year-old punk with a piece-of-crap car who had to be absolutely crazy about skydiving to have shown up at the drop zone that day.

They weren't actively searching for teammates and I wasn't looking to be found. But our shared passion for skydiving had put us on a collision course. If they hadn't always had their net out, considering anyone they met as a possible teammate, then we probably would have missed each other.

Woody, Fang, and their teammates were the last holdouts that day. They were practicing for the U.S. National Championships by working on particular 4-way moves and techniques and were still hoping that a hole in the clouds big enough for them to fit through would break open so they could squeeze in a jump. I watched them in awe. They really knew what they were doing.

As sunset was approaching, one of their teammates gave up and left. Not long after, the hole they were hoping for appeared in the clouds. They asked me if I wanted to go do a jump with them. I was bursting at the chance. How lucky I was to have shown up on that day. Woody and Fang were by far the best and most experienced jumpers I had ever met, and they wanted to show my sorry butt how to do 4-way.

I had no idea what I was going to discover at Greene County when I started driving down from OSU that day, but this was better than I could ever have dreamed. My love of skydiving and a gut decision had brought me to the drop zone. Maybe luck had nothing to do with it, but I felt like the luckiest guy in the world.

We did the jump, and it was absolutely amazing, like nothing I'd ever seen before. Wow! Woody and Fang could really fly. They were so smooth and controlled. On every skydive I'd done before, we had a little bit of a plan but, for the most part, would just jump out of the plane and see what happened. Not these guys: they had a plan and they made it happen. Each move was sharp, calculated, and right on target.

This was true flying. This is what I'd always wanted to do. Watching them in the air showed me what was possible. We actually did several formations, despite me banging around like a pinball every time we let go of grips on each other. I wanted to fly like they did.

###

THE SUMMER WAS approaching, and after having been to Greene County every weekend since the first, the drop zone owner, Jim West, offered me a summer job packing parachutes, washing planes, mowing grass, picking up trash, cleaning bathrooms, sweeping floors, answering the phone, and doing anything else required. My payment for this work would be $100 a week, a bed in the bunkhouse or a spot to set up a tent, and all the jumps I had time to make.

"All the jumps I can make?" I asked him. That is what he said, all the jumps I could make. He was certain that common sense and the time constraints of doing all my assigned tasks would restrict me from actually being able to make all that many jumps. He had no idea.

I bought a second parachute system for $150. That way I'd always have at least one ready to go. I made every jump I could. The type of jump or who I'd be jumping with didn't matter at all. If a plane took off, I was on it.

My grandparents were visiting my folks in Columbus and drove down to Greene County to check out my new line of work. Grandma was nearly speechless, for maybe a second.

"This is where you work? What could you do here in the middle of the cornfields? Why would you want to jump out of a perfectly good airplane anyway?" Then she looked at the airplanes. "You fly in that? It doesn't look like it will get off the ground." She shook her head in disbelief and disappointment. "Danny, this is not something nice Jewish boys are supposed to be doing."

But Gramps thought it was cool. He watched in amazement, as if looking through the eyes of a little kid. He knew that I knew he was digging it. I was sure he wanted to go and wished I could share it with him. Unfortunately, in 1981, the sport wasn't forgiving enough for a seventy-one-year-old man to learn to jump, even one as strong as my grandfather. He put his powerful arm around my shoulder and pulled me in tight. He could see the excitement in my eyes and was happy I had something I loved so much. I recognized his expression of approval, his unspoken encouragement, and was so glad to have that from him.

On the busy Saturdays, my primary job was to repack the student parachutes. Fortunately, we had so many that we could usually make it through the day without repacking them. But if I didn't keep up during the day, then by sunset there would be nearly one hundred parachutes piled to the ceiling that had to be packed and ready first thing Sunday morning. I didn't care. I would jump all day and spend the whole night packing, often finishing the last parachute just in time to get on the first lift the next day.

I started the summer with eighty jumps and finished the year with over eight hundred. That year, I also became a licensed instructor and jumpmaster. And boy could I fly. It was still only the beginning.

11
The College Years

IN MY SOPHOMORE year at Ohio State University, at nineteen, I was hanging out with some friends one night when my right lung collapsed. A "spontaneous pneumothorax," as the doctor at the hospital called it, indicated that there were weak areas in my lung tissue. I was told that playing sports and accidentally getting hit in the chest could easily cause another collapse.

I described to the doctor the "opening shock" that skydivers experience when their parachute opens. He said that the parachute opening would definitely put too much pressure on my chest.

Hmm, this was a problem. There weren't any exercises or diet he could suggest that would strengthen the lung tissue itself. The only line of defense would be to build up my upper body as a shield for my lungs.

You have to be in reasonable shape to excel at skydiving, but of the things I would need to do to advance in my sport, I hadn't considered that a regular workout routine at the gym would be one of them. It didn't sound like fun, and I didn't have any interest in being disciplined about something that wasn't going to be fun.

Theater sure, skydiving yes, but going to the gym every day? Only if I absolutely had to.

Well, I had to. It was time for me to discover that no matter how much I loved a sport or activity, truly excelling and being the best I could be was not going to be all fun and games. Building up my upper body became a necessary goal. It wasn't one I would have chosen, but it was one I couldn't succeed without. If I wanted it badly enough to do what it was going to take to make it happen, then I guess I was going to become a regular at the gym.

As soon as I was able, I started going to the gym and lifting every day. Everything happens for a reason? Maybe, but for the life of me I didn't know what the reason for this could have been. Not yet.

###

WHEN I STARTED college, my only goal was to graduate with a degree in theater. But as it turned out, the time and effort I wanted to devote to skydiving left very little for acting. Both require no less than a 100 percent commitment to excel in, and I didn't want to put 50 percent into either.

Skydiving won out. I continued with school but no longer had a specific degree I was aiming for. Without a clear goal, it wasn't long before I wasn't particularly concerned about what my grade point average was either. For that matter, I didn't really care if I learned anything or not. I just wanted to do my time and finish my four years of college with a diploma of some sort.

At Ohio State University there were 55,000 students of which 30,000 were women and 10,000 were freshmen that had just been let out of the house for the first time. High Street was the very appropriately named main drag on campus, and the drinking age was eighteen. As if all of that wasn't enough of a distraction for me, on every sunny day (and many rainy ones) I drove an hour to go skydiving.

I convinced myself that my goal of graduating would require little effort and no real sacrifices from me. During my first three years of college I usually took twelve credit hours of classes per quarter, the minimum required to be considered full time. I went to class only as often as I absolutely needed to in order to get by. When I did show up at class, I was frequently late and would try unsuccessfully to sneak in to the backseats unnoticed.

In preparation for tests I crammed weeks' worth of lessons into one night. I dreaded showing up for class on test day. The professors and other students could see how terrified and unprepared I was. They looked at me with an expression of disgust, knowing I was getting just what I deserved. At best I remembered enough of the material to squeeze by with a passing grade and forgot it all as I left the room.

At the end of my junior year, I was called in for a meeting with a dean. She asked me what I'd been doing for the last three years and went on to inform me that I wouldn't be able to graduate after my senior year. At the pace I was going, it would take me at least another two years to collect enough credits in any one particular subject to actually earn a diploma. "Don't worry," she said sarcastically, "if you continue on this road, after six years of going to school full time you'll be able to proudly complete college, with an impressive 2.2 grade point average."

Damn, she was good. In one sentence she made me realize that I had just wasted three years of my life. It may have been fun, it had its moments, but that was not a path I wanted to continue down. I walked out of the meeting and immediately committed myself to graduating within one year, with a degree in Aviation and a 4.0 grade point average in my remaining classes.

This was an ambitious goal. I set the bar much higher than I ever had before, but I wanted it badly and I thought I could do it.

To accomplish my goal, I would have to take twenty or more credit hours every quarter. This was twice as many classes as I had ever taken before and more than the school would generally allow. At our next meeting, the dean laughed at me. She had meant to motivate me in our previous meeting, but this was reaching far beyond what she assumed I was capable of. I begged her to let me try. She grudgingly gave in.

Reaching this goal would require a much greater commitment to school and learning than I had ever made before. For starters, I would have to sacrifice many of the things I enjoyed, beginning with skydiving, followed closely behind by partying, barhopping, and socializing. I had learned from being so disciplined about going to the gym that sometimes you just have to do what you have to do and hoped I'd be able to work out my brain as hard as I did my chest.

I may not have been as bright as I thought, but I wasn't stupid either. I knew I would have to do this on my own, but that didn't mean I couldn't ask for help.

I told my professors what I was trying to accomplish and asked them for help and advice. I participated in class by asking questions, offering answers, and involving myself in all discussions and debates. It was apparent to my professors that this was a new me. They seemed almost inspired by my newfound drive and were truly excited to help in any way they could. My goal became their goal. They were teachers after all. My success became their success. By helping me to reach my goal, in some way they would also be reaching theirs.

Through my active participation in class, I met other students that were as motivated as I was. We started to schedule a few hours a week for studying together. Sharing, discussing, and explaining concepts and principles from our classes helped the learning process tremendously. Reading it on my own gave me the general idea. Explaining it to another person proved to me that I actually knew the material and made clear the parts I still didn't understand that required more studying.

There are only twenty-four hours in a day. If I was going to take this many classes and get As in all of them, I would have to make optimal use of my time. I was always the first person to class and sat in the front row. Immediately after class, I would go to the library and review the lessons we covered in an effort to let them sink into my head before running to the next class to absorb more new information. I would do additional work late into the evening and get up early in the morning for more.

After having studied until two o'clock in the morning and waking up again at six to get back to the books, I felt better than when I stayed out late with my friends and then slept in too late to go to class. This was playing to win, and I could feel myself becoming a winner.

The classes I had to take my final year were the ones that I had been avoiding the first three years. I didn't love the subject matter, but I did like the challenge. I had committed to the goal and this is what I *needed* to do to reach it. Just like going to the gym, there was no getting out of it. I may not have enjoyed the studying per se, but I loved showing up for the test confident and ready. There was no practical purpose for taking some of the particular subjects. I would probably never use them again for the rest of my life. But I needed them to graduate. It had to be done, so I did it. Lesson learned.

I couldn't wait for test days. The professors could see how relaxed and confident I was. They looked at me with an expression of pride, knowing I was getting just what I deserved. I aced them all, every single class.

Getting a college degree would be considered a solo event. Initially I set the bar very low toward achieving this goal. I was uninspired, unmotivated, and committed nearly nothing toward this effort. I didn't ask anyone for help, and if I had, no one would have been inclined to give it to me. "No one wants to help someone who doesn't want to help himself"—a quote I had heard from Gramps many times.

When I raised the bar and truly aimed to be the best student I could possibly be, it was no longer a solo event. True, no one could do it for me. But my passion and commitment toward my goal was contagious. I asked for help, and the people who were capable of helping me wanted to. My solo event felt much like a team effort.

Never before had I aimed to achieve such an ambitious goal. I had always been an average student, and I had just spent the first three years of my college career in the lulls of mediocrity. I was satisfied with just having fun and getting by. I had taken pride in doing the least I could do, as long as I could get away with it. I had no idea of what I was truly capable of because I had never pushed myself to find out. I didn't realize what I was missing out on. Never again.

In the spring of 1984, after having attended school for four years and two extra quarters, I graduated from Ohio State University with a degree in Aviation and Atmospheric Sciences. Being so intensely committed and driven to achieving a goal like this was incredible.

I felt like I came to life in a way I never had before. *In the course of making the decision to aim for this high goal, planning how to accomplish it, doing the hard work, and finally watching it come to fruition, I became a winner.*

On the day of graduation, I made the decision that I would never accept mediocrity from myself again. After experiencing what it felt like to play to win, mediocrity—with all its good times and parties—didn't seem like much fun anymore. From here on I would try to push myself in whatever I did to be the best I could be, and often better than I thought I was capable of being. Having accomplished this goal, I knew that I could do anything I set my mind to.

During my senior year of college, my professors and classmates made a significant contribution to my success. Studying and discussing material with classmates enabled me to have a deeper understanding of the topics. Knowing I wasn't the only one on the battlefield provided moral support and encouragement. Through my professors' efforts, I learned the information in a shorter amount of time. The questions plaguing me and stalling my learning were answered without delay. Knowing that they cared about my progress, and that my success would be personally rewarding to them as teachers, brought a great deal of enjoyment and motivation to the entire process. It made me very happy that they were not only proud of me, but also proud of themselves when I did so well.

There is no doubt in my mind that the experience as a whole was far more rewarding because I had these individuals' support than it would have been had I been completely on my own. I would have reached my goal either way, but it would have taken me much longer and would not have been nearly as fulfilling if I had to do it alone. In every way, the experience and success was far better being part of a team.

After graduation, I got in the car and drove to the drop zone. I had already set my sights on winning the National and World Skydiving Championships. That I couldn't do alone and I didn't need to—my team was waiting for me.

12

Greene County Fusion, My First National Competition, and Learning How to Reproduce My Peak Performance

I WOULD GUESS THAT for many of us who fall in love with an activity, the degree to which we enjoy it is directly related to our continued improvement. If we reach a point where we stop getting better, we often begin to lose interest. To continue improving, we usually need a goal of some sort. Aiming for this goal usually involves striving to become better than we are, the best we can be, or sometimes even the best there is.

This isn't limited to big-league sports, it's human nature. Our son Landen has loved to play with Legos since he was five. He started off doing the smallest, most simple ones. Now he wants the biggest and most complicated. Or sometimes he'll choose to do a small one but try to do it faster than the last time. Doing a harder project or doing the same project faster are both examples of working toward becoming better. There is no award for it; nobody else cares. He just does it because he thinks it's more fun that way.

It was the same thing when Landen was first learning to ski. As soon as he was able to stand up all the way down the bunny hill, he wanted me to time him. As soon as he had a time he wanted to beat it. And Landen is no more competitive than my father.

Having a goal based on improving our skills at anything, even Legos, by definition makes us competitors. We are always competing with ourselves, sometimes against others. Sometimes solo, sometimes as part of a team. Whichever gives us the best opportunity to continue improving at what we love and, by doing so, having more fun and being more fulfilled.

Six months after my first jump, I was introduced to 4-way formation skydiving. I watched a film of the top teams in amazement. I knew I could fly like they did if I just had the chance to try and learn.

Finally, Woody and Fang asked me and my friend Mark Badillo to join their team and compete with them at the 1983 U.S. National Skydiving Championships. I didn't join the team thinking we could win. There was no chance of that. I joined the team because I knew the fastest way to improve was being on a 4-way team with people who were better than I was. For me, improving was the definition of fun. So I joined the team for the pure fun of it.

After months of preparation for the U.S. Nationals, our team, Greene County Fusion, had made about 150 practice jumps. During these jumps I had a chance to try flying moves I had never attempted before and the opportunity to get them wrong enough times that I could finally figure out how to get them right. My flying advanced more in those 150 jumps than in the previous 500. I couldn't wait to get to the nationals and show what we could do.

Fusion wasn't aiming to win. That year at the U.S. Nationals, there was a total of twenty-eight 4-way teams, seven of which were made up of the best skydivers in the country and expected to finish way ahead of everyone else. The only chance we had of winning was if all seven teams had a bad meet, a really bad meet.

The two top teams both trained in California. The Mirror Image 8-way team was the current world champion in that event (8-way has the same rules as 4-way but with eight people and a fifty-second time clock). The Visions 8-way team was their closest rival, and the

U.S. Army Golden Knights 8-way was not far behind. These three 8-way teams all split into six 4-way teams and made up the top of the pack in our event.

Then there was Tom Piras. Tom's 4-way team, Desert Heat, had won the U.S. Nationals is 1981. That same year, the world championships was being held in South Africa, and the United States was boycotting in protest of South Africa's apartheid system. Having missed the opportunity to compete for the world championships in 1981, Tom had set his sights on winning in 1983 and had put together a new team that he thought could do it. After his 1981 national victory, he and his friend Bob Hallet opened up a new skydiving center in Deland, Florida. Over the coming years, competitive skydiving and 4-way training in particular would start to take off. Deland would become the epicenter of it and Tom the single, undisputed leader.

These seven teams were in a league of their own. Our loose goal for the meet was to finish eighth—"the best of the rest," as they say. We didn't know what that would take or even what any of the rest of the teams were scoring, so we didn't have anything to really base this goal on. But it sounded like the highest we could possibly hope to finish, so why not?

###

WE WERE CLIMBING to altitude in the Cessna 182 for the first round of my first national championships and my heart was pounding. After a twenty-five minute ride, we finally reached ten thousand feet. The pilot told us we were two minutes away from exiting. I was getting nervous. Actually, I was so terrified I thought I was going to puke. The fear wasn't about safety. I was an experienced-enough skydiver to be far beyond worrying about that. The terror I felt was all performance anxiety. I was almost praying not to screw up. I didn't want to let Fang and Woody down. I didn't want to embarrass myself in front of my peers. With each second, I could feel my heart racing, my hands sweating. The little voice in my head came back. "S—t, Danny. What have you gotten yourself into this time?" The fear got bigger and the voice louder as we were getting closer to exiting, closer to decision time.

Suddenly, it came to me. I'd been here before, like déjà vu. The feelings I was experiencing, sitting in the plane, getting ready to exit for round one of the competition, felt *exactly the same* as standing offstage, preparing to walk into the scene during a play. I immediately applied what I had learned in acting to competitive skydiving. I reminded myself I could do it, that I had practiced the moves hundreds of times before and visualized them thousands. I told myself, "Just relax. Wait for the pilot's exit command and just climb out onto the step. You've practiced enough. It will be fine. Just climb out, just climb out." My heart was still pounding and my hands were sweating, but *I knew that all I had to do was trust that if I calmed down, relaxed, and just let it happen, I would perform to the top of my abilities.*

I calmly kept telling myself, "Just climb out, just climb out."

The exit command from the pilot was like my cue to go on stage. I took one more deep breath, climbed out the door, and let it happen. The instant we left the plane and the wind of free fall hit my face, the fear was gone, just as it was when I came out from behind the curtain and the stage lights hit my eyes. It was like some kind of magic spell came over me and I immediately started flying. It seemed to happen automatically, instinctively. Almost as if I was just along for the ride as I watched my body, mind, and soul do what they had practiced doing. If I started thinking too much about it, I got in their way, so I just let it happen. We rocked.

There could not be two activities more different than acting in a play and competing in formation skydiving. But the mental state necessary to reach my peak performance was the same in both. The process for preparing for that mental state was identical whether it was getting ready to walk onstage for a show or exiting a plane in competition. If the same process worked for acting and skydiving, it should work for anything.

After one year of training with the team, my flying had become faster, sharper, and more precise than I ever imagined was possible. I was flying like I had dreamed of as a five-year-old boy chasing birds in Hawaii. Facing my fears and being tested to perform at my best under the pressure of competition was incredible.

When the final results were posted, Fusion came in seventh place, beating one of the Mirror Image teams. Within the thirty-five-second working time, we had averaged just over eight points (formations) per jump. By definition, we were now one of the top teams.

It was at that moment that everything changed for me. If we could do that well our first year, it was possible to win the nationals. If we could win the nationals, it was possible to win the world meet. I could be a world champion.

I had never before thought much about "winning" anything or even made much of an attempt at winning anything because I didn't think there was anything I could actually win at. But the idea of being the best in the world at the sport I loved grabbed me like nothing ever had before. Now that I believed I could win, I wanted to.

13
Going into Business

COMING IN SEVENTH and beating one of the top teams at the 1983 nationals was better than we had ever hoped to do. Fusion had reached the level of the top teams after only 150 practice jumps, roughly half as many as our main competition had done. If we could make as many practice jumps as they did, we might be able to medal, even win. Our best chance was to keep our team together and to add more training days to our schedule. With the extra days and a little luck on the weather, we hoped to be able to come close to their speed and accuracy.

I had been working at the drop zone since 1981. In addition to being a jumpmaster and instructor, I had also become a licensed parachute rigger and a single-engine pilot. I could run the place by myself if I had to. I loved every aspect of the business and took great pride in the job I did there.

Jim West, the owner of the drop zone, asked me if I wanted to buy it. This seemed like the perfect plan both in terms of pursuing a career and for how best to approach my top priority, training to win the nationals. I would have my own business doing a job I loved, and I'd be able to arrange it so that I could do as many training jumps as the other members of Fusion would agree to, something that a "regular" job may not have allowed.

Decision made. At twenty-two, rather than using my new college degree to enter the normal workforce, I became a full-time professional skydiver and the owner of my own skydiving center.

Jim was the only person to ever have a franchise of drop zones. He had made several deals like this and had enjoyed quite a nice living from them. The way the contract read, the purchase of the business would be spread over a nine-year period of healthy monthly payments and would include three planes, one hundred old student parachute systems with round canopies, and parachute rigging tools. The monthly payments would also cover the monthly lease on the airport, clubhouse, and hangar, which Jim owned. At the end of the nine years, everything would be paid off and the business would be mine. The one part that wasn't in the contract, but that Jim had assured me of, was that at the end of the nine years, I would be able to continue to use the airport and buildings for a minimal rental fee.

My brother Cliff, now a law student at New York University, advised against it. He explained to me that as the contract read, after paying for nine years, Jim would have no obligation to continue providing me a place to operate. He could legally kick me off or charge me a fortune to stay. I would own the business, but it wouldn't be worth much without an airport to run it from, and airports aren't easy to come by. My father agreed with him.

Jim wasn't willing to make any changes to the document but promised me that between friends like us, a contract was merely a technicality. Of course he would let me operate the business there and would never do what Cliff said the contract allowed him to.

Having had the good fortune of being raised in a family where unconditional love and trust were a given, I had become a very trusting, if not naïve, person in my twenty-two years. Jim had taken me under his wing when I only had fifty jumps. He had taught me to fly and given me the opportunity to excel at the sport I loved. I trusted him like he was family.

At this point in my life, I was beginning to buy into the idea that there are few things in the world that are not entirely under our control, and that we must have faith and trust that the world will allow these things to work out for us as they should. Signing an ill-written contract would prove not to be one of those things.

But for now I had it all. I was running the business, jumping with Fusion, and having a ball. My drop zone was at the forefront of developing new skydiving instructional programs. We were one of the first centers in the United States to retire the round military-type parachutes and replace them with state-of-the-art systems using rectangular, winglike "ram-air" canopies for our students. (That made the purchase of the student equipment from Jim a complete waste of money, but I felt allowing new jumpers to use that old crap would be negligent when this new and far, far better equipment was available.)

We started taking first-time students on tandem jumps or accelerated free fall (AFF) instead of static line. On tandem jumps, the students are directly attached to their instructor under a parachute system made for two. AFF students would wear their own parachute system but jump with two instructors holding onto them until they deployed their parachutes. Then a third instructor guides them from the ground, communicating by radio.

All of these contributed to completely revolutionizing the sport. Previously, most new skydivers were athletic men between eighteen and thirty years old who were strong enough to carry the heavy equipment and withstand the punishing landings. The new lighter-weight gear and soft landings opened up the sport to men and women of all ages, sizes, and levels of physical conditioning. With static-line training, one instructor would teach a class of twenty students. With tandem and AFF, there are one or two instructors per student. This more nurturing, personalized attention changed the mood of skydiving training completely. And we drew the staff that had the personalities for it.

David Layne was an old friend of Jim West's from England who had moved to Xenia a few years earlier with his wife Rita, eight-year-old son James, and six-year-old daughter Caroline. The Layne family had been a presence on the drop zone for a few years before I actually took it over. The Greene County Sport Parachute Club was a family business with a club atmosphere back then, and like other members of the "club," the Laynes contributed to keeping the place moving.

I had become very close with Rita, David, and their kids. Once I started running it, the drop zone became the Greene County "Skydiving" Center. In many ways, it was still a family business, and the Laynes were my family. David became the chief instructor, Rita ran the office, Caroline helped Rita every way she could. And James, well, James went crazy about skydiving.

The school bus dropped James at the drop zone every day, and he would be there until sunset or past. For all practical purposes, the drop zone became his second (or maybe his first) home. In addition to his drop zone "chores" of cleaning planes, mowing grass, washing bathrooms, and running the snack bar, he sat in and observed the first-jump courses, listened to the jumpmasters as they talked on the radio to the students, and even learned to pack parachutes. When Fusion was jumping, James would watch us prepare for the jumps and listen to us review them after landing. By the time he was thirteen, he knew everything about everything and could easily have taught the class if we let him. He wanted to jump so badly.

James became an expert in skydiving training, free-fall skill, and canopy flying long before he ever made a jump. There weren't official skydiving "coaches" during that time. Anyone who knew anything willingly offered help to anyone who knew less than them. James would see student and novice skydivers who were struggling, and in the casual, comforting tone of a lovable thirteen-year-old, he would offer tips and advice to them. Because James was so genuinely caring and nonthreatening, they would often benefit more from James's input than from the expert skydivers and licensed instructors.

Working at the drop zone presented James the opportunity to learn many things more important than the technical aspects of skydiving. He learned a great work ethic. He learned how to get along with a wide variety of characters and to not let the little stuff get the better of him. He learned what to stand up for and what things were not worth fighting about.

According to the United States Parachute Association (USPA), no one under the age of eighteen could learn to jump. But occasionally exceptions were made for sixteen-year-olds who had parental permission. The only parents who would usually give their kids permission were also skydivers. Letting kids under sixteen learn to skydive was pretty much unheard of. The equipment was just too heavy, the first jumps too punishing, and the price of making mistakes too daunting. But the new tandem rigs and state-of-the-art AFF equipment changed that completely.

It took lots of convincing from me and begging from James, but we finally got an eager "thumbs up" from David and a hesitant "okay" from Rita. We took James on his first tandem jump when he was fourteen. Of the thousands of people I'd trained to skydive, James was the best.

As a general rule, kids become comfortable and take on new sports more quickly than adults do. This was especially true with sports like ice skating, skiing, skateboarding, gymnastics, and skydiving. Kids have several advantages. First, they are only doing it because they love it, not because they're trying to prove something to themselves or someone else. For the same reason, they couldn't care less about making mistakes and don't fear looking like a dork. Plus, they're fearless. Last, unless there is an obsessive coach or parent involved, they're not trying to win anything so they don't fear losing.

At fourteen, James had all of this going for him. But it wasn't just that. In the mideighties, there were no vertical wind tunnels to practice in and very little free-fall video being used. Without these tools, it was much more difficult to figure out the body mechanics of flying and how to coordinate our body movements to make us go, stop, turn, move forward, backward, sideways, up, and down. We did the best we could during the average forty seconds of free fall we had on a jump, but there was minimal data and feedback for us to work with. We didn't know how to teach skydivers the finer skills of "body flight" mechanics back then because we really didn't know what they were. Some people just "had it" and some didn't. James had it. Woody and

Fang thought I was the ultimate natural flyer because I could "just do it" without thinking. Well, that's at least what they thought until they saw James fly.

James was so smooth and effortless, so relaxed. Sometimes we'd watch what he would do with his body to make a certain move and it didn't make sense to us. In free fall, straightening your legs and pointing your toes should move you forward, while doing the opposite and bending your knees so your feet are on your butt should move you backward. But how we said it worked and what should happen in the air didn't matter to James. He seemed to have his own intuitive methods. I would try to copy his flying but couldn't even come close to the same results.

The only problem James had learning to fly was that he was so small. In addition to flying his own body, he also had to control the huge parachute rig on his back, a piece of equipment which was wider and longer than his torso and almost half his body weight. Even when we tightened down the rig as much as we could, it still slipped and slid all over him. In free fall, it would shift to one side and try to drag James across the sky. He would naturally do whatever was required with his body to compensate, hold himself still, or even drag the rig along and fly in the other direction if he wanted to. When we finally found a rig that fit him, it was like letting a bird loose from the chains that had held it down. His flying became even more phenomenal.

James blasted right through the AFF program. By the time he was sixteen, he had over a thousand jumps and had earned his instructor and jumpmaster ratings. He would fill in on the team anytime one of the members of Fusion wasn't around, and even at that level, he continued to amaze us in the air, effortlessly doing flying moves the rest of us had worked for hundreds of jumps to learn, and he did them faster than any of us. James and I would often speak about the day when I'd have him on my team. We'd win it all for sure.

None of James's success in skydiving ever went to his head. He was extremely confident but never arrogant. Even though in no time his flying ability had surpassed all of his childhood idols, he never thought that his expertise as a skydiver made him any better a person than anyone else. He only used his uncanny ability to help others enjoy the sport as much as he did and to become the best they could be at it.

James was the closest thing I'd ever had to a little brother. With the extra elements of having ten years' difference between us and an employer-employee factor built into the relationship. We were buddies, but I was also his boss. He was my student who in time became more like a partner. We spoke about things at work and at school, about jumpers and friends, about girls, and about becoming champions together someday.

I had always been the little brother, the youngest in school, and the new guy on the team. As the youngest sibling, I was completely carefree. I didn't have anyone to watch out for other than myself, and no one looking up to me that I had to be conscious of being a good (or bad) influence on. I had never been a role model or mentor of any kind, and I hadn't recognized how important it was to be aware of what I said and did and how I said and did it. I discovered that my best intentions could create the opposite results if I presented them with the wrong words or actions. I also realized how much I could learn from someone younger than me who was my student. I learned more about coaching and communicating through working and playing with James than I ever had in any other way.

I loved James like a brother and wanted everything for him that he dreamed of. Because we shared so many of the same dreams, I was in a position to have a direct effect on helping to make his dreams come true. It was an amazing feeling to realize how important I was in James's life. I always wanted to come through for him and never let him down.

The weather in Ohio forced us to nearly close the drop zone down in the winter months. With little or no work that time of year, I had found a drop zone near Tallahassee, Florida, that needed a plane. I flew one of my Cessna 182s there for them to use while things were slow at home.

The first time I was there I met a young jumper and pilot named Mikey Traad. What a character this guy was. He was going to the Florida State University in Tallahassee, premed, and by twenty had earned a commercial pilot license and had made over two hundred jumps. He had the loud, goofy, playful, youthful enthusiasm of a twelve-year-old but the abilities and brains of a person much older than he was.

Like James, Mikey was a natural at anything in the air. He was an excellent "seat of the pants" pilot and a skilled skydiver. I took an immediate liking to him and invited him to work at Greene County during the summer break when he was out of school. Mikey would always jump into the conversation when James and I would talk about putting our team together. He was nowhere near up to James's level, but he made it clear that he was going to be as good as the "kid" someday. My net was always wide open looking to catch future teammates, and I loved the idea of having these two on my team. With Mikey and James under my wing, I was quickly becoming the senior member of the group, quite different than the role I was accustomed to.

So picture this: You come out to the Greene County Skydiving Center to make your first skydive. You're nervous but you've always dreamt of making a jump and you've finally decided to go for it. You show up at the drop zone and are welcomed by the twenty-five-year-old owner who introduces you to your sixteen-year-old instructor. After the class, you climb into a little Cessna 182 with Mikey, your twenty-year-old pilot, at the controls. It may have appeared we were operating on youthful enthusiasm alone, but this young staff had more experience and talent than most who were twice our age. It didn't take long before even the oldest, most cautious students realized it. When they returned to continue their training, they often wanted to jump only with James and from a plane that Mikey was flying.

All of our jumpers and staff weren't this young. But this young core-staff team injected a level of excitement into the drop zone that helped it take off. The place was busy, we were having a great time, and we were on the cutting edge of a fantastic sport that was truly coming of age.

During the same time Fusion had continued to progress. Year by year we kept plugging away as we continued our climb to the top. At both the 1984 and 1985 national championships, we came in fifth. Tom Piras and his team from Deland, the Air Bears, won in 1985 and went on to become the world champions of 4-way that year.

Mark left Fusion after 1985, and we picked up Marilyn Kempson for the coming year. Our perseverance paid off. After the last round of the 1986 nationals, we were tied with one of the U.S. Army Golden Knight teams for second place. All the other teams watched as they sent two planes up with only our two teams on them for a jump off round to break the tie. We went head-to-head, point for point. We tied again and were called to do another jump-off round. Every jump was like the first round of a one-round meet. It all came down to those thirty-five seconds. I had never felt the competition intensity at this level. I was scared and I loved it.

After two jump-offs, as the sun set on the final day of the championships, Greene County Fusion had averaged eleven points per jump and finished still tied for second place with the Golden Knights. We won our first medal, and Marilyn became the first woman ever to win a medal in 4-way at the U.S. Nationals. Finally, we had arrived.

After our 1986 finish, Fusion was sure that 1987 was going to be our year. The world championships were held every other year on the odd-numbered year. In order to become the U.S. National team and to represent the United States at the 1987 world meet, we first had to win the 1987 U.S. Nationals.

14

The Game Changer

THAT YEAR, THE world of competition skydiving changed dramatically. Two teams acquired unprecedented financial support and upped the ante.

The owner of TAG Heuer was a Saudi Arabian–French skydiver himself. Skydiving and competition had become a passion of his, and he decided to sponsor the French national team. This was a passion, not a business venture, and money was no object. He provided them with training tools that included their own airplane, two sets of parachute equipment for each person, professional parachute packers, a ground-to-air video cameraman, an air-to-air video cameraman, physical trainers, and unlimited training jumps. TAG purchased a house in Deland, Florida, for the team to live in, covered all their expenses, and even paid them salaries. The French team set up their winter training camps and started jumping full-time and making in excess of one thousand training jumps a year.

TAG hired Tom Piras as their coach. This was the first real professional coaching job in the history of formation skydiving. I was shocked one day when Piras called me at the drop zone in Ohio and asked me to move to Florida to be his assistant coach, and possibly jump on a team together. Wow! I could be paid as a coach and be on a team with the best in the world. I had never imagined an opportunity like this could even exist, not to mention present itself to me out of the blue.

But I couldn't do it. As great an opportunity as this was, I couldn't just pack up and walk away from my business, and I certainly wasn't going to leave Fusion when we were finally within reach of our goal.

The Golden Knights increased their training plans to try and match the French.

At that time, the sport was still thought of as being too great a risk for commercial sponsorship, considering the minimal media coverage (actually none) it received.

We couldn't figure out a realistic approach to getting sponsorship, and without the possibility of any financial support, there was no way that we could match the training of the French and Golden Knights. 4-way training was their full-time employment; it was all they did. We had jobs, responsibilities, and very limited financial resources.

Within the constraints that we established for ourselves, Fusion trained harder than ever. We picked up an air-to-air video cameraman so that we could much more clearly review our training jumps and better evaluate new and old techniques. Fang built a ground-to-air video system to let us see exactly what the judges would see. We traveled to Florida for a one-week winter camp in Deland and trained side by side with the French team, trying to learn (steal) any ideas from them that we could.

When spring came and we were back to training in Ohio, the jumps started off at a whole new level. We were looking better than ever. In practice, our scores were skyrocketing and our confidence was soaring. We had stuck with it for five years and were now closer than we had ever been to reaching our goal.

But things sometimes change in an instant without any warning. A few months before the nationals, Woody injured his back and had to stop training. Though he managed to be ready to jump in time for the competition, the team never recovered. We placed fifth. The Golden Knights won the nationals in 4-way that year but were beaten by the new dominant French team at the world meet.

15

Wanting to Be the Best: Winning

BEFORE WOODY WAS injured, we had done over a 12-point average in practice. The Golden Knights won the nationals with 12.5, and the French the world meet with 13.4. We were so close I could taste it. Even with relatively minimal training and no outside financial support, we were within range of winning. I was pissed off and now wanted to win more than ever.

What was it going to take to make it happen? It occurred to me that when we had planned our training in the past years, we hadn't truly asked ourselves, "What is the most we can do, the biggest effort we can put in, that will give us the best chance of winning?" Subconsciously, but in reality, we had asked ourselves, "What is the least we can do that may position us to where there is some chance of winning?" Not a question that is likely to lead to victory, and I promised myself to ask the right questions from then on.

My dream, and Fusion's goal, was to win the National and World Skydiving Championships. How could we possibly match the training regimen of the Golden Knights and the French? No longer was jumping only on weekends going to be good enough. If we wanted to give ourselves the best chance, or even any chance of winning, it would require much more from us. What was it going to take?

We broke it down to the bare essentials.

- To make the number of practice jumps we would need, we would have to train full-time, which meant we'd need to move the team to a location with better weather year round.
- To move away and jump full-time, we'd have to leave our jobs.
- To come up with the necessary funds, we'd need to sell whatever worldly possessions we had and borrow the rest. Even then we'd barely be squeezing by financially.
- In order to save as much money for training as possible, we would have to minimize our expenses by living in our vans or camping on the drop zone.
- Even with this ambitious, bare-bones plan, we were coming up way short of matching our competitors' training conditions. We still wouldn't be able to afford a coach, second sets of parachute equipment, professional packers, ground-to-air video, physical trainers, and salaries. We would be the equivalent of a playground team going up against professionals.
- There was no financial reward for winning the nationals. Being 4-way champions wasn't likely to create any new employment opportunities for us. Win or lose, at the end of the year, we would be completely out of money.

All this effort and sacrifice purely for love of the sport. And quite a love affair it would have to be because there was no "purse" or monetary prize of any kind awarded to the winners for either the national or world championship.

Did we want it badly enough to do what it was going to take to make it happen? If we wanted any chance of winning the national and world championships, this was our only option, the only road to follow. There was certainly no guarantee we would win. But there was an absolute guarantee we wouldn't if we did any less.

The answer was *no*. Fusion was finished. The team had had a great run and shared an incredible few years together that none of us would ever forget or would trade for anything.

This was our collective dream, but the plan demanded more than my teammates were willing to sacrifice. They had put out a lot, but they didn't want it quite badly enough to go to this level of effort and commitment in pursuit of their goal.

We all have our limits and we need to know what they are. For each of us, there could come a time when we should step away, and it is important that we know when we have reached it, when it is better to put our attention toward a different dream with its own goals. They had reached theirs. I hadn't yet. But with the rest of the team stepping out of the game, the situation changed for me.

Now I was on my own. I had a dream that required a team, but no teammates, a plan that required funding, but no money, a sport that required sunshine, but it was raining. After my senior year at OSU, I thought I was ready for any challenge. But at that time I had everything I needed. It was just a matter of buckling down and getting the work done. Now I had nothing.

16
Dreaming Big

I WAS NOW INTO my fifth year running the drop zone. Soon after I had signed the contract and taken over the business, Jim and my relationship had started to steadily decline. It was becoming apparent to me that Cliff had been right. I was certain that after completing nine years of payments for the purchase of the Greene County Skydiving Center, I would be without an airport to operate from. I asked Jim to revise our contract to guarantee that this wouldn't happen, but, as I expected, he declined. I was going to have to move on.

I started negotiations to end our agreement. It was decided that after making every monthly payment for four and a half years—half the contract—I would only be able to keep one of the Cessna 182s and seven of the new state-of-the-art student parachute systems I had purchased. According to Cliff, the way the contract was written I was lucky to get that.

I love every aspect of skydiving and had enjoyed the challenge of running my own business. This deal, as raw as it was, still left me with the minimal essential equipment necessary to open up another skydiving school. But I wanted to fly faster and to be the fastest. I wanted to win the world championships, and I knew I could do it if only I could figure out how to create the right opportunity for myself.

I spoke with friends and family about this. Almost all of them thought the idea of finding a new team and training full-time was ridiculous. I was being a crazy dreamer.

"Be realistic, Dan. You will have no chance of winning this year. The top teams are starting at a level you've only dreamed of, and they are already training right now."

"You don't have a team and you don't know where to find a team. You'd be starting from scratch."

"You won the silver medal, that's good enough."

"Open a new drop zone or use your degree to get a normal job."

But not everyone agreed with them. Gramps knew I loved skydiving and competing more than anything else I'd ever done in my life. It was largely because of him and his parents that I had the privilege of having a selfish dream like excelling in a sport at all. In their lives, most of their dreams were limited to survival, providing shelter, feeding a family, and getting by. The idea of pursuing something for no reason other than that I loved it so much and couldn't imagine doing anything else was almost something he couldn't fathom.

He wasn't going to tell me what to do. It would have to be my decision. But he was certainly not going to be the one to hold me back, if anything, just the opposite. It was clear that he would have loved to have had dreams like this when he was my age. That wasn't possible. He had worked so hard so that all of his children and grandchildren would have these freedoms and opportunities. In some way I almost felt like I owed it to him to go after the dreams that he had given me the chance to have. For me to have the chance and the courage to go after my dream was the definition of his success. He wanted me to.

Following my dreams had served me well so far in my life, but never had I dreamed so big. Never was the plan so unclear or the outcome so distant and seemingly out of reach.

Then I remembered the promise I had made to myself, that I would be sure to ask the right questions. "What should I do?" didn't seem like the right question. Instead, I substituted it with what sounded like a better question: "What do I want to do more than anything else?"

If this was going to be the last year of my life, how would I want to spend it?

The answer was crystal clear. More than anything else, I wanted to have one good shot, one chance of winning.

A couple of years earlier, a good friend of mine had given me a copy of the book *Illusions*, by Richard Bach. We all find valuable input and wisdom from a variety of sources and people. The ideas in *Illusions* had always worked well for me.

You are never given a wish without also being given the power to make it true. You may have to work for it, however.

That was it, cut-and-dry and straight to the point. It was possible. I loaded up my van with all my worldly goods, two pairs of jeans, one pair of sweats, five T-shirts, three long-sleeved shirts, one shirt with a collar (just in case I needed to go formal sometime), tennis shoes, five pairs of socks, five pairs of underwear, two bathing suits, two towels, a shower bag, a jacket, forty-three cassette tapes, sunglasses, two twenty-five-pound dumbbells, and my parachute equipment.

I climbed into the driver's seat, closed the door, buckled my seatbelt, put the key in the ignition, started to turn it and . . . paused.

I knew this was it: decision time. If I started the van, there would be no turning back. If I drove away in pursuit of my dream, I need to be 150 percent committed to not letting any obstacle stop me. It was all or nothing. Did I have the courage to turn the key and follow my dream? The fun-loving, enthusiastic, Lover of Life Dan spoke to me again: "Turn the key, Dan, turn the key. Just turn it."

I was as scared, sitting safely in my parked van, and as worried about my future as I was on my first jump. But if I wanted a shot at my dream, this was the only possible course of action. Turning the key would be the first step to setting things in motion that could open up the possibility of becoming a world champion. Not turning the key and retreating would probably forever put this dream out of reach.

I turned the key, started the van, and headed south. The feeling I had at that moment was exactly the same as the moment of decision time when I let go of the plane on my first jump. I was flying.

The only thing I felt bad about was leaving James. He wanted to leave with me, but he was still in high school. I told him this didn't mean the end of our dream, that he should stay at Greene County and continue working for Jim. Someday, when he was old enough, we'd have the chance to put our team together and go for the gold.

17

A Goal with No Plan

I HAD A VISION and a goal, but no specific map of how to reach it. It was fall of 1988, and the 1989 national championships were only ten months away. If I was going to have to start a new team, and I was, the ideal situation would be to put together a team made up completely of top-level, world-class competitors. A team with this caliber of teammates would be at a high performance level right from the beginning. To get past the Golden Knights, we'd have to be.

The best skydiving teams in the United States were from Florida or California; those were the only places I would find talent and experience like this.

Tom Piras was single-handedly leading the sport and taking it to new levels. Over the last few years, he had developed new training tools, strategies, and techniques that had led the U.S. Air Bears and the French TAG team to consecutive 1985/1987 world championships. His success continued when, along with Jack Jefferies, Tom's new protégé, their team from Deland won the 1988 national championships. There were 4-way teams from around the world that were starting to train more seriously, and every serious team was training in Deland.

After being led to victory at the world championships by Tom, the French team chose to no longer work with him. As for Tom, he planned to beat the French, and his 1988 national champion team, the Deland Gang, was his first step toward building a team that could do it.

Back when Tom had called and asked me to move to Deland to be his assistant coach, Fusion was still going strong and the drop zone was busy. I chose to decline the offer, but had done so somewhat reluctantly. It was two years later, but seeing that he had called, I had a strong feeling an opportunity may still be there for me. And what a great opportunity it would be. I'd learn from the master, and being the new guy on the winning team is every competitor's dream.

There was one small little detail that I felt might be a problem. As much as I respected what Tom had accomplished and wanted to learn from him, I wasn't sure I could handle being on a team with him.

I had seen Tom at several training camps and competitions. Many times I had witnessed him insult and demean other people, other competitors, and even his teammates. I could have understood his behavior if he did this to try to get some kind of competitive advantage by "psyching" out his opponents, but most of the time it wasn't about that. He seemed to just enjoy it. He seemed to believe that his skydiving expertise and competitive success made him a better human being than anyone else. How would I survive with this guy?

It would only be a year. I could put up with anything for one year. This was clearly the fastest way to the top and, based on logic, probably the only way to win that year. Did I want to win badly enough to do what it was going to take? Yes or no? "Follow your gut, Dan. Follow your instincts."

I did, and the answer was *no*. The chance to win would be worth a lot of sacrifices, but not this one. I couldn't be a teammate with someone who could treat people the way I had seen Tom do. I couldn't be a partner, standing side by side, sharing my dreams, and depending on someone whom I disrespected on such a core level. Everyone has to have a certain ethical and moral code they live by. This code draws a line that is their definition of basic human decency, a line that they won't cross under any circumstances. I might not have been a saint myself. But that was my line.

After having made this decision, a strange thing occurred to me. My goal was to win the national and world championships, or so I thought. Going to Deland would have been by far the best chance and quickest path of getting the gold medal. But I hardly considered it. I easily dismissed the closest thing there was to a guaranteed gold medal and instead chose to look for other uncertain possibilities that didn't yet exist. There must have been something more than just "winning" that I was after. I wondered what it might be.

18

When I Started Following My Gut

WE ALL GET gut feelings. As young children, these feelings determine most of our actions and choices. But over the course of growing up, we begin to ignore them. As adults, we often let these gut feelings, our instincts, go completely unnoticed.

When I drove away from Ohio, I didn't have a clear map. There was no counselor who could say, "Go to this school, get this degree, and it will provide this future for you." I didn't know anyone who had accomplished or even attempted what I was trying to achieve now, so I had no proven path to follow.

I followed my gut and turned west to head to the Perris Valley Skydiving Center in California, the skydiving mecca of the West Coast. Perris was the home of the Gumbies, another top team that Fusion had frequently gone head-to-head with at the national championships.

I had become good friends with them, and our two teams had even joined forces and medaled together in both the 8-way and the 10-way events at the nationals. I was hoping they shared my dream and would be chomping at the bit at the chance to train full-time and go for the gold like never before.

At first my plan was to take a few weeks and explore the United States on a great cross-country road trip. Thirty-six hours later, I was blasting through Arizona in the middle of the night, trying to get to Perris as quickly as I could. I really don't know what came over me; I just kept driving. I didn't want to stop. If I was going to find my new team and win the nationals ten months later, there wasn't time to stop.

None of the top teams were from Arizona, so it wasn't on my radar at all. Deep in the desert, between Tucson and Phoenix, I saw a sign for the town of Coolidge and remembered that Piras's first champion team, "Desert Heat," had come from a drop zone there.

I didn't know anyone from Coolidge, never thought of stopping there, and had no idea what I would find. But after driving all night, an incredible desert sunrise was just starting to brighten the horizon. A sight so beautiful, it deserved much more attention than I could give it in the rearview mirror. I broke right, got off at the exit ramp, and headed east toward Coolidge before I had time to think about why.

Listening to my gut like this became like a game. I didn't sit quietly waiting for it to speak to me. Doing so would have involved too much time for analysis, and that would defeat the whole idea. Instead, I'd just get a feeling and instinctively choose to act on it or not. It was like playing a game and I was a Jedi Knight who could sense what to do at any moment.

Following my instincts didn't exclude logic or reasoning, but it did add a higher value to what "felt" right. It required me to trust that in the pursuit of my dreams, opportunities would present themselves, and I needed to recognize them when they did.

I felt an impulsion—this was the place to be now. I'd been driving for a day and a half. If this place offered nothing else, I knew it would at least have a shower, and that was reason enough for the detour.

Coolidge is way off the beaten path. I was thirty miles off the freeway and deep, deep into the desert wilderness before I saw any signs of it. Finally, I arrived at the almost abandoned World War II training airport at about five thirty in the morning. Before I did anything else,

I found the shower they have available for jumpers who are camping on the drop zone. After getting cleaned up, I took a little walk around the drop zone to check it out. There were very few people up this early in the morning, so being a complete stranger, I drew some attention.

The drop zone owner, Larry Hill, was the first to welcome me. After a short introduction, he proceeded to tell me how he had just moved from a different location to open Skydive Arizona in Coolidge. He explained that competition 4-way teams were training more than they ever had before, and he had big ambitions to turn Skydive Arizona into the biggest training center in the world.

He was right. Competitive skydiving was just starting to take off around the world. The most motivated teams were few, but they were very motivated. Teams had started traveling away from their local drop zones to hold training camps at more well-equipped skydiving centers with better weather. The team "market" was showing signs of becoming big enough to make a significant factor in building business at the right drop zone.

He went on to say that Skydive Deland had been the only operation that was making the most of this opportunity, but not for long. The weather in Arizona was far better for team training than Florida, and Deland had little for facilities compared to the operation he was planning to build. The only thing Deland had going for it that Larry didn't was Tom Piras. Larry knew that if he wanted Skydive Arizona to become the next big training center, it would require having a top team, with a top-name player, to draw in the other teams.

But the top names were very few and *all* either from the pro teams or Deland. He had it all figured out, but that one missing piece of his puzzle was going to be hard to find.

While we were talking, we had been joined by local hotshot Jim Hotze (that is actually his real name). Jim introduced himself and asked if I'd like to make a jump. Of course the answer was yes. Then he asked if I had ever done any 4-way; another resounding yes. He went on to tell me about his 4-way ambitions. He had been trying to put a team together for the nationals championships for a few years but still hadn't ever made it to the meet. He currently had one other guy and was looking for two more.

This wasn't possible. I couldn't believe it. Larry and Jim had no idea who I was or what I was doing in Arizona. We were the early-morning boys talking over coffee before the drop zone woke up and came to life. I had just showed up, been out of the shower for less than thirty minutes, and had hardly said a word. I didn't have to. It was almost as if I had called ahead looking for anyone who was seriously interested in competitive 4-way and they were waiting in the middle of the desert for me when I arrived.

It wouldn't have been any better had I planned it myself. They were just as shocked when I told them who I was and what my goal was. They had both heard of Fusion and remembered hearing about our jump-off, medal-winning performance at the '86 nationals. I was the closest thing to a 4-way champion Coolidge had seen in years. Larry and Jim were looking for me as much as I was looking for them.

Unfortunately, Jim's teammate, Jeff Root, wasn't going to be at the drop zone that day so we made a plan to jump together two weeks later. In the meantime, we would try to find a fourth person to fill the potential team roster.

Talk about crossing paths. All three of us had basically woken up that morning, thrown our nets out at the first sight of possible teammates, and caught each other hook, line, and sinker. But it didn't stop there.

When I left Ohio, Mikey had moved back to Tallahassee to finish school. I sent my one remaining Cessna 182 with him so the drop zone there could use it on the weekends. I called him to see how things were going. He told me he was leaving Florida and had decided to finish school in Tucson. Mikey was moving to Arizona! I asked him if he could fly out the coming weekend to jump with us and possibly join our team. He was all over it, had already planned a trip, and could just as easily make it for then.

> Every person, all the events of your life are there because you have drawn them there. What you choose to do with them is up to you.
>
> —Illusions

I didn't know what we would end up choosing to do with each other, but I was certain that we must have all been drawn there that morning.

I had only been in Coolidge for a few hours and already the possibility of a new team was forming. It would be an inexperienced team that would have a huge way to progress before even being close to where our competition was starting from. Not ideal at all, but after the series of bizarre coincidences that morning, this was definitely a possibility that had to be considered. The most promising options were still in California.

I arrived in Skydive Perris and immediately met up with the Gumbies. I had called ahead to tell them I was coming. They actually had five team members at that point. I made six. We rotated different people in and out and made several jumps that day. Each and every jump was fantastic. Unquestionably some of the best 4-way skydives any of us had ever done.

This was exactly what I was hoping for. If I could put a team together with these guys, we would start from a level even higher than where Fusion had finished and with no limit to where we could go from there. I told the Gumbies about my big plans. I wanted to pick the best four out of the six of us (hoped I'd be one of them) and train full-time until the nationals. With a team of this caliber and an intense training plan, I knew we'd definitely have a good shot at winning.

They were very tempted. They wanted to be competitive, to be contenders, and good enough to possibly win. But like my teammates from Fusion, they weren't willing to leave their jobs and go full-time. Training weekends was the most they were willing to put toward that effort.

Would that be enough with a team of this caliber? Could we do it with only half as much training? It was possible. But doing the least we could do to have a chance at winning wasn't enough for me. Not anymore. I was in 150 percent. I wanted to be sure when we arrived at the nationals, there was nothing left. Sure that we had put it all out there, put it all on the line. And I wanted to do it with teammates that wanted it as badly as I did. I headed back to Coolidge.

Mikey, Hotze, Jeff, and I did about eight 4-way jumps that first day. Hotze and Jeff were decent flyers, had lots of natural ability, and certainly showed potential. But it was quite obvious that they had never done any serious team training. The jumps were mediocre, a far reach from the skydives I had just made with the Gumbies. Not even up to the level I had reached with Fusion five years earlier. We would have a ton of work to do before we'd even be close to medal contention. Did they have any idea of what it was going to take? Did they want it badly enough?

They all told me how this was their dream, how they'd wanted to do this for years and would do anything they had to do to make it happen. But would they put their money where their mouths were?

If they really wanted it that bad, all they had to do was answer one simple yes-or-no question. The same question I asked of Fusion and then the Gumbies.

"Will you quit your jobs, move to the drop zone, live in your vans, jump every day, and come up with the $20,000 it is going to cost you over the next ten months to pay for training, eating, and competition?"

There was no hesitation from any of them. The answer was "yes."

19
The Coolidge Fource

WE NAMED OUR new 4-way team *the Fource.* (It was ten years later but I still loved *Star Wars*). We started off at about 6-point average. At the 1987 world championships, the French had won with a 13.4 average. We figured that we'd have to average at least thirteen to win the nationals, more for the world meet. I could see the potential the team had and the effort my teammates were willing to put into it. I knew what I had gotten into, but it was still painful to be skydiving at a level so much lower than what I had done with my previous team. We had a long way to go, so we got right to work.

I managed to acquire videos of the top-three teams. They had different styles and techniques, but each provided valuable tools that we could put to use. We developed our own training plan utilizing pieces of what we saw as well as things I had learned with Fusion.

Within a few weeks, our vans were parked between the saguaro cactuses in the rugged desert terrain surrounding the airport. Mark Price had joined the Fource as our video flyer. We were on the first lift every day, which was usually close to sunrise, and on the last one, which was usually around sunset. We each had only one parachute and were packing for ourselves. We were jumping from Cessna 182s, a 1950s Twin Beech, or a 1940s DC-3. Both the Twin Beech and the DC-3 were old radial engine airplanes that spit out oil like a can of spray paint shoots paint. Our jumpsuits were covered with it. They both sounded like old pickup trucks backfiring on the first start every morning. With these slow planes and without the help of professional packers, it usually took all day to get eight jumps in.

But we were off and running.

20
Finding Work

THERE WAS A large Japanese group of about forty people jumping in Coolidge that winter and amongst them the Japanese National 4-way team, one of the few national teams that wasn't training in Deland. They saw the progress the Fource was making and asked me if I'd coach them. Since I hadn't ever actually coached a team, and communication between us was difficult, I wasn't sure exactly what it was they were asking of me.

I told the Japanese team that I'd be glad to "help them out." They said, "Not help out, coach?"

I didn't understand the difference between "helping them out" and "coaching them," so I asked them to explain exactly what they meant. They wanted to train like the Fource was training. They would be jumping for two weeks and wanted me to plan out all the specifics of their camp. To tell them which type of jumps they should work on and when, and to help them prepare and review each jump as they went. The Fource was training side by side with them from the same planes, so it should be relatively easy to work with them while we were also training. I told them I'd be glad to "coach" them.

They then asked what I would charge them for this service. That question caught me totally off guard. They were willing to pay me for this? I was planning to do it just because I was a nice guy. But I was going broke fast and definitely needed the money. At that point, Piras and very few others were the only people that had ever been paid to coach. I didn't know what to say or what coaching services were worth. I asked them, "What would you pay me for this?" They asked if $100 a day would be okay. $100 a day! I could eat for a month on $100. I took the job!

That Japanese team had a great camp. An Austrian team came in to train, saw the Japanese team's progress, and asked me to coach them.

A little while later, during a short break in the Fource's training, the University of Colorado team hired me as a coach. Troy Widgery was the captain of the team. Everyone thought he looked like Tom Cruise in *Risky Business.* While busy with his studies, he also found time to start his own business called Sky Systems, making and selling Tube Stoes—fancy, durable, tubular rubber bands used when packing a parachute to stow the lines in and control their release during deployment.

After having the business open for less than a year, the entire skydiving industry was under the impression that Sky Systems was a huge operation with a big factory and international production. When I traveled to Colorado to coach his team, I discovered the truth. The entire business basically amounted to Troy, a big supply of superglue, a pair of scissors, and a special tool he designed to "stow" one end of the tube into the other. He asked me to keep it under wraps, afraid it would cut into sales if people knew the truth.

A born marketing strategist, he had personally put his team together and had taken great care in the team-selection process. His other three teammates were all beautiful, blonde, college coeds. I did my best to maintain a professional approach.

I imagine it was because I could see right through his cool façade, to the true Troy who was plenty cool enough on his own, that he and I immediately hit it off.

Meanwhile, the Fource was making huge strides. Other teams saw this, wanted to achieve the same results, and offered to pay me to show them how. I had hoped I would coach teams someday, but I had no idea the opportunities would come this soon. They just materialized without me actually planning anything. Apparently, I had sort of created a job for myself. The coaching jobs kept my gas tank and stomach full so I could spend everything else I had on team training.

The Fource was jumping nearly all day every day. Jump, land, pack, debrief, prep, jump, land, pack, debrief, prep, jump . . . We didn't miss a load. It quickly became apparent that my new teammates had lots of natural ability and unlimited potential. With talented rookie players like that, it is common to make huge gains right from the beginning as the team first finds out what they are capable of. We were seeing the results and we liked what we saw. The clock times of our moves were getting faster, and the scores were consistently going up. But it was only the beginning, and there was still so much more to do.

###

Soon after I had started jumping, Gramps had his first fight with cancer. Cancer had never met a tougher man with a stronger desire to live than my grandfather. Each time it returned, he beat it back, only to have it return again.

There came a day when he was rushed by ambulance to the hospital, but the doctors told him that nothing more could be done. They didn't think he was stable enough to go home and didn't know when he would be. The next day, I called their apartment to check in on my grandmother and was shocked when Gramps answered. He told me that he had enough of being in the hospital, so he just got up and left. He hadn't been able to walk in, but through his determination, he walked out. That's my gramps for you.

I flew out to New York the next day. The eighties had been a very rough decade for him, but this was the worst I'd ever seen him. I was shocked by how physically weak he was, so small and frail. As weak as his body was, his mind was still sharp and his attitude and spirit as strong as ever. I was sitting in my grandparents' living room reading while he was napping when I heard his faint voice calling me. He needed help getting up to go to the bathroom. He was so weak I ended up having to pick him up and carry him in my arms.

The man who had carried me since birth, who had been there for me anytime I ever needed him, who in my eyes was the biggest, strongest, most powerful man on the planet, and I was carrying him to the john. It killed me to see him like this. Both of us laughed it off. Even in this condition, he was still trying to heal with humor.

I stayed with him for about a week, and miraculously, little by little, day by day, he became stronger and even stood taller. It wasn't long before he and Grandma didn't need me to stay with them. Soon after that, he was basically back on his feet and was even traveling to visit his kids and grandkids. *He wanted to live and refused to lose.*

###

I RETURNED TO the Fource. We trained with the same intensity and effort after three months into it as we had the first week. But the initial pace of improvements a new, talented team sees when they start training doesn't last forever. We were quickly flying as a team up to the potential of the individuals. Once that happened, we leveled off. The move times and scores were up and down. We weren't advancing at the same rate as we had enjoyed in the initial months of training. Sometimes it felt like we weren't advancing at all. Mistakes became more obvious and improvements few. Self-doubt often took the place of confidence, and at times, frustration stepped in where youthful enthusiasm was dwindling. We kept at it, put our noses to the grindstone. We had to fight through the disenchantment of getting stuck at the plateau. Jump, land, pack, debrief, prep, jump, land, pack, debrief, prep, jump . . .

21
Discovering Arizona

AFTER MIKEY MOVED to Arizona, I wasn't comfortable leaving my Cessna in Florida anymore. It wasn't working enough anyway, so I went back to Tallahassee and flew it across the United States to Arizona. I was hoping Larry Hill would buy it, but he already owned one Cessna and had no reason to have a second one.

The only way I was going to be able to come up with the funds I needed for training was to sell the Cessna. All the money I had was in the plane. I wanted to sell the plane as quickly as I could but decided to take it for a flight all around Arizona while I still had the chance. I filled it with gas, loaded up my cooler, and took off before sunrise. I had just flown across the entire Southern United States, but no state I had flown over even came close to the awesome majesty of this place.

Flying over Southern Arizona looked like I was on the moon. It was flat and empty, with only a few scattered hills that broke the barren landscape. Passing Phoenix, it quickly became apparent that northern Arizona had a much different look to it.

Coming over the foothills of the central Arizona mountains, I had to climb higher and higher to maintain at least three thousand feet above the ground.

Farther ahead the mountains changed shape and turned a deep red color. I was approaching Sedona. I had heard about this ancient Indian holy ground but had never been there before. What an unearthly sight. The towering red rock mountains of Sedona reached up from the ground as if trying to touch the sky. I couldn't help myself. I had to bring the plane to a lower altitude so that I could fly around and alongside of them.

The entire area seemed to be bursting with life and energy from everything: the hills, trees, mountains, valleys, canyons, and sky. The Force must be strong here. I promised myself that I would come back in my van and spend some more time there.

There was more of the awesome beauty of Arizona to enjoy as I left Sedona and flew up through Oak Creek Canyon towards Flagstaff. Continuing north, I could see the Grand Canyon out in front of me. If you ever wake up one day and feel a bit cocky and full of yourself, go fly a single-engine Cessna over the Grand Canyon alone. I have never felt as small and insignificant as I did in this tiny airplane surrounded by this enormous, beautiful canyon. As I reached the far east side of the canyon, I descended into the Painted Desert and flew at about ten feet off the ground and 130 mph for the next one hundred miles.

I pulled up as I was approaching the Superstition Mountains. Flying high above, I looked down into the canyons between the mountains and saw a series of lakes I never knew about. From west to east were Canyon Lake, Apache Lake, and Roosevelt Lake. I saw an old abandoned runway that ran north to south, perpendicular to and ending almost right into Roosevelt Lake.

The runway had big Xs painted on the ends, which are meant to signal that it's closed. But it didn't look too bad, so I did a slow flyby just a few feet above and alongside of it to check it out. It was fine to land a Cessna on, so I put it down there and then walked to the lake for a little picnic and swim. Another beautiful place I promised myself I'd have to come back to.

I took off and climbed fast to get over the mountains. Once I cleared them, I was nearly able to coast all the way back to Coolidge and arrived right as the sun was setting.

It was an incredible day. I saw things and places I had never seen before and discovered lands I couldn't wait to visit again. I had never seen anywhere as beautiful as the places I saw that day. I was so glad I had taken the flight, knowing this could be my last chance for a while because I really needed to find a buyer for the plane as quickly as possible.

At nearly the same time, Larry was landing in the Twin Beech after returning home from a skydiving event in Rocky Point, Mexico. We both parked our planes and walked across the ramp, talking about our day. We stopped dead in our tracks, staring dumbfounded as we were hit with a very unusual sight.

Larry's Cessna had crashed into the back of the wing of another Twin Beech that was parked on the ramp. Both planes were still sitting there as if they had just hit. The nose and propeller of the Cessna stuck halfway into the back of the wing of the Beech, and both planes were badly damaged.

One of the jumpers came running up to tell Larry what had happened. It turns out that the pilot of the Cessna and a World War II aviator had loaded up the plane with four jumpers and tried to start it. He couldn't get the propeller to turn, so as is commonly done, he got out of the plane to "pull it through" a few times.

One important thing to do before pulling the prop through is to be sure that the key is "off" and the throttle is pulled back. He forgot that part. When he pulled the prop through, the engine started. Fortunately, he was able to dive out of the way before the propeller ripped his head off.

Unfortunately, the plane went to full power and started rolling for takeoff. The jumpers pulled back on the control yoke, thinking that might slow it down, but it doesn't work that way. The plane was quickly accelerating but fortunately ran into the Twin Beech before it got up enough speed to take off.

As luck would have it, no one was hurt, and all involved would forever have one hell of a story which they were already at the campfire embellishing as we spoke. We could hear their celebration, and I couldn't help but see the humor in it. I did my best to mask my feelings, considering that the aircraft owner would probably not think it was as funny as I did.

Larry stayed amazingly cool, basically unruffled. While still looking at his crashed plane and without missing a beat, he said to me, "So, how much did you want for your Cessna?" I handed him the keys and told him I'd trade it for my jumps. The deal was done.

###

WITH ONLY A few months left before the nationals, the Fource had broken through the plateau and launched from there with the same accelerated pace of improvement we experienced early on. In May, we finally surpassed the highest level Fusion had ever achieved and were doing jumps faster and smoother than what I had done with the Gumbies. It felt great to be able to measure the results of our hard work with a time clock and a scoreboard.

22

1989 National Skydiving Championships

IN THE MIDDLE of May, the Fource had left Coolidge, escaping the 115 degree heat, and headed to Skydance Skydiving Center in Davis, California, where we could enjoy a cool, comfortable 99 during our final training push. At a competition there, a few weeks before the nationals, we averaged 13. Our young team had come of age. We were finally putting up the scores it was going to take to be competitive with the top teams. We were ready.

Seven hundred seventy-nine jumps, 882 peanut butter-and-jelly sandwiches, 222 nights in the van, and three trips to Apache Lake later, the Fource was driving out to Muskogee, Oklahoma, for the 1989 National Skydiving Championships.

The 1,782-mile road trip from Davis to Muskogee gave me the chance to look back at the decisions I'd made and the amazing year those choices led to. I had sold everything I owned, my soul included, and spent every cent toward this effort. We had made the necessary sacrifices and worked our butts off. The Fource would be a force to be reckoned with at our first nationals.

I had followed my dreams and trusted that the answers and opportunities I needed would present themselves, and they did. I felt like

I had recognized every good opportunity and made the most out of it. Considering the way everything had fallen perfectly into place, I had no doubt we would win. We had earned it and it was meant to be.

Right out the gate, it was a three-team race between the Fource, the army's Golden Knights, and Deland Heat and Air captained by world champion Irv Callahan with Jack Jefferies. Everyone at the meet expected Deland and the Knights to be the forerunners. But no one had any idea that our rookie team from the desert would be able to go head-to-head with the big boys.

It felt like we were trading punches in a boxing match. We won a round, the Knights won two, Deland took the next one.

Some of the jumps were as good as any we'd ever done. Even the ones that came up short of our best weren't too far off from it. Jump after jump, we were holding it together. It looked like it was going to go right down to the finish line.

Seven rounds into the ten-round meet, we were ahead of Deland and closing in on the army. As we were getting closer to the finish, the tension was mounting, but we were staying on it, slugging it out. In the eighth round, the jump was great, right on pace. Suddenly there was a hesitation: one member of our team "brain locked" and forgot what point it was and took the wrong grips on the formation. Another team member didn't see we had the wrong point, and he moved on to the next formation while the rest were still trying to correctly build the first one. Everything went to hell, and the confusion that followed cost us a lot of time and points. Deland went ahead. The two remaining rounds weren't enough to get the points back and change the standings.

The Fource finished in third place for the bronze medal with a 12.9 average, only a few points behind Deland. The army team was too strong for either of our teams. The Golden Knights took the gold.

The Golden Knights also won the 8-way event and were selected to represent the United States in both the 4-way and 8-way events at the world meet. Having tried and almost losing in both events at the 1987 world meet, they didn't want to spread themselves too thin and risk losing everything. They chose only to do the 8-way and handed over the U.S. 4-way team slot to Deland.

The Deland team represented the United States at the 1989 world meet, but they couldn't keep up with the dominant French team, who blew everyone away by scoring a 15.2 point average.

23
What's It All About?

THE LOSS WAS crushing for the Fource. In training, we had given it all we had. Everything had come together so perfectly, like magic. I really believed it was meant to be: it was my fate—our fate. I was so sure we would win. To lose it all by just a few points in the last two rounds. I couldn't believe it. It was over. We were out of money and out of time.

Skydivers had taken over the Muskogee airport that week. There were tents and trailers everywhere, and the closing festivities were coming to life all over the place. I was so looking forward to these post-meet parties, certain they would be the Fource's victory celebration.

After the final round, people congratulated me and said things like, "You guys were the best team here," and "I can't believe how far you came in only one year." "Amazing what you did with this team, Dan." But as I saw it, we just had our butts kicked, and I was a sore loser.

The more I thought about it, the more pissed off I got. What the hell was I thinking anyway? I should have opened up a new skydiving school or quit skydiving altogether, and gone back to school. My dream had come to a dead end.

I threw my gear in the van, jumped in the driver's seat, and turned the ignition key.

"Roll with It" by Steve Winwood instantly came on the radio.

It was perfect. I smiled and shook my head and laughed a bit at myself. When I had left Ohio, I had thought I was 150 percent focused on winning. Had I gone to Deland, I might have gotten on their team and would have been planning for the world meet right now. Looked like I had been right; that was by far the most likely route to winning the national championships and going to the world meet this year.

Instead I decided to go to Arizona and start a rookie team, which was a long shot at best. What was it I was after aside from that victory?

Maybe the real purpose was to truly prove to myself that if I confidently went after my dreams, everything would work out and come together as it should. Perhaps the real purpose was to give the world a chance to demonstrate to me that it deserved my confidence, faith, and trust in it.

I didn't know what was going to come next, but decided to calm down, roll with it, and be confident that the answers would come to me. When they did, the choice would be mine. It didn't take long. I quickly made a few decisions.

I decided that I liked having faith in the magic of the world, *and* I wanted to win the damn world meet too.

I decided I liked believing in the power of the force, *and* I wanted to fly faster than any team ever had.

I decided that I was capable of being the best, and I wanted to prove it in competition.

In my eyes there was nothing contradictory about these goals at all. They seemed to fit perfectly together to me.

24

The Fource 1990–1991

WHAT WAS IT going to take this time?

The next world meet wouldn't be until 1991. To be selected as the U.S. team we'd have to win the 1991 U.S. nationals. So taking another shot at winning the World Championships was going to require a two-year commitment this time. Since we didn't have enough money to pay for one year of training, paying for two years wasn't any worse.

As much as I was on a mission to win the world meet, Larry was on a mission to build the best skydiving training center in the world. He knew that even with the best weather, airplanes, and facilities, he still needed a winning team, and the Fource was his best bet.

Skydive Arizona was starting to become more well known in the industry. Teams from around the world recognized what we had done with the Fource, coming from nowhere and in less than a year becoming competitive with the top teams. Since most new teams were also starting from nowhere, many of them wanted to know how the Fource accomplished what we did. More and more often, I was getting requests from teams to coach them.

Despite the progress of both the drop zone and the team, neither could afford to pay for the costs of team training. But I had a feeling that somehow, between Larry and me, we could find a way to make it happen. That's what you do when you're on a mission.

I was right. Larry had big plans for building up his facilities, and he needed manpower to do it. He offered to let the Fource jump for free if when we weren't jumping, we would work as extra hands toward any job he needed doing, including construction, aircraft cleanup, and maintenance and basic janitorial services.

That first year, we had each found a way to come up with enough money to support ourselves, so when we finished training at the end of the day, we could retire to our vans, trailers, campfires, and relax. Days off had been ours to do with as we pleased. Now at the end of our training days and on our days off, we would be elbow-deep in drop zone projects that could range anywhere from yard work to airplane motors to cleaning toilets.

Did we want it badly enough to do what it was going to take?

Yup, the Fource was in, but with a few changes. We had to replace Jeff. When we were training in Skydance prior to the nationals, there was a local team training there called the Blade Runners. One of the team members was George Jicha. George was also from Ohio, seven years older than me, and in active duty in the military. We didn't get to spend that much time together during the weeks we were in Skydance, but I can usually tell a lot about people by how they act with their team, when they're training, and in competition. And from what I could tell about George, I wanted him on the Fource.

After the nationals, George had mentioned to me that if the Fource continued and I had an open slot on the team, he would be interested in filling it. I didn't see how a career army man, already at the rank of major, was going to be able to drop everything and join our little band of gypsies.

But a dose of army discipline would definitely do the Fource some good, so I called his bluff. By phone, I told him about the plan and what was going to be involved in making it happen. George entered inactive army reserves and moved to Coolidge. Wow, now that guy wants to win. Or he was just nuts.

Our cameraman, Mark Price, was also ready to move on. I had met Richard Stuart, an Australian skydiver who had also shown interest in being the cameraman on a full-time team. Team training could become pretty intense at times, and I was sure that Richard's easygoing attitude, quick wit, and wacky sense of humor would be a good addition as well. If nothing else, it would certainly add balance to what the "major" brought to the team. And since Richard already lived in his van he affectionately called "Henry," I knew he'd fit right in. One call and he was ready to go to.

It took us a few months before we had everything arranged and were back to training.

That year, Piras was back on the Deland team with Jack Jefferies. They were also aiming for the 1991 world meet, and they had collected the best flyers from the rosters of their past few years of teammates. The Golden Knights returned as strong as ever with mostly the same lineup. The final scoreboard at the end of the 1990 nationals was a repeat of 1989: Golden Knights number 1, Deland number 2, the Fource number 3. We still got the bronze medal, averaging 14.2 to the Golden Knights' 15.4.

We now had two years under our belts and had built a strong team. The year 1991 was going to be our winning year. We had also decided that, win or lose, it was also going to be our last year.

The world meet was scheduled for July in Czechoslovakia. This was earlier in the summer than was usually the case, so the United States Parachute Association planned to hold an early "selection meet" to pick the U.S. team in May.

We were ready. For a month leading up the meet, we were skydiving smoother, better, and faster than we ever had before. We arrived at the nationals with more confidence than any year past.

We came out swinging from the first round and outscored everyone. After five rounds we were 5 points ahead of Deland and 7 ahead of the Golden Knights. Jump by jump, we were knocking them out. We just had to stay steady and strong. This was it. Finally, at my eighth national championships, the gold medal was clearly within reach.

The way the rules were in 1991, if on a jump someone misses a grip or takes the wrong grip, the team would receive a three-point penalty (now it is only a one-point penalty).

Round six was off to a great start. We came out the door and kicked it right into gear, perfectly in synch. The points were going by fast. On each formation we picked up grips simultaneously and broke them together almost instantly. But, building one particular formation in the sequence, one of us picked up a grip on the right leg that was supposed to be on the left leg, three times. We lost nine points in one round and moved into third place.

We came back on fire in the following round and broke the world record of 22 with a 24-point jump. But it wasn't going to be enough. The "Deland Gang," with Tom and Jack, won the gold, the Golden Knights were second, and we finished in third for another bronze. (Man, I hate bronze.)

My run on the world meet gold medal had come to a dead end again, and short of even achieving the first step, winning the U.S. Nationals. Like Fusion, the Fource had run its course. It was time for its team members to move on.

The skydiving the Fource had done was fantastic. We may not have won the meets, but we had reached levels I had previously only dreamt of and were flying as well as any team in the country and nearly as fast as the French. We had reached close to a 17-point average—17!

The faster we became, the more fun it was. I still wanted to fly faster and to be the fastest. I wanted to win. But at the moment, I didn't know where to begin or whether I had the energy to start all over again. I didn't regret any of my decisions. It had all been worthwhile, and if there was anything I would have done differently, I didn't know what it was. I wished so much that we had won, but I was okay with it. Maybe my time to turn in a new direction had come.

25
The World of Competitive Skydiving Had Changed Forever

THE WORLD OF competition skydiving had changed dramatically over these three years. When I first started skydiving, competitors were recreational jumpers that put a little more into the sport than most other jumpers did. The French and the Golden Knights then broke away and showed what a team could do if they treated skydiving like a professional sport. Skydivers and competitors around the world watched them in awe, wishing they could fly like that.

But being sponsored as they were, these teams stood alone. At times this stirred up animosity from the recreational competitors who couldn't afford the intense full-time training as the sponsored teams and resented having to compete against them—amateurs against professionals, as they saw it. We would frequently hear them saying "Well, if someone gave me free jumps, I could be a world champion too." They obviously never had the courage to pursue their dreams. If they had, they would have known that no one is going to hand your dreams to you on a silver platter. No matter how much support you have, if you want to win or be the best you can be at anything, you're going to have to work for it.

The Deland teams weren't sponsored to the degree the French and Golden Knights were. But after being led by Tom through a successful series of national and world championships, they were also considered to be in a class by themselves.

But no team had ever tried to achieve what the Fource did our first year. Three of our four team members had never competed before, yet in ten months we were matching the scores of the best teams in the world. The response from teams across the globe was "If these guys can do it, so can we." They were inspired by our success and no longer had an excuse for not being competitive with the top teams. If they weren't competitive, it was because they didn't want it badly enough to do what it was going to take.

Teams around the world started training harder, hiring coaches, and spending lots of money doing it. Most teams would train at their home drop zone on weekends and also travel for one- or two-week training camps to the drop zone where their coach of choice was located.

Mostly because of the Fource's success, and despite our losses, I was in high demand, and coaching had developed into somewhat of a profession for me. I had teams coming to Arizona to train with me and had traveled as far as England to work with teams there. Most recently, the British National 4-Way team had asked me to be their coach at the world meet in Czechoslovakia.

Drop zones started recognizing how their local teams could motivate other jumpers. Skydiving centers with a big team presence would see their customers making eight to ten jumps a day instead of four or five.

Passion, drive, and enthusiasm are contagious. They're also good for business. Knowing that they could have a positive influence on the rest of their clientele, many drop zone owners became much more supportive of their home team.

Soon after the Fource's final meet. I was presented with an offer from Melanie and Pat Conatser, the sibling owners of the Perris Valley Skydiving Center in California. They had recently taken over the business from their parents. Skydive Perris was the biggest drop zone on the West Coast, if not the USA. It was the perfect facility with the ideal weather to accommodate intensive team training, but they had captured very little of the new competition team market because they didn't have a top team or reputable coach. The Gumbies were the biggest team training at Perris, and they had fallen behind the pack.

Tom Piras, Jack Jefferies, and I were the busiest coaches in the world. We drew the most teams, and therefore business, to whatever drop zone we were located. Tom and Jack had long been in Deland, and it didn't look like they'd be leaving anytime soon.

If Perris wanted to build up their piece of the competitive skydiving team market, Melanie and Pat knew I'd have my own following of teams that would come to Perris to train if I was there. They also realized that to make the most of this opportunity, Perris needed to have a top local team, ideally the winning team. They asked me to come to Perris to lead this effort and offered me a paid position on staff with this as my job description.

I couldn't even have imagined having an opportunity like this when I left Ohio. No job like this had ever existed, so I had never even imagined looking for one. *This opportunity came looking for me. It was my passionate pursuit of excellence, of victory, of being the best in the world that made me into a highly sought-after coach and created this opportunity.*

It was the *pursuit* of victory, not the victory itself. I still hadn't ever won the nationals or competed at the world meet. I hadn't yet achieved what I had worked so hard for. But look what I had gained and what had developed through my efforts. Other than my personal satisfaction, I don't know how it would have been any better if I had won the world meet. This was more than I had ever thought possible.

Maybe this really was the way the world works its magic when you dare to follow your dreams. But I still hadn't reached my goal, and there was no way I was going to quit now.

I said good-bye to Larry, for now. I was moving to California to start a new team in Perris.

26

Perris Airmoves

FROM BOTH THE business and competitive perspectives, it would have been ideal for me to recruit as many other top-ranked competitors as possible to join the new team. This would ensure that we started off at a very high level right from the beginning and would have brought other experienced coaches to Perris that should soon be attracting an even bigger piece of the team market there.

But that wasn't the deal. The deal was that Perris would cover the cost of the jumps and that I would get to pick the team. And I knew just who I wanted.

After eight years of competing, I had become quite particular about who I wanted to be on a team with. One thing I learned early on from Fang and Woody was to always have my net out looking for any possible future teammates. Even when the Fource was going strong, I was continually building a list of people I may want for my next team should I ever have one or possibly even to replace a current teammate if something unexpected happened and a team member had to step out. My net was wide open, so it didn't take too much to get on the list, much more difficult, however, to stay on it.

Up until now, my criteria were as follows:

1. Anyone who demonstrated the athletic potential to learn to fly at a champion level. (A lot of people made it past this.)
2. Anyone who loved the sport of 4-way enough that they would be willing to put in the hard work that would be necessary to excel, regardless of the level of financial support. (This shortened the list by quite a bit. There were far more people with potential than there were individuals who wanted it badly enough to put in the work necessary to reach their full potential.)
3. Anyone who loved 4-way so much they'd be crazy enough to quit their job, move to the drop zone, and sell their souls to do it. (That pretty much removed all the sane people.)
4. Anyone who had some way, any way, of coming up with the money. (The number of jumps and weeks of training had become so much and the investment so big that few people who passed 1, 2 and 3 were able to get by 4)
5. After meeting the first to fourth requirements, it would have been perfect, the best, if they also happened to be great friends of mine. But it was rarely possible. Most of my friends had more sense than I did, and as much as they may have loved skydiving, they didn't love it enough to put forth the insane commitment I was asking for. If they had joined the team without being equally committed, our friendship would probably have suffered for it. I had been fortunate enough to have had several teammates that, through the course of being on a team together, had become very close friends. But choosing my best friends as teammates right from the beginning was a luxury I hadn't often been afforded.

This time it was different. With the opportunity from Perris, I was able to remove number 4, which opened up the possibility for a few very close friends who wouldn't have been options otherwise.

On the very short list remaining were three people. And a team with them on it would be the start of my ultimate dream team. James was first on the list, and I called him the second the plan at Perris was set.

We had been talking about being on a team together since he was a kid. At first he was too young. Then, when he was finally of age, the financial investment was too great. Now he was twenty and the costs were covered. The chance we had always dreamt about was finally coming true. I knew he'd be on his way to California before we hung up the phone.

I was shocked when the line went silent. James was torn, didn't know what to do. He had been dreaming about this for so long without seeing any progress that he had stopped believing it could ever happen. This childhood dream had slowly faded away into a distant memory. Since he assumed it could never happen, he had given up on it. Instead he was doing what is expected out of a responsible young man and working toward his future.

James had already earned his pilot's license and his multiengine rating. He was thinking about starting school at the university. He swore that he still loved skydiving, the idea of being on a team together, and going for the gold. There was nothing else he'd rather do, nothing he could even imagine being anywhere close to as awesome of an experience and as much fun. I could tell he wanted to come. But he was scared to take a break from his studies and professional advancement, things he thought he "should" be doing.

I understood his dilemma but still couldn't believe it. "James, it's going to be less than two years. You can get right back on track after the world meet. You can go to college and get a degree anytime. But if we don't do this now, we may never have another opportunity like this again. When you're a professional pilot, sitting on your butt, looking out the window of a 747 with the plane on autopilot, you will be wishing you had done this when you had the chance."

He knew I was right. I asked him the question I had asked myself. "Forget what you should do. What do you want to do?" And on that note the decision was made.

After a long talk with Rita, and a promise to return to Ohio after the world meet, he packed up his pickup truck and headed to Perris Valley.

Troy and Richard didn't take as much convincing. The mere mention of it and they were on their way.

Troy's marketing strategy had worked; the skydiving community still believed that Sky Systems was a big operation with research and development programs that were discovering new and improved ways of producing essential skydiving equipment and accessories. In reality, the total inventory had increased. No longer were Tube Stoes all they had to offer. The extended product line included goggles with Tube Stoes around the edges. The total production line had also doubled. Troy now had twice as many employees as he did previously. That amounted to two, including Troy and a roommate from college. It wasn't a piece of cake, but it wasn't going to take too much for Troy to pack up the entire operation and move it to Perris Valley, where James would be there to replace the workforce.

I had clued Richard into my conversations with Melanie and Pat soon after we started talking. At the mere mention of the possibility, Richard acted like he knew with absolute certainty that we were moving to California. I told him I wasn't sure yet, I needed to think about it before I committed to another team. I needed to call James and Troy. He didn't buy it for a second. He laughed at the idea that I might even be considering not doing it. I guess he knew me better than I knew myself.

With James, Troy, and Richard, I had more than teammates with the potential to fly at a champion level who loved 4-way so much they were willing to sell their souls to do it. I had three guys I loved like brothers and couldn't wait to share my dreams with.

To fill the one remaining position, I was planning to hold tryouts. Tom Falzone had competed at the nationals the last two years, and his teams had finished in the middle of the pack. Tom was actually the first person to approach me about starting a team in Perris. It was Tom who had convinced Melanie and Pat that Perris needed a top team and a well-known coach to build up the team business. Tom had the drop zone's best interest in mind, but more than anything, he wanted to be on the team. I could definitely relate and had no problem with the way he was also trying to work the situation into an opportunity for himself.

But I hadn't jumped with Tom and didn't know him well enough to promise him a slot. The deal was that I would pick the team, and I wouldn't know who the best person would be until we completed the tryouts. Many people showed interest, but I narrowed the prospect down to six individuals. As it turned out, Tom rose to the occasion and outperformed all the others.

Perris Airmoves was up and running.

27
California Dreaming

THERE WAS ANOTHER reason that made this the perfect time for me to move to California. There was this girl . . .

During the summer months after the nationals, when the Fource took time off, I had been working at a skydiving school in the town of Hemet near Perris. Coolidge is way out in the desert, and as much as I enjoyed the wilderness feel, crystal clear skies, and starlit nights, it was nice to spend a few months with the busier pace and a few million more people that Southern California offered.

As was usually the case on Saturday mornings, I would teach the forty-five minute tandem jump course with the first-jump students of the day. Being in Southern California, it was not uncommon to have a few attractive young ladies in the class. Any man with a heartbeat would have taken notice of this, but especially one who lives most of the year in a van on the airport in Coolidge, Arizona.

There were two very pretty girls in the class one day, Kristi and Val. They were cousins and both about my age. I could tell immediately that Kristi was going to be a handful. She was nervous, which is to be expected. She was covering her nerves with a cute but sarcastic sense of humor. I was busy that morning running the whole school and thought she might be more of a challenge than I felt like dealing with that day, so I took Val on the jump and another instructor took Kristi.

After the jump, we were all hanging out and hearing about what a great time they had. The nerves now gone, Kristi was more relaxed as was I. She said she was planning on coming back and going through the AFF course, but we hear that from people all the time and often never saw them again. I thought about asking her out. I would be going back to Arizona soon, so if I was going to, I'd better do it right away. But I didn't, and away she went.

I kicked myself for letting her escape. What the hell? I have the confidence to walk out on stage in front of hundreds of people to perform in a play or exit an airplane and skydive at the top of my game during a competition, but I didn't have the guts to get the words "Kristi, do you have any plans next Friday?" to come out of my mouth?

The next Saturday, I was away from the drop zone and didn't arrive back until the afternoon. As I came into the school, I saw Kristi walking in, having just landed from her first AFF jump. A second chance! I love second chances and wasn't counting on getting a third. "Ask her out, Dan. Ask her out."

I tried to restrain my excitement as I very coolly walked over, welcomed her back, and asked how her jump went. Several hours later, we were still in the parking lot talking.

I attempted to steer the conversation to be more about her, but Kristi's newfound interest in skydiving kept bringing it back toward me.

I asked her where she lived and what she did. Kristi had an apartment is Orange County. She loved kids and art and had opened her own business in mall kiosks selling personalized children's toys, lunch boxes, book covers, and that sort of thing. She would customize each piece for the individual child by painting their name and a little picture on it. I was impressed that she was doing what she loved and making a living at it.

She asked me where I lived and what I did. I was afraid she wasn't going to be quite as impressed with my answer: "I live in my van in the desert. Don't really have a job. I work doing janitorial services, washing aircraft, lawn care, and building maintenance, but I don't get paid as such. I trade the work for free jumps. I need the jumps because I'm on this skydiving team and we're trying to win the national championships. It's a sport no one knows exists, and there is no award for winning, but I'm addicted and just can't quit. I've been at it for several years, but we keep losing."

Despite my fears, we hit it off right away. For two people that basically just met, we were strangely comfortable speaking with each other about anything, and the conversation easily expanded from your basic skydiving chitchat to more personal things. I even went as far as to give her a copy of *Illusions*, complete with a play-by-play, quote-by-quote presentation of why I liked it so much.

I didn't let her escape this time. Our date was set. I would meet her at the mall where she worked a few days later.

I hadn't been on real "date" for years. I wanted to be as cleaned up and presentable as possible, but by the time I was done working that day, it was already late. Usually I would shower at the gym in the morning, but there was no chance for that now. Instead I showered with a garden hose. It wasn't as bad as it sounds. I was able to completely clean up with shampoo, soap, and all. I just did it while standing in the grass with the hose in my hand. It was pretty hot that day and my van didn't have air-conditioning. To stay clean and not break too much of a sweat on the drive, I went shirtless and kept all the windows open.

I parked at the mall and got out of the van half-dressed with my hair going everywhere; I must have looked crazed. I straightened myself up standing in the parking lot, pouring water from a jug over my head, then combing my hair and brushing my teeth in the side-view mirror. Any passerby had to think, "This guy is a class act."

Fortunately for me, my life didn't require much of a wardrobe selection. I'd been saving the only shirt I owned with a collar for a special occasion, and it hadn't seen the light of day in a couple of years. I dug into the van and found it under the bed, permanently folded, with quite a layer of dust and desert sand on it. Wished I had thought about this before I was in the mall parking lot. I pulled out the shirt, shook it off as best I could, and headed into the mall.

Dinner was terrific. The level of comfort we felt earlier wasn't a fluke. We joked, laughed, and were able to speak as freely with each other as we would have an old friend. I even ended up telling her about my trip to come see her, which she found quite comical.

Kristi was back on the drop zone two days later to continue with her AFF jumps. I was the scheduled pilot that day, so I didn't get to make the jump with her. But I did get to watch her leave the plane and begin what looked like a perfect skydive before she had fallen too far away for me to see.

After the last load of the day, I landed, tied down the plane, and immediately went looking for her to see how the jump went. Her instructor told me that the jump went great except for one small item. She had broken her ankle on landing and was at the hospital.

I rushed to the hospital to see how she was doing, her knight in shining armor. It seemed her pride was more severely damaged than her leg. But I could tell it hurt. They put a cast on it and released her late that night.

Kristi's car had a stick shift so she was stuck in Hemet for a couple of days. Following in line with the "everything happens for a reason" philosophy, and being a guy, I tried to see this as an opportunity. I may be a skydiving bum, but that doesn't mean I'm not a gentleman.

Hemet isn't the greatest of towns, so I offered to let Kristi stay with me that night in my van. She ended up staying for two days before I took her back to Orange County.

During that time I was the kindest, most respectful, and honorable gentleman I have ever been in my life. I hoped Kristi was more impressed with this than my lifestyle. A week later, I was back in Arizona training with the Fource.

Kristi and I stayed in touch and over the next year made several trips back and forth to visit each other. On her last trip to Arizona, I picked her up at the airport and drove her directly to Apache Lake.

We had an incredible couple of days walking, hiking, swimming, boating, and sleeping under the most beautiful starlit sky. By the time we drove out of the Superstition Mountains, it was official. We were in love. The only thing separating us was the miles. My move to California would take care of that.

28
Let the Training Begin

JAMES ARRIVED FROM Ohio with everything he owned tied down in the back of his little old white pickup truck. Troy came in towing a trailer with his personal belongings and Sky Systems' equipment behind his Porsche. It was obvious from the first moment that these two were going to become quite a pair.

They moved in together with a few other young jumpers in a house about fifteen minutes from the DZ. The house, which came to be known as the "High Chaparral," had an old busted-up barn they set up as the Sky Systems factory and warehouse.

Richard had been living on the drop zone at Skydive Arizona (now located in the town of Eloy) with the rest of the Fource teammates. He moved into a trailer park, affectionately referred to as "the ghetto," right next to the Perris Airport. Tom had a house near by the drop zone, and I rented a room in a small house owned by one of the Gumbies, my friend Kenny Masters. To me it was like living in a mansion.

I was twenty-nine and in my prime as a skydiving athlete. Now, in my ninth year of competition, I was making a living doing a combination of *all* the things I loved most. If I had been asked to design my "perfect world" when I drove out of Ohio, this entire situation would have been exactly what I described.

When James and I were working and jumping together six years earlier, I had often thought about the man he would grow up to be. Now at twenty, I couldn't have been more proud of my little brother.

His out-of-this-world natural flying ability and the ease with which he learned new moves and skills was amazing, and at times even intimidating to Tom and Troy, both of whom were great flyers, just not as good as James. For that matter, there was no one on the drop zone as good as James, including me. The Southern California community is often looked upon as being fairly superficial, and for good reason. The Perris "Skygods" had taken great pride in being the top dogs and best jumpers on the world's largest drop zone. Their egos could handle it all right when I arrived in Perris as a top national competitor and raised the bar. But they didn't take too kindly to it when this farm boy from Ohio showed up and outshined them all.

Everything James learned by working at Greene County served him well now. As a man he still had the loose, fun-loving, comforting tone of that thirteen-year-old boy and came off as genuinely caring, non-threatening, and always respectful when he should be. Where other jumpers saw their skydiving skill as the source of their identity and self-worth, James knew it was just a game and not one of real significance other than being the most fun game ever.

He still knew how to get along with a wide variety of characters and to not let the little stuff get the better of him. And this was all little stuff. No matter how they tried not to, the Skygods couldn't help but like him. Their attitudes loosened up, and the atmosphere on the DZ soon became more fun than any place I had ever been a part of.

Most of the members of Perris Airmoves had at first been viewed as imports to Perris. But after only a few months, we had become the home boys and home team.

The deal was for Airmoves to train Monday through Friday and to work at Perris as instructors, jump organizers, and coaches on the weekends. I had teams coming from all around the world to train with me, and there were half a dozen new teams made up of local jumpers that had been put together, mostly inspired by Airmoves' contagious love and enthusiasm for the sport. It was coming together just as Pat and Mel had hoped.

Kristi had closed her business and decided to go back to school and complete her degree in education. She had a couple of hundred jumps by then and was working part-time in both the public school system and the office at the Skydive Perris Skydiving School. She moved out from Orange County to be closer to the drop zone and her other job (and me, I think).

Kristi and I enjoyed the time we spent together on the drop zone, but even more so when we were away from it and without all the distractions of my team and work. Kristi had her own life and goals she was focused on, so she wasn't standing around waiting for me. But that didn't stop me from calling her and trying to get her to fit any time she had into the few openings on my schedule. I suggested that if we had a place together, at least we'd get to see each other in the evenings when we were done with our day. However, Kristi was adamant that she would never move in with me unless we were married. And that wasn't something she was pushing all that hard for either. Not yet anyway.

Everyone could see the progress Airmoves was making. The team shared all we were learning with anyone that was interested. This was something rather shocking to other team jumpers who, up until then, had been quite secretive. All the other teams benefited directly from it. They could tell we were going to be serious contenders at the nationals, and they were cheering us on.

James brought another very rare quality to Airmoves. Something the entire team needed, especially me. Even as a very experienced and incredibly talented skydiver, James had managed to maintain that fearless, childlike enthusiasm. He didn't have anything he was trying to prove to himself or anyone else. Like a kid, he instinctively knew that in order for the team to get to be that good, we were going to have to make some big mistakes and sometimes look like dorks in the process. Allowing ourselves the leeway to do that would be a huge part of the fun we'd have.

I knew all this as well, and if you asked James, he'd probably tell you he learned it all from me. But after so many crushing losses at the nationals, I just wanted to win the damn meet. My intense focus on winning that gold medal was clouding my ability to see the complete path to getting us there. Jumping with James again reminded me of this, and right away, everything else became clear as day once again.

In the process of training with the Fource and coaching so many other teams, I had developed a model for a detailed, step-by-step training plan that worked as the foundation for any team beginning at any level. We had specific goals for every day and on each jump. The plan started with building a strong foundation and layering the details on top of it. The training was more efficient, more productive, and I had a much better picture of the ups and downs that would occur and how to use them to our advantage when they did.

Airmoves was improving at a rate I had never seen a team grow before. We began training in November at a 9-point average. By my thirtieth birthday in February, we had made two hundred training jumps. At a competition in Arizona, we met up with the Golden Knights and had the first chance to show our stuff. We averaged 14.5 to their 15. We were moving up fast and still had eight months to go before the nationals.

On March 1, James turned twenty-one. The team and a big entourage of friends went to Palm Springs to celebrate. The evening, which went well into the next morning, gave James and me a chance to and reminisce about when we met, his first jump, all the great times and experiences we shared over the years, and how it had all come together so perfectly now, a dream come true. Who would ever have known the day I left James behind in Ohio it could possibly have worked out like this? James told me he couldn't believe he had almost said no and thanked me for not letting him off too easily. It was the kind of evening that the phrase "I love you, man" gets said a few (dozen) times.

A new team, led by Jack Jefferies, was training in Deland. Different from the previous Deland teams, Jack's team like mine had three team members who hadn't competed at a high level before. One of them was quite well off and financed the entire project with Jack hired as a team captain and coach. The way I saw it, this time we were starting from an even playing field. It wasn't just Perris Airmoves against Deland Vertical Speed—it was me against Jack as team captain and coach.

Vertical Speed competed at a meet in Florida. We called Deland to find out what the particular sequences of formations were for the meet jumps and their scores. As soon as we knew, we went right up and did the same jumps so we could see where we stood against them. They averaged 14.7. We did a 15.2.

We were five months into our training. We started off at 9, and after six months and 350 practice jumps, we were averaging over 15. We had already gone head-to-head with some of the top teams in the country. It may be the most overused cliché in the world, but in every sense, we were truly "living the dream." But life can change in an instant, without any warning.

29

"Skydiving Plane Crashes in Perris"

AS RECALLED BY *Mary Pat Avery, a friend and skydiver from Perris Valley*:

It was 11:10 AM on a beautiful spring day, with the perfect temperature and a gentle breeze. Two planeloads of skydivers had already gone up. The plane landed and needed to refuel before the next load, on which Airmoves would be doing their second training jump of the day. It was a busy day for a weekday, with two 4-way teams training, as well as the Skyhawks, the *Canadian Forces Parachute Demonstration Team.* Add to that the various assortment of first-time jumpers, and people perhaps playing hooky from work just because, and it would be another full planeload, with twenty-two people. Like usual, Airmoves would board the plane last so that they could be first out once they reached an altitude of 12,500 feet AGL, above the ground. (Student jumpers, because they open higher than regular jumpers, always jump last out of the plane, and therefore are first in, closest to the pilot.)

The night before, earthquakes had rocked Southern California, which, at Perris Valley, resulted in a broken gas line that was used to pump fuel for the aircraft. No problem. They simply called in an outside vendor to truck in fuel.

THE CALIFORNIAN

25¢ THURSDAY APRIL 23, 1992

Skydiving plane crashes in Perris

Sixteen people died when this twin-engine DeHavilland DHC-6 Twin Otter crashed after taking off from Perris Valley Airport Wednesday.

JOHN GEORGE/The Californian

At least 16 die as craft falls on takeoff

■ TRAGEDY: *American, Dutch teams were practicing for upcoming competition*

JOHN HALL/The Californian

PERRIS — Sixteen people have died as a result of a Wednesday morning crash of a plane filled with skydivers at Perris Valley Airport.

Fifteen were pronounced dead at the scene and another died about three hours later at Riverside General Hospital. Six people, including at least two from Southwest County, survived the crash and remain hospitalized with injuries ranging from serious to critical.

The bodies, scattered on the ground around the split-open craft, were covered with white tarps as dozens of people — some with video cameras, binoculars and others carrying small children — tried to get an eyewitness view of the graphic

The plane taxied out and took off. About two hundred feet off the ground, a strange noise caused everyone on the ground to stop what they were doing and look up towards the end of the runway, just in time to see the plane disappearing behind a building. Many people, including the Skyhawks, dropped everything and sprinted for the site.

I was a weekend jumper at the time when a skydiving friend called me. He said in a chilling voice, "Turn on the TV." I did, and there was the plane I'd jumped out of so many times on the screen, sticking nose first into the ground with the tail straight up. The nose completely demolished, the wings ripped off. A television announcer was standing in front of the plane. "There were twenty-two people on board. We're not sure if there were any survivors."

It was national news. Rita Layne was sitting with friends in Ohio trying to get information. Friends were on the phone trying to piece together information on who was on the plane, who made it, who didn't make it.

Seven survivors had been taken to the local hospitals. Miraculously, all of Airmoves survived. But Dan was in bad shape. Witnesses at the scene felt sure they were going to lose him. He was making a horrible wheezing sound, combative, struggling for breath. They somehow managed to stabilize him enough to get him to the rescue vehicle. He was rushed by helicopter to Loma Linda hospital, along with Troy and one of the members of the Dutch team TOMSCAT.

James, Tom, a local skydiving cameraman named Wayne Flemmington, and another member of Tomscat went to Riverside Hospital.

At Loma Linda Hospital, the doctors didn't know if Dan would make it. He had been crushed. He had a broken neck, cracked skull, collapsed lung, bruised intestines, and was barely hanging on. It was literally a minute-by-minute watch.

Two hours into this, another devastating blow came from Riverside Hospital. A skydiver announced the news.

At the scene, James Layne had appeared to be one of the least injured. But they didn't realize his aorta had burst. He had taken the thirty-minute ride to the hospital by ambulance and the paramedics were having increasing trouble stabilizing his blood pressure. Upon arrival, they rushed him into surgery where doctors worked on him frantically for two hours. But it was to no avail. We lost him; James was gone.

The waiting room was at first silent, absorbing this latest unthinkable news. And then the tears started streaming down faces. People hugging one another. Reeling from the blow. It was more than they could bear. Oh God, what if they lost Dan too? No no no . . .

Dan's mom arrived at the hospital the next day; his father Howard, brother Cliff, and sister Cara were close behind. Mimi Brodsky-Chenfeld was an amazing woman. Someone mentioned that she had lost her first husband at the same age Dan was now—thirty. And yet, this woman somehow had the presence of mind to ask Dan's friends how they were doing.

On the third day, the doctors were having trouble once again stabilizing Dan's blood pressure. They brought him back for exploratory surgery to try to figure out what was going on. Kristi was in tears talking to someone on a payphone in the waiting room, "They don't think Dan's going to make it," she sobbed.

Amazingly, Dan survived another night. And then one more. And then one more. He remained in critical condition, in a coma, and on life support, but at least he was alive, for the moment.

A memorial service was held at Perris Valley ten days after the crash. Hundreds of people gathered for a day of remembrance. Skydivers and families of the deceased. Even the local fire station who had responded to the call sent trucks to honor the dead.

The father of the only woman who had been on the plane, Jackie Downs, twenty-seven, was there, and the local news did a piece on him making his first skydive. "My daughter loved going to the playground when she was a little girl. Now I'm going to go to her playground. This is what she loved, this is what she loved to do."

There were several "ash dives," skydives on which the ashes of the deceased are released in free fall. Several people spoke. Tom and Troy were honored as survivors who were present for this gathering. They looked lost and desolate. Troy and James had become close, close friends during this time. Other people were honored and singled out, and a woman sang a beautiful rendition of "Amazing Grace" for the gathered crowd.

Towards the end of the day, Melanie Conatser came to the microphone with a surprise announcement. Dan B. C. had been taken off life support and was breathing on his own for the first time. A wave of applause spread across the area. It was the first glimmer of life and hope in a day that had been all about loss and sadness. But Dan still remained in a coma.

Dan stayed in the coma day after day, week after week. Kristi held vigil by his bedside as the one-month-mark passed. We didn't know if he'd ever wake up or who he would be when and if he did.

Doctors had no idea what Dan's prognosis would be. Would he be a vegetable? Had the broken neck paralyzed him? How severe was his brain damage?

As much as everyone was praying and pulling for Dan to come through, equally worrisome was the thought, "What is he going to do when he finds out that James is dead? He's going to be devastated."

Finally, Dan woke up. Somehow he already knew.

###

"You need to go get control of the situation."

I woke up a different person in a different world than the one I remembered, and the memories of my old world were scattered at best. I remembered training with Airmoves, possibly because my talk with James had been a reminder of that. But I didn't recall that I had moved to California or what year it was. Being unconscious for so long, heavily medicated, weak, and totally fatigued made it difficult to keep things straight. I tried to concentrate, to focus, but couldn't hold my mind on one line of thought for very long. It was all so unbelievable, so confusing.

It hurt too much to lie down horizontally with the halo brace on my head so I would stay more upright in the hospital bed. This was less painful, but I rarely fully slept. With the combination of sheer exhaustion and hard-core narcotics, I would sometimes pass out, but there is a difference between being sedated and in true deep sleep. When I was unconscious enough to actually experience a moment of waking up, I sometimes forgot what had happened. I'd be out of breath with relief, sure that it must have all been a terrible dream. But the pain and physical restraints would quickly remind me that it was true even before I visually recognized where I was.

Waking up when the crash was already history and having no memory of it actually occurring made it very hard to believe. I know it drove Kristi crazy, but every day I would ask her to explain it to me again and again to be sure I had it straight. One at a time she would go down the list of the friends we had lost. I could never remember everyone, so each time she told me, it was like learning about someone for the first time all over again. The mention of each person's name was like a dagger in my chest. But only by hearing it all from the beginning could I be sure I understood the situation for what it truly was.

At my request, friends had brought to the hospital news articles and video of TV footage about the accident. There it was on the front page of several newspapers: the plane in pieces, dead bodies covered up by blankets and tarps, James and I lying in the front of the picture being worked on by paramedics. The evidence couldn't have been more conclusive. But without having any memory of it at all, it was still so hard to accept as reality.

My conversation with James was the one constant, clear memory I had. His words, his orders to me—"You need to go get control of the situation"—were always on my mind. But before I knew what that meant, I had to have a better understanding of what the situation was.

The one thing I did understand was that my focus needed to be on healing and recovering. But it was difficult to put my efforts toward this because I had trouble remembering what exactly was wrong with me. Every day when I saw the doctor, I would ask him to explain my condition to me again.

He would start at the top of my body and work down. He'd speak slowly to me, as if explaining a very complicated topic to a six-year-old. I wasn't so brain damaged that I couldn't tell that. I guess it might almost have been comical to anyone listening to nearly the same conversation day after day.

Doctor: "Hi Dan, how you doing today?"
Me: "I'm fabulous." What else was I going to say?
Doctor: "What did you do yesterday?"
What, was he kidding? I thought about it for a second, then realized I couldn't remember. "Shot hoops, you?"
Doctor: "Not much. Do you remember what year it is?"
This must be the standard test question. I could swear someone had told me, but I couldn't think of it.
Doctor: "It's 1992."
1992? No way. That means I'm, uh, wait a second—'62, '72, '82, '92—I'M THIRTY? Man, thirty sucks. It was way worse than I had ever imagined it was going to be.
Doctor: "You do understand that your neck is broken, right?"
With the cage on my head, that one was hard to forget. "Yeah, I got that part."
Doctor: "You also cracked your skull and had a very severe blow to your head. You are probably going to experience some memory loss, especially short-term memory. It can make things seem very confusing at times, but I expect it to start getting better before too long."

Memory loss? Did I have memory loss? I didn't know. I didn't remember if I'd forgotten anything. One thing did pop into my head though. I had to ask him, "My memory, will it last thirty-five seconds?"

He looked a bit confused, obviously wondering why in the world I would ask a question like that. But rather than opening up that can of worms, he instead offered an easy answer.
Doctor: "Thirty-five seconds? Well, sure, I guess it should be okay for thirty-five seconds."

Whew, that's good. I'll need at least thirty-five seconds worth of memory if I ever get to start doing 4-way again.
Doctor: "The primary reason that you are short of breath is because one of your lungs collapsed. That is why you have the chest tube."
And I thought I was just out of shape. I tried to figure out where the chest tube was, but there were so many tubes coming out of me I couldn't tell which one went where and I couldn't turn my head to see. I had to ask him. "Which lung collapsed?"
Doctor: "Your left one."
"Damn it. That was my good lung." Somehow I remembered that it was my right lung that had collapsed in college. Strange, the things I could or couldn't remember. No kind of consistency to them at all.
Doctor: "It is a very good thing you were in such good shape. You must have gone to the gym a lot (as if trying to remind me). If you hadn't been so strong, your injuries could have been even more severe. We might not be having this conversation."

The doctor went on to say that while I was in a coma, he wasn't sure of the extent of the brain or nerve damage, and at that point he didn't know if there would be any paralysis or if I would ever be able to walk again. He was very relieved that there appeared to be minimal infringement on my spinal cord, and it looked at this time that the nerve damage was not too severe.

Depending on the condition of my neck after they took the halo off, he was hopeful that I would be able to return to a normal life. "Normal" in that I should have the physical capabilities to take care of my own basic needs and possibly even to participate in activities that didn't present the opportunity for any jarring motions or sudden impact to my neck, back, or head.

Smooth walking, swimming, bike riding, or golf should be okay. Basketball, football, tennis, skiing, water skiing, and certainly skydiving would be too much. The constant impact from any running sport would take its toll overtime, and the risk of sudden impact from any skiing sport is too great. The opening shock skydivers feel when we deploy our parachutes, a knee to the head while doing 4-way, and anything less than a tiptoe landing would be out of the question. "Don't even think about it," he said. Someone must have warned him that I would be.

I realized I might not have been thinking straight, but the doctor's diagnosis didn't seem to add up. If my nerve and brain damage were minimal and ultimately shouldn't cause me any real problems in normal life, and everything else was expected to heal well enough to get by on, then why was it I couldn't skydive? My neck may be somewhat fragile, but so was my lung for the last eleven years. I had still managed to build up a shield and protect it well enough to withstand a plane crash. Why couldn't I do the same with my neck? Sounded to me like I should be able to make a full recovery, or at least close enough to one.

I was glad to be alive and to be able to move my fingers and toes. But it occurred to me that if I did decide to skydive again, there would be nothing stopping me. I put that thought in my pocket and saved it for later. There were more urgent matters to deal with.

"You need to get control of the situation."

I would speak with James's mom, Rita, frequently. Sometimes I would call her, sometimes she would call me. As much as I had been comforted by my conversation and visit from James, she was going through absolute torture. Her pain was more devastating than I could possibly fathom. She had lost her son. And nothing I could say that James had told me to share with her could bring her any comfort. Every day I hoped that somehow he would figure out a way to tell her himself. Maybe that would relieve me of the guilt I felt.

I had talked James into coming to California. Rita didn't want him to go. At first James wasn't even sure he wanted to. Why didn't I just leave it alone? Why did I have to push him? Was it because I was so selfish? Was it because I wanted to win so badly and I knew I couldn't do it without him? Oh God, what had I done? Lying in a hospital bed gave me way too much time to think. And these thoughts were haunting me. Thank god James had come to speak with me, and to tell me it was okay. Otherwise, the guilt may have been more than I could take. It was far more painful than any of the physical injuries.

The following weeks were foggy. Memories from the months before the crash were vague and scattered, and those from earlier years didn't all line up correctly in my head either. Even memories of what I had done just a few hours ago would sometimes escape me.

The problem with memory loss is that you don't realize that you've forgotten anything until someone tells you about it. I would get excited when friends would tell me about something, and the memory of the same incident would be reawakened in my mind. But I would get even more frustrated when they told me about something that I should remember but didn't. Without having the memory in my head, I would question whether they were telling me the truth. Were they testing me? Why would they test me? Maybe they were trying to manipulate or control me?

I could see their surprise and disappointment when they realized a special time we had shared together was gone from my mind. They would pull back from these conversations because they didn't want to scare me or show their deep concern for my mental state.

I received a phone call one day from a close friend. He was so glad to speak to me, so glad I was alive. He said he'd been thinking about me, praying for me. For the life of me I couldn't place him. How could I forget someone who is so close? How screwed up in the head am I? I acted as though I knew him, to be nice. He closed out our conversation by saying, "Dan, I want to help you. You deserve to be compensated for all your pain and suffering. I'm with —— Law Firm and I can make sure you're taken care of for the rest of your life."

The schmuck was an ambulance-chasing lawyer. I had never met him before in my life, and he had me thinking he was one of my closest friends and believing that I was severely mentally limited because I couldn't remember him. I was so pissed off I nearly came unglued. I was fragile enough and didn't need anyone screwing with my mind like that. I was cussing at him for five minutes before I realized that he had hung up the phone, probably four and a half minutes earlier.

I had to cool down so I started opening up letters and cards I had received. All very kind, very caring, I felt better after reading them. Even remembered most of the people they were from. As I was picking blindly through the box of mail, I came across a bill from the hospital. Not being insured at the time, I thought I'd better see the damage my being damaged had caused. It was for $478,000. Never had I ever seen a bill with that many zeroes on it. I wiped my eyes and squinted, trying to be sure I was seeing clearly. I was.

It took me all day with a calculator to figure out that if I paid it at $100 a week, it would take 4,780 weeks, 1,104 months, or 92 years to pay it off. Instead, I wrote them a check for the entire amount. If you've never written a check for $478,000 before, you should try it sometime. It's fun, especially if you have less than $50 in the bank. It was the first time I'd laughed in a long time.

There was a jar of water on a shelf in the room. It had been there as long as I could remember. Other items on the shelves were in constant movement. Get-well cards were put on the shelf and then tossed in the box when new ones came. Medical devices were moved from one spot to another or replaced. Books, newspapers, and magazines would come and go; the same with flowers and plants. A small TV VCR unit was set up and then taken away. But this jar of water never moved. It was always in the same place, like the sun with all the planets moving around it.

Finally I asked Kristi what it was. She said my teammate George Jicha from the Fource had come to see me only days after the crash. On his way from Casa Grande, Arizona, to Loma Linda Hospital in California, he took a five-hour detour to drive up to Apache Lake. He and I had escaped there a few times, and he knew how much the place meant to me. He filled the jar of water from the lake and brought it to me.

I was glad to remember Apache Lake and what a special place it was. And even happier that I remembered George and the brothers we he had become as a teammates.

People were all very supportive. They were compassionate, sympathetic, nurturing, polite, cautious, gentle, and helpful. They were too nice. Why were they acting like this? Many treated me strangely, differently than they had done before. They looked at me like they didn't recognize me and seemed to guard every word, like they didn't know what to say. Their behavior led me to think there must be more wrong with me than I thought there was.

I asked friends to bring in video and photos of Airmoves training. I needed to solidify the memories in my head and reassure myself that they were real.

One video showed the team arriving for training on the first day. All of us excited to be there, smiling and gesturing to Richard and the camera as we walked by. A raised fist. A finger pointing "number 1." A quietly confident nod and wink.

The jumps were pretty good right from that start. But more impressive was watching how we immediately improved by leaps and bounds and almost on a daily basis. The learning curve was more like a launch angle, and we were going straight up like a rocket. We never reached a plateau, never took a step backward. I'm sure we would have at some point, but I guess we never had a chance to get that far.

I think I watched every jump we'd ever made, all 350 of them. It was true. We were living the dream and on our way to winning the gold, just like I remembered it.

I finally got to the end of the last tape, our last jumps on the day of the crash. The jumps were the smoothest and fastest yet. Then the tape started skipping, the picture breaking. It shook like an old antenna TV losing the signal, then slowly dissolved to nothing but all black. It was over.

My memory was real. But it was of an old reality. I found myself now in a different reality, and I was a different person there. Before the crash I was strong, confident, independent, self-reliant, focused, and playing to win. I was clear on what my goals were, how to achieve them, and the human being I was and wanted to become in pursuit of those goals. Not anymore. Not even close.

Crystal clear in my limited memory was a quote my grandparents had on their wall:

God grant me the serenity to accept the things I cannot change,
the courage to change the things I can,
and the wisdom to know the difference.

As a child, I hadn't understood. I did now.

If I was going to get control of this situation, the first thing I had to do was accept the things I couldn't change and not waste any more time wishing they were different or trying to change them. The facts were that I had woken up in a world where I was weak, fragile, mentally foggy, totally dependent on others, and unclear of who I was, what my goal should be, and what my future would hold. James and many other friends were gone. My memory was scattered, and I wasn't sure how much of it I would ever get back. Perhaps if a spiritually advanced healer of some kind had found himself in a similar situation, he could have changed it. But not a simple skydiver like me, I couldn't. This was it.

Getting control meant changing the things that I could. Getting control was not giving in. Getting control was demanding that life would be everything I wanted it to be. After having experienced what it was like to live my dreams, I wasn't willing to settle for anything less.

There was lots I couldn't do, lots I didn't remember, and more that I didn't know. But I knew one thing. I needed a goal, something to focus my energy toward. Something I loved and wanted to aim for.

If it could no longer be skydiving, then I would need to find something else. But what? At the moment, I couldn't imagine what it might be. I couldn't even pretend to imagine. I was lost.

I needed an answer, and I needed it right now. I couldn't afford the time to discover a new dream or a new passion. I needed something to go for, to get me through, to distract me—anything—as long as I could get started on it right now.

It came to me. There was only one thing I absolutely knew how to do. So I'd better do it. I had no choice. I had to rebuild the team and go to the nationals.

Could it actually be done? Could I do it? Who knows? Who even cares? It didn't really matter if I could or not. *It mattered that I chose to believe I could.* And I did believe it. Otherwise, it would have only been pretend. And for the first time in my life, I didn't want to pretend.

Did I want it badly enough to do what it was going to take? Sure, why not? This is what I knew how to do, a goal I could sink my teeth into. Since my teeth were about the only part of me that was still working, I thought it would be perfect.

My doctors and friends insisted that my skydiving days were over. The skydiving community had accepted this as the best-case scenario even before I had woken up from the coma. Their doubts made me want to go for it even more. That was what getting control of the situation meant to me. These were the things that I could change, and I promised myself to have the courage to try and change them.

Friends came to the assumption that my head injury was so severe that I simply wasn't capable of recognizing reality. Out of sheer pity, they went along with it, not wanting to discourage and demoralize me after all I had been through. Maybe I wasn't thinking completely straight. But I easily saw through them. So I went along with them going along with me, even though I knew they didn't think it could possibly happen.

I called my surviving Airmoves teammates. We were all in different stages of recovery, but I had a plan. Troy had had surgery on his broken and dislocated hip. Both Troy and Tom had broken bones in their backs. Tom's shoulder was also badly damaged. I wanted to start training as soon as we could make it happen. I wanted to train as hard as we could and go to the nationals, playing to win. They also thought I was out of my mind, but at least they didn't mind telling me so. But they humored me and left the possibility open. Since I was the one in the worst shape, they told me to call them when I was ready to go. When I was ready, they'd be there.

Whether it ever actually happened or not didn't really matter. I felt better already just having taken the first steps. I wanted to keep the momentum building, so I didn't stop there. I called Mikey and asked him to join the team in James's position. Also to appease me, he went along with it. But then I gave him a date. The plan was for me to get the halo off in about six weeks. The way I had it figured, I'd need a couple of weeks to strengthen my neck, and then I'd be good to go. I told Mikey and the rest of the team to be in Perris, ready to start training, in the beginning of August.

Now the dream had a date. Now it felt real. At least the intent was real. This I understood; this was how I was used to operating.

My physical condition hadn't changed. I was still weak, fragile, mentally foggy, and totally dependent on others. But I had decided who I was, what I aimed to do, and what my future would hold for me. At the moment of decision time, the instant I decided to take the team to the nationals, or even just try regardless of the actual outcome, everything changed. As far as I was concerned, I was on a mission. I was back.

30
Out of the Hospital

I DIDN'T HAVE MEDICAL insurance, and to my surprise, the bank wouldn't cover the check I wrote for $478,000, so the hospital was kind of eager to get my sorry butt out from under their care as soon as possible. As far as I was concerned, it couldn't have been soon enough. (As it turned out, the drop zone insurance offered to pay all my medical expenses if I promised not to sue them. Since I wasn't going to sue them anyway, I jumped on the deal.)

After a week or two in rehab, I was released, with the doctor's orders for full-time assistance at home for at least a month or so. My parents wanted me to go back to Ohio with them so they could take care of me. But staying at my folks' house with them looking after my every need didn't sound like the best recovery strategy. If I couldn't completely take care of myself, I wanted to at least try to be as independent as possible. I wanted to be at the drop zone, with my friends and with Kristi. And then there were my plans with the team. The halo should be coming off in a little more than a month, and I intended to be in the air shortly after.

Skydivers take pride in having excellent spatial awareness. It is not only an essential skill to develop as a competitor. It is a survival skill that you use in free fall, under parachute and after landing. A prejump safety briefing will almost always end with instructions that basically amount to "Keep your head on a swivel." In the hospital I hadn't recognized the complete constraints of the halo on my visual awareness because in the hospital there generally wasn't much to look at or anything that I needed to be aware of. But once I was back in the real world, I felt more closed off and claustrophobic than ever. The ride home from the hospital exacerbated that even more.

I think that we are all backseat drivers to some degree. We can't help but pay at least a little attention to the road. We can see when all is clear or recognize when there could be an impending accident and prepare for either. Sitting in Kristi's car, I couldn't turn my head or twist my torso at all. I could only see straight ahead, directly in front of us, and even then as if I was looking through a small window. I had to completely rely on others. Having faith was harder than ever. By the time we got back to the house I lived in, I was exhausted.

Now that I was home, I felt insecure. At the hospital, at least I knew I had support of any kind any second I needed it, so much so that I took it for granted. At home it was different. The nurses had been giving me sponge baths, and I wasn't exactly sure how I was going to go about bathing by myself. Driving with a halo wasn't possible and riding a bike would have been catastrophic, so I wouldn't be able to get around without help.

I hadn't gained any significant weight and was still tipping the scales at about 130. I couldn't pick up anything heavier than a large book unless I was sitting down; otherwise it might tip me over. I needed a cane to walk for the extra stability it provided. This was all going to take a little getting used to. But I really didn't want to get used to it.

Kristi stayed with me for the first few days to help me get settled in. Kenny worked in Redondo Beach and only stayed at the house on weekends, so without Kristi I would have been there by myself. I tried lying down in my own bed to sleep at night, but that wasn't going to work at all, so Kristi put a bunch of pillows under me to raise my upper body similar to how it was in the hospital. I did my best to make it through the night but was too uncomfortable.

The next day, my friends Brenda and Sandy Reid, the owners of Rigging Innovations, Airmoves' equipment sponsor, brought me a La-Z-Boy chair they had. This was far better than a bed, but I wouldn't exactly call the state I was in at night "sleep." Under normal conditions, I used to roll around in bed throughout the night and adjust myself to the most comfortable position I could find. With the halo on, I couldn't budge. I had to become very accustomed to lying still and quiet. That was the best I was going to do.

The doctor had given me a supply of pain medication and sleep aids, but after two months of daily doses of a variety of narcotics, I was done with the drugs. I did all I could to keep my focus on healing fast and healing well, and I needed all my strength to do it. Sedating myself didn't fit into that plan.

With my capabilities so limited, I put my efforts toward the few things that I could actually work on. One of these was exercising with a breathing tool the doctor had given me to strengthen and expand my lungs. It had a gauge that read from 1 to 10 and measured the power of my lungs when I breathed into it. Level 2 was the highest I could get it up to. I liked that I could measure the results and calculate the exact level of improvement and was determined to blow the top off this thing. I used it almost any time I was sitting around and would blow into it until I'd nearly passed out. I improved, but only by millimeters. Improvement it was nonetheless, and the millimeters slowly added up.

One of my greatest fears was of sneezing. I was certain that one sneeze and the weak lung in my chest would pop like an old balloon. I'd always had fairly bad allergies and had to use all sorts of seasonal medicines. For my entire life, on any given day I'd be blowing my nose and sneezing several times. But in my condition, if I felt a little tickle near my nose, I'd panic and start scratching, grabbing, and slapping myself in the face in anticipation of letting one loose. I don't know how it happened, but amazingly enough, I didn't sneeze for months.

Another immediate goal of mine was to stand up to pee. I know it doesn't sound like much, but men aren't supposed to sit down to take a leak and it pissed me off (no pun intended) that I had to. I just couldn't do it successfully standing up. I couldn't look down, see my feet or anything else, so I couldn't aim. I also couldn't bend over at all, another required maneuver for proper targeting. I think of myself as someone who is fairly confident with his masculinity, so why the idea of having to sit down to pee, bothered me so much I don't know, but it did. Though I somehow got away without sneezing for a couple of months, I still had to pee, so there was no getting around it.

Kristi had a few pairs of very light dumbbells that I started exercising with. The ten pounders were too heavy for me, so I worked out with the fives. Brenda and Sandy came back with more help; this time they brought a stationary bike. That was the perfect workout machine for me as long as I was careful getting on and staying on. I needed to lock both my hands tightly on the handlebars all the time just to stay stable. If I loosened my grip at all, I was sure that I'd have been on the carpet instantly. Trying not to fall off was a total upper-body workout. I could feel it in every muscle I had.

People generally think it is knees and ankles that take a lot of abuse in skydiving, but there is much more wear and tear on the neck and shoulders. I was concerned about how fragile my neck was going to be when the halo came off. The doctors had warned me the neck muscles would be so weak that once the halo was removed, it may feel like my head was going to fall right off. I tried to figure out a way to exercise my neck, but when you can't move the body part you're trying to work on, the options are very limited. But there was one thing, isometrics—exercises in which muscles are briefly tensed by putting pressure against an immovable object.

The halo was pretty damn immovable. So I thought I may as well get some use out of this piece of crap as exercise equipment. Throughout the day I would try to pull and push my head against the resistance of the halo. I'd go up and down, side to side, and rotate left and right. I'd feel a sharp pain when the halo screws would start pulling against my skull. At that point I'd stop pushing and just try to maintain the level of pressure as long as I could. (I'm told it looked pretty masochistic and was either horrifying or hilarious to watch depending on how sick your sense of humor was.) A few seconds was the most. But I could feel my neck muscles working and see them tightening when I watched in the mirror.

Kristi helped me with everything. I couldn't stand up in the shower, so I'd sit in a chair and Kristi would help me bathe. She drove me wherever I needed to go. She would cook and clean and run errands for me.

Before the crash, when Kristi and I had spoken about moving in together, it was always an absolute "no" with her while the topic of marriage, on the other hand, received a "maybe." For me it was the exact opposite. But under the circumstances, she gave in. We set up the La-Z-Boy chair next to the bed so we could hold hands at night while we lay there talking.

Kristi is loving and kind, but make no mistake, she's a tough cookie. During my recovery she was always there for me and would do anything I needed her to do, but nothing more. Where other people might feel pity for me and would go out of their way to help in any way they could, she would only do for me what I couldn't do for myself.

At first that amounted to everything. But she kept tabs, and as I became capable of doing more, she made me do it. It wasn't long before I was hearing, "Wash your own damn clothes," or "What's the problem? Is that halo so tight that you can't put the dishes away?" Or "Figure out how to bend down and pick up the newspaper, or I'll help you figure out a way."

She was never mean, but always challenged me to be the best I could be and pushed me to do everything for myself that I could do. It was the recovery version of pulling out all the stops and giving it all I had. It was playing to win, and if I was going to stick with my plan to be jumping on schedule, then nothing less would do.

I'd recline in the La-Z-Boy chair for hours but would rarely ever get to sleep. Out of frustration I'd get up, sit down on the couch, and turn on the TV. My favorite thing to do was watch Airmoves' training jumps on video. I loved just thinking about doing 4-way. My memory was still vague at that time. Watching and visualizing the jumps would show me that I hadn't lost it. My mind and body still knew what to do even if they couldn't do it right now.

As I'd watch the jumps, I'd start dirt diving, practicing the moves in front of the TV, visualizing each move, fantasizing as if I was there at the moment. I'm not really sure at what point visualization transforms into fantasy; as a matter of fact, I'm not sure I could tell the difference between the two. My best visualizations were the ones that were the most clear and involved all my senses, more than just sight. I could feel which muscles were used to make a move, I would feel the grips in my hand and hear the noise of free fall, I would feel the emotion, determination, and heart that went with each point.

In skydiving, visualization is an essential part of training. Ours is a sport where the actual time on the real playing field is extremely limited. Consider the math. Airmoves had hoped to make eight hundred jumps that year. That would have been about 11 hours or 660 minutes of actual free fall time. We would have to bust our butts all year to get 11 hours of practice in. If I wanted to excel at most other sports, I could do 11 hours in a day if I chose to.

Visualization had always been part of our training. But I had never done it to this extent.

I started going to the gym as frequently as possible. There wasn't much I could do there at first, but it felt great just to be back in the sweaty hole. Kristi would usually drop me off for an hour. One day she wasn't able to come back and get me, so I told her I would call my teammate Tom for a ride. But Tom was with his mom at the moment and I hated to bother him. I couldn't bear to call Kristi. This was one of the first moments in months she actually had a few hours to herself. I was so sick and tired of being completely dependent on Kristi and my friends that I decided I wasn't calling anybody. I decided I'd get myself home.

The gym was just off the exit on the freeway, and Kenny's house was about ten miles down. I walked out of the gym, made my way down the exit ramp to the freeway, and stuck my thumb out for a ride.

It didn't take long before a kind soul pulled over. He looked out the window with his mouth wide open in shock. He couldn't believe there was some guy with a cane and a halo brace hitchhiking down the freeway. He seemed even more surprised when we started talking and actually had a normal conversation. I think he was expecting for me to be completely deranged. Nonetheless, he took me all the way to Kenny's house and watched me go in before he drove off.

This was one of the first moments of becoming independent again, and I needed it. I was quite proud of myself. To Kristi and my friends, of course, it just proved I really was deranged.

Gramps was still hanging in there, but he was staying in Columbus more often and not able to get around quite as much. Having to be on oxygen twenty-four hours a day adds another degree of difficulty to any extensive traveling. But as soon as I was out of the hospital and doing a little better, he was on a plane to California to see me. My uncle Mike, aunt Laura and uncle Bob and their kids—my cousins Bill and Jean—all lived in San Diego. Gramps flew in there, and Kristi drove me down to meet him.

Gramps and I were quite the pair walking down the sidewalk along the beach. Gramps had a cane in one hand and was pushing his oxygen tank with the other. I also had my cane but with a cage on my head to boot. He was still the strong, proud man he always was, but he didn't carry that attitude with the same 6'0" stance that he used to, more about my height or a little smaller now. I, on the other hand, had better posture than ever, seeing that my head was being pulled straight up by the halo.

Other walkers cleared the sidewalk when we were coming by, bikers went twenty feet around to miss us. The closest anyone came was when the dog they were walking pulled them over to sniff us. It was a great day. When we were together, it couldn't be any other way. We laughed about these circumstances the same way we'd laughed off any other problems we'd shared.

I wanted, needed, to be at the drop zone. Given my still being underweight, fragile, walking with a cane, and sporting a far-from-manicured beard, it took several double takes for most people to recognize me the first time I showed up there. As they realized it was me, they ran up to say hi. I could tell they were glad to see me, but I could also tell that many of them didn't know what to say or how to treat me. The last thing I wanted was any sympathy or special treatment. I had received enough special treatment by being allowed to live and not being hurt any worse than I was. I was the luckiest man I knew. But just as with friends that visited in the hospital, when these friends treated me like this, it made me think again that I must be in way worse shape than I thought I was.

One of our full-time local jumpers was Ivan Henry, a veteran Los Angeles County sheriff and basic badass. As most of my other friends walked away, Ivan put his arm around my shoulder and quietly said, "I better not hear one word of whining out of you, you're lucky to be here." This was music to my ears. I just about kissed him. Thank goodness, finally—someone that wasn't feeling sorry for me and wouldn't accept me feeling sorry for myself. As a competitor, this is the kind of thing you want to hear, words that motivate you. It also made me think I must not be in that bad shape if Ivan is so quick to give me a hard time.

From then on I was on the drop zone every day. It felt great to be there with my friends, helping out teams, and helping run the place. People started treating me more like I was myself because I was acting more like myself. I would still have lapses in my memory, but they were fewer.

I was putting all the effort and energy I possibly could toward exercising and regaining my strength, but my digestive system had not been working properly since the accident and I wasn't eating enough to fuel this effort. It may have been smarter to have listened to the doctors, rested more, and allowed my body a month or two of time to heal. But anything I had ever accomplished in my life I did by busting my butt, and the idea of recovering by sitting back and taking it easy didn't work for me. It may have been the better plan for my physical recovery, but my mind, soul, attitude, and spirit required a more aggressive strategy.

I recovered as my strategy would dictate. My mind, soul, spirit, and attitude were doing great. But I was physically deteriorating with the overtraining and undereating. Sheer exhaustion was weakening me.

Finally I hit the wall. I hardly left the couch for days. I knew something was really wrong when Kristi even backed off on her motivational harassment. I needed to keep making progress. I had a goal to reach. But I was so weak and tired that I couldn't do anything. I didn't know what to do.

Despite the total physical fatigue I was experiencing, I still couldn't sleep. I lay in the La-Z-Boy chair that night wondering what to try next. I couldn't just sit around the house; I'd been sitting too long already. But there was no way I could possibly continue at the pace I was going.

I had an idea. I waited as long as I could for Kristi to wake up. When it seemed like she was going to sleep in all morning (it probably wasn't past six in the morning yet), I started stumbling around and making noise. As soon as she was awake, I asked her, "Baby, can you take me to Apache Lake?"

31
Back to Apache Lake

WE THREW A few things in the van and headed out. There wasn't any particular reason I had come up with this plan and nothing specific I was after. I just didn't want to be stuck in the house any longer, and going to the drop zone was too much for me to handle right then. I needed to get out from behind closed doors and hit the road. As soon as we were out of the traffic and on the open highway, almost immediately I was able to relax back and enjoy that feeling of total freedom—the freedom to go where we want, stop when we wanted, and stay until we felt like leaving.

I had driven the road to Apache Lake dozens of times, but never from the passenger's seat. Even with the halo restricting my sight, I was able to enjoy the drive in ways I had never been able to before. I didn't feel like I was looking through a small window at all. I could see everything.

Kristi pulled over as we broke through the mountains and had our first view of the lake. It was beautiful beyond belief, just like I remembered it. Like a person who had to swim through miles of rough water and had just made it to the shore, I was hit by a wonderful feeling of peace. I felt totally safe, totally secure there.

We drove down and parked in the campgrounds next to the lake and found a nice spot to sit while we had a little lunch. It was so good to be back. We sat together for a while, enjoying the warmth of the sun and the colors it brought out in the mountains.

After a little while, we got up and took a walk. I was still using the cane, especially on rough terrain, but was starting to rely on it less and less.

The walk ended at the marina, so we decided to rent a small pontoon boat and go out on the water for a few hours. After successfully departing from the tie-downs and maneuvering away from the pier, there was no longer anything to run into, so I asked Kristi to let me take control of the boat. She was happy for the chance to finally be a passenger, and it felt great to me to be steering, to finally be allowed to be physically in control of something again.

Kristi sat in the front of the boat, leaning back, enjoying the sun, with her hair blowing in the breeze. She looked so beautiful, more relaxed than I'd seen her in a long time. I remembered our last trip to Apache Lake and how it was there that I realized I had fallen in love with her. But I loved her now more than ever.

That evening we watched as the sun set in slow motion. The length of the lake runs east and west. If you position yourself in the right spot, looking west, the water almost meets the sky and the canyon walls rise sharply on both sides. During a mid-July sunset, the sun descends on a path left between the mountains. Each second is an individual picture all its own as the sun settles down for the night and the sky and rocks slowly change color. But to see the full beauty of it all, you can't look away. Shadows slowly formed and grew, as the blue faded from the sky and a full array of oranges and reds replaced it. As the last bit of sun set below the horizon, everything darkened and the first faint stars slowly came into view and continued to brighten until the entire sky was covered with them.

Every second was fabulous. Each one a moment and picture I wanted to remember forever. I visualized it again right then to be sure this was a memory I could enjoy for much more than a fleeting thirty-five seconds.

The sun was set and so was I. I had all the beauty I could take in one day and was hoping to go to our room in the little hotel by the lake, have a glass a wine, and pass out to some mindless entertainment on TV. If I was lucky, a good old Clint Eastwood Western would be on.

I actually got some sleep that night, woke up the next morning feeling great, and let Kristi lie there undisturbed until she woke up completely on her own. We went to another spot near where we had parked the van when we first arrived, took out the cooler and had muffins, yogurt, and grapes for breakfast. Afterward Kristi sat back down by the rocks while I walked over to the lake to put my feet in the water.

I left my cane on the side and walked in ankle deep. The water felt so good. That perfect temperature, warm but still refreshing. I stood there feeling the rocks under my feet and looking around at the incredible canyon walls that surrounded me.

I walked in a little farther, the water now up to my knees, massaging my legs. A gentle breeze rolled across my chest and the sun shone down, heating up my back.

Soon the water was up to my waist. A few minutes later, all that was sticking out were the tops of my shoulders and my head. It was so relaxing, so calming, I couldn't quite remember if I had walked into the water or if the water had risen up to me.

I closed my eyes and slowly exhaled until my lungs were completely empty of air, then took another slow, deep breath. For the first time in months I felt so light on my feet, almost floating as much as I was standing. I let my arms rise to the surface and turned my palms upward toward the sky so that only my fingers were out of the water, and took another long, slow, deep breath.

I stood quietly in this place I loved. I could feel the breeze in my hair and on my face and fingertips. I felt the warmth of the sun on my hands, head, neck, and shoulders. I heard birds flying, fish jumping, water running, and leaves blowing. The water felt like the hands of fifty angels massaging my body and giving it renewed strength and energy. I felt fish on my sides giving me little pecks like kisses.

I was standing there calmly, quietly appreciating the beauty and breathing in all the wonders of this marvelous place, when I thought I became aware of something happening to me, an actual physical change in my body. With each breath I thought I was getting stronger, bigger.

I wasn't sure what was going on, but I felt like something was strengthening me, fueling me, healing me. One breath at a time, I tightened a muscle and felt it swell with power. My arms and biceps hadn't woken up in a long time, so I started with them. Then my fists and forearms, my chest and shoulders, until my entire body felt like I just finished a full workout.

I had never experienced anything like this before and certainly didn't expect to now. I was just walking into the water to get my feet wet. I didn't even know what to call it. Praying or meditating maybe, but being a person who hadn't ever done much of either, I wasn't sure.

I had lost all track of time. With each breath, each peck, and each breeze, I felt like I was being further rejuvenated. Finally, when it seemed to me that I had absorbed as much power from the forces of nature as I could, I took one more breath and slowly opened my eyes. I turned and walked back out feeling like a completely different man. Not frail or fragile at all. I felt strong, confident, and unstoppable yet very peaceful.

Did I actually experience a measurable physical change to my body while I was standing there? Was I truly stronger when I walked out of the water than when I walked in? I can't say. But I was absolutely sure at that moment that if there was a bench press next to the water, I could've proven it to be true.

Who knows? Who cares? It didn't really matter if I was actually stronger or not. *It mattered that I chose to believe I was stronger.* At that moment I believed it without any doubt, and I've continued to believe it to this day.

Kristi was still sitting on the side, watching me as I walked out of the water. I guess I'd been in there for over an hour. She could tell something wasn't normal and asked me, "What happened to you?"

I said, "I don't know. But let's go home." I knew at that moment that I'd be ready to go, ready to jump.

Once we made it out of the mountains and onto the freeway, I asked Kristi to let me drive the van. It was easy. I could see everything. Riding in the passenger's seat when I was first released from the hospital, I felt claustrophobic. But from the driver's seat now, I had the whole road out in front of me, and what wasn't in front of me, I was still completely aware of.

I felt like I could see out of my ears and saw things in the full range of my field of vision that I would never have noticed before. Like a person who can't see whose hearing improves because more is required from it, I was using senses I didn't know I had to help me see places my eyes couldn't reach.

Wearing the halo for the last few months had done wonders for my peripheral vision. I had no doubt that this would have a direct benefit of increasing my aerial awareness as well. Finally, similar to doing isometrics using the halo for resistance, I was glad to have figured out a way to get some specific skill training accomplished out of all this.

32
Losing My Halo

OVER THE NEXT couple of weeks I really started making progress. I came up with a customized routine at the gym, was gaining weight, gaining strength, and one millimeter at a time had finally blown the ball out the top of my breathing machine. I had a doctor's appointment to have the halo removed, and in anticipation of our 4-way team training finally beginning, Mikey moved out to Perris. He and Troy were the first of the team to get back in the air, about three months after the accident. It was great to see them jumping, and I couldn't wait to get the cage off my head so I could join them.

Kristi drove me to Newport Beach for the appointment with Dr. Steven Dennis, a orthopedic surgeon I started seeing because he gave it to me straight when it seemed like some of the other doctors spoke as if their main priority was avoiding a lawsuit. To my surprise, Dr. Dennis walked into the room with nothing but a screwdriver in his hand.

He told me to brace myself because it was going to feel very strange and my head was going to suddenly become quite heavy, I might not be able to hold it up. But I had kept up with the isometric exercises and was confident that my neck would be strong enough for the job.

His face was only a few inches away from mine and his eyes seemed huge as he put the screwdriver to my head. He looked like a mad scientist, gritting his teeth as he started turning the left screw. The kind of image you see in a nightmare after watching a Frankenstein movie. I could hear the screw grinding in my skull like someone ripping their fingernails down a chalkboard, but the chalkboard was inside my head.

Finally it was off. He was right, my head felt as heavy as a bowling ball. But as long as I thought about it, I could hold it up fine. Slowly I nodded my head up and down, tilted it side to side, and rotated it left and right. It all seemed to work. I almost shot off the chair in excitement. After having woken up with the halo on, my memories of what it was like before seemed very distant. I had forgotten completely how good it felt to do the simplest thing like nod, shake my head, or just roll my head back when having a good laugh. I felt like I had been released from jail. I asked him if I could start working it out that day and what exercises I could do.

He told me to settle down, take it easy, and not to get ahead of myself. Let's see how it feels after a week or so of normal use before putting too much strain on it. He gave me a soft-collar neck brace and sent me on my way.

I felt great. Walking out of his office, I realized that without being so top-heavy, I was much more balanced on my feet. My head was out of the cage, and I could move it slowly with limited mobility but in all directions. It felt so good I could hardly let it sit still and was always moving it at least just a little. I was sure that with gentle stretches and light weights, in no time I'd have the neck of a pit bull that would protect my spine the same way working my chest out so much had protected my lungs. I slept like a rock, horizontally in my own bed, for the first time that night.

The following morning I got up early and headed to the drop zone. The rest of the team was already there when I arrived. We laid out the training schedule all the way to the nationals. The way I had it figured out, I'd be able to start jumping in two weeks. That should give us time to make about two hundred jumps before the meet. This wasn't a lot, but it was going to have to be enough.

Tom, Troy, Richard, and Mikey couldn't believe it. We were actually going to do it. It wasn't all a joke. I hadn't been kidding when I called them from the hospital bed and told them we were going to the nationals. I had managed to convince myself we were going to make this happen since the moment the decision was made. But now, for the first time, we all believed it. Perris Airmoves was going to the national championships. And we weren't just going. We were playing to win.

I stood up and gave Troy an enthusiastic high five. As our hands smashed together, my head bent forward. It went past about thirty degrees, and my entire body went numb. I froze. Slowly I lifted my head up. The numbness stopped. I cautiously bent my head forward again. When I got to the same spot, my body went completely numb.

For the first time in a long time I was scared again. Unlike the adrenaline-junkie stereotype people assign to skydivers, I personally don't like to be scared. I was afraid that I'd hear something and instinctively turn my head to see it. Afraid I might turn it too far, too fast, past the point where I became numb. I was terrified of what would happen then.

I put 100 percent of my attention on not allowing my head to move at all. I didn't want to let it turn, nod, or budge, not even a little. I tried to ignore everything around me. I never realized how much effort it took to *not* pay attention to anything.

I returned to Dr. Dennis's office that same day. Kristi and I didn't have to wait long for the results of the scans, and he didn't have much to say. Only, "We need to operate."

I was furious beyond belief.

Me: No. No way. Not now. It's too late now! Why didn't we do it a month ago?

Dr. Dennis: We didn't know a month ago. But there's no question now. Just walking around, you're at risk of becoming a quadriplegic. It wouldn't take much of a hit at all to cut right through your spinal cord.

That shut me right up. But I couldn't believe it. We had come so far, I was sure we'd make it to the nationals. But I wasn't going to risk being paralyzed. I had to draw the line somewhere. How great a risk was it really?

I asked how long it would take me to be ready to jump after surgery when I wouldn't be at any greater risk than normal of becoming paralyzed.

Dr. Dennis: Dan—

Me: Doc, look. There're no lawyers here, no tape recorders. Just us. Please. What's the absolute minimum this could take to heal?

Dr. Dennis: I advise you never to jump again.

Me: Yeah, I know. Thanks for the advice. How long?

Dr. Dennis: It's over, Dan. You are not jumping.

Me: How long?

Dr. Dennis: *If* everything heals at record pace, *if* everything fuses perfectly together, the area where the surgery was will be strong enough after ten weeks. You won't break it there. But your neck will still be very weak, very fragile. If you're stupid enough to jump out of an airplane, I will not be responsible for what happens to you.

Kristi: There's always next year, Dan.

The thought of pushing it to next year wasn't an option for me. I still needed a goal now, not later, not next year. How did we know we'd even have next year?

As we walked out of his office, I only had one thing on my mind. The nationals was eight weeks away. I knew Dr. Dennis was pushing the limits to tell me ten weeks. Eight weeks would be stupid, basically suicidal. I was out. But that didn't mean Airmoves couldn't still be in. They could still win. It was still possible.

33
The New Airmoves

I CALLED KIRK VERNER. Kirk was on a team from Illinois called the Magnet Men. The Magnet Men came onto the competition scene in 1989, the first year of the Fource. In 1991, they had finished just behind the top three teams. I knew Kirk was a great skydiver, had a lot more experience than the rest of Airmoves, and had also been coached by Jack Jefferies, our main competition, which added the benefit of bringing some valuable insights with him. But most importantly, I thought he'd say yes and immediately drop everything to do it. I called him at once. He was in Perris three days later when I went into surgery.

On my way to Hoag Hospital in Huntington Beach, I had stopped by the drop zone and watched the team preparing for their first jumps together. I was relieved to see them back at it, even if I couldn't be in the air with them. I told them to get to work and I'd be back with a new neck in a few days.

The first moment I came to after surgery, I knew it had been a success. A piece of my hip bone had been used to replace the C5 vertebrae; it was locked in place with a metal plate. I could tell immediately when I opened my eyes that my neck was much more stable. With nothing in my recent memory to measure it against, I hadn't realized what bad shape my neck was in after the halo was removed. I thought it was fine; anything was better than having that thing on my head. I had to wear a hard neck brace that went from the back of my head and around my chin all the way down my torso. It was much more cumbersome than the soft neck collar, but it was certainly no halo.

I stopped by the drop zone to see the team on my way home from the hospital. They were training hard. Like any other team sport, four great skydiving athletes don't necessarily add up to one great team. Before they become a team, they'll need to learn how to work together and to read each other on and off the playing field. Everybody can make the moves, but making them together, at the exact moment they need to be made (and consistently doing it with the right attitude), takes time, training, and a coach to plan and guide them through the process. I couldn't jump, but I was eager and ready to step in as a coach and the team was counting on me to do so. It was obvious that there was a lot of work to be done before the competition, and I was confident we had the energy and desire to do it, if we only had the time.

It was a powerful thing to be a part of the team even if I wasn't jumping. I knew I was going to sleep well that night.

Two hours later, I was lying on the bathroom floor in a fetal position, barely able to struggle up to my knees to puke my guts out in the toilet. Nothing I had experienced since the plane crash was more painful than this. I didn't know what was going on, but I could've sworn someone had blown up a stick of dynamite in my abdomen.

Kristi came running in to see what was wrong. I knew I had to go to the hospital, but Hoag was too far away so she took me to the closest facility there was. They shot me up with Demerol, let me lie there for a couple of hours while the pain subsided, and sent me home. When the drugs wore off, I was on the floor again. This time Kristi took me to a different local hospital where they immediately admitted me.

They correctly diagnosed that I must have had some kind of bowel obstruction caused initially *by* internal injuries when my body was crushed in the crash with the job being completed when I went under sedation for the neck surgery. They tried to put a nasogastric tube down my nose but were not successful. Without the relief the tube would provide, my gut was still killing me and regular shots of Demerol were the only thing that got me through it. But frequent doses of heavy narcotics never cured anyone of anything. While I was still able to think straight, I told Kristi not to tell the team what was going on. Instead, I told her to call and tell them I needed to rest at home for a few days. They should keep jumping and I'd check in with them soon. I knew we couldn't afford to miss one day of training.

I couldn't eat, so the only nutrition I was getting was through an IV. I was delirious from the drugs, in a constant mental fog, forgetting where I was, and hallucinating half the time. I couldn't sleep, which made my mental condition that much more fragile. They switched me from Demerol to morphine. As soon as it would start to wear off, some level of clarity, along with the pain, would return. Just as I was getting the least bit of a grip on where I was and what was going on, they would immediately shoot me up again. This went on for days. I felt like a prisoner, trapped and totally helpless.

In the middle of the night, four days after being admitted, the nurse was late with my scheduled pain medicine. As the last dose started wearing off, I remembered that in my fog I had wondered where I was and if I was dead. That maybe this is what death is like. As I started coming back into reality, I realized that I must have been there for a long time and that nothing was being done to help me. My condition was getting worse. With the constant drugs and the sleep deprivation, I was beginning to lose it. I thought that if this continued, I was going to die there.

I didn't want another shot. I stared at the door, afraid to blink, readying myself to fight if the nurse came through it with a syringe in her hand. I would welcome the pain if it would allow me to think straight. I was searching for the energy I had experienced in Apache Lake, looking for the power of the Force, but at that moment, in that hospital, I couldn't find it.

At three in the morning I called Kristi and begged her, "Baby, get me out of here. I'm scared. I'm afraid if I pass out, I'm never going to wake up again."

All I could think to do now was try to stay as alert as possible. I refused the morphine shots because as long as I was feeling the pain, I knew I was alive. Finally I heard some unusual rustling noise and activity in the hall. Then Kristi's voice commanding the nurse, "I am here to have Dan Brodsky-Chenfeld released." The nurse resisted and tried to stop Kristi, telling her that she hadn't heard anything about this from the doctor and she needed the paperwork first. Kristi told her to go get the paperwork herself and came charging into my room with a hired ambulance service. She had called Dr. Dennis and already arranged to have me admitted into Hoag Hospital for evaluation. Thank God, the cavalry was there to save me.

As they loaded me up on the stretcher, the doctor came barging in, yelling at Kristi, "What do you think you're doing? You can't just come in here and take my patient." Kristi didn't miss a beat. "We're taking him."

The doctor responded, "If he leaves this room, I am not responsible and I want it on record that it is against my medical advice." Kristi fired back, "We don't have time for your medical advice," and we were out of there like an Old West jailbreak.

Two hours later we pulled into the emergency room at Hoag. A colleague of Dr. Dennis's was waiting for us. He took one look at me, put an NG tube down my nose in about two seconds, and within minutes I was being put under and going into surgery.

By now I had lost all the weight I had gained back since the crash, and the little muscle mass I had built up had again withered away to nothing. Between my neck and my abdomen I was stitched together across my entire body.

But for the first time I could remember I finally felt fixed. The blockage had been removed from my gut, and my neck felt weak but not broken. Much of the pain I had learned to accept as normal was gone. The fine sewing work did cause a bit of discomfort, but mere

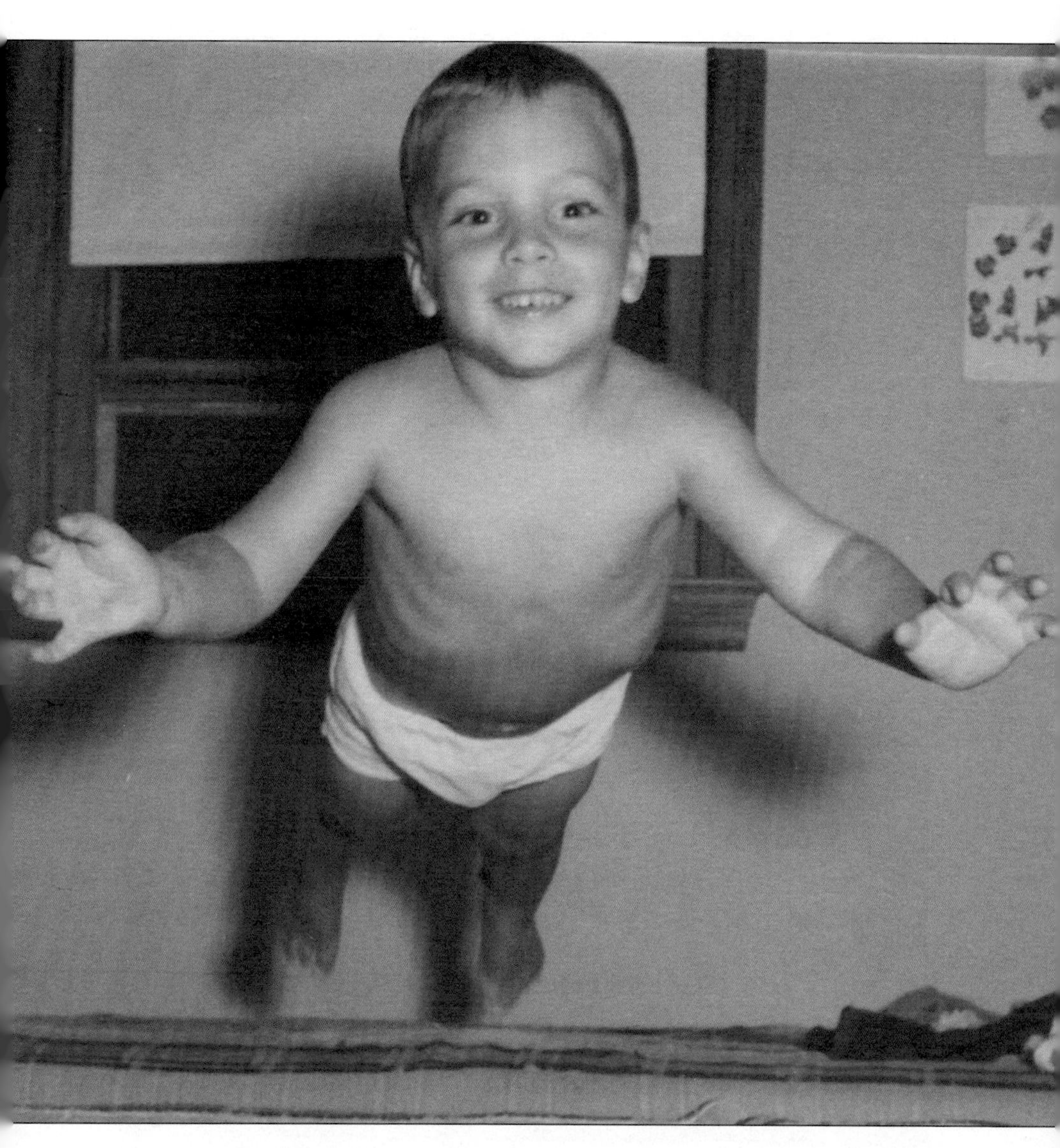

Dan, age five, "flying."

Grandma Iris, Howard, Mimi, Dan, Cara, Cliff. Quite the fashionable family.

Cliff, Grampa Joe, Dan, 1981.

Dan packing his parachute, 1981.

Dan taking James Layne on one of his first jumps, 1985.
Photo credit: Jim Fangmeyer.

Greene County Fusion, 1986. Dan, John Woody, Marilyn Kempson, Jim Fangmeyer.

Larry Hill presenting Dan with his Quadra Diamond Wings award for 4000 jumps, 1989. Kevin Vetter looks on.

Perris Airmoves, 1992, shortly before the crash. From left to right: Dan, Tom Falzone, Richard Stuart, and James Layne; not pictured, Troy Widgery.

From left to right: Dan, Troy, Tom, and James. Perris Airmoves, 1992; not pictured, Richard.
Photo credit: Richard Stuart.

Peter Phun / *The Press-Enterpr*

Rescue workers attend to the injured after an airplane carrying sky divers crashed yesterday after taking off from Perris Valley Airport.

16 die in Perris plane crash

The Press-Enterprise • Thursday, April 25, 1992 • A-5

PERRIS CRASH: *Worst in county's history*

Steve W. Grayson / The Press-Enterp

Rescue personnel work at the scene of the crash of a twin-engine plane loaded with skydivers near Perris Valley Airport.

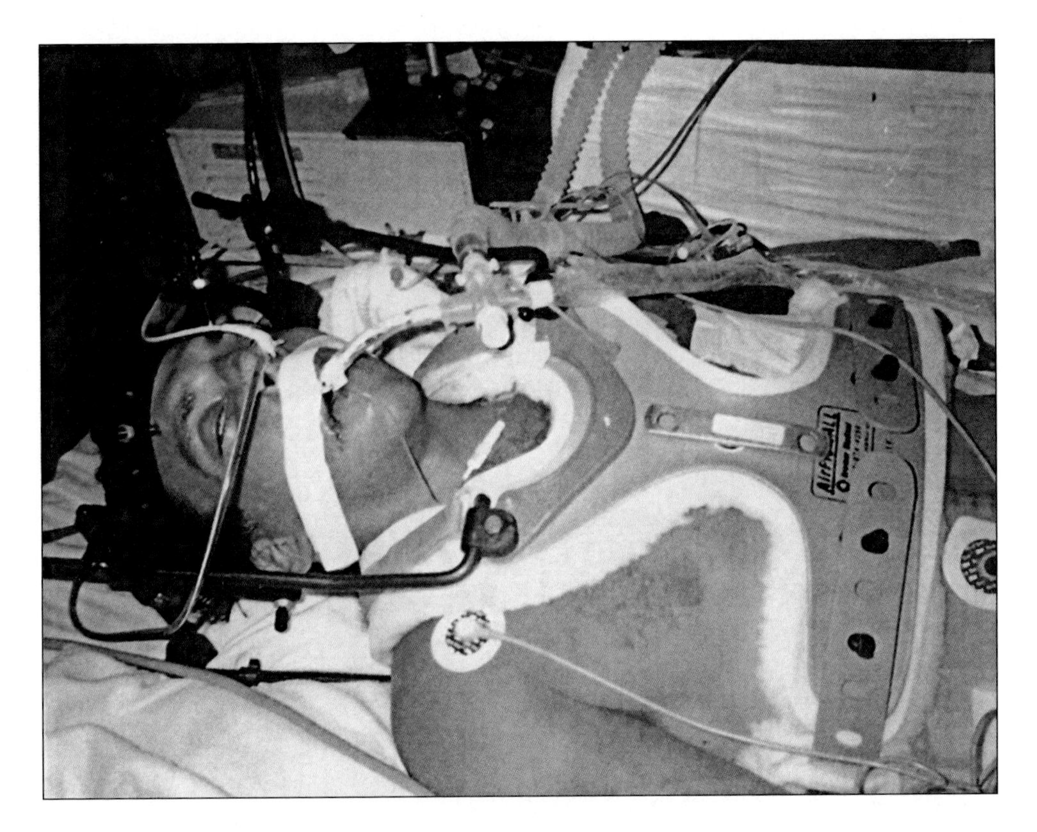

Dan in a coma a few days after the crash.

Dan and Kristi being silly at a 1991 trip to Apache Lake.

Dan and Kristi at Apache Lake a few months after the crash.

The U.S. team, Arizona Airspeed, landing during a training jump for the 1995 world championships. From left to right: Dan, Jack Jefferies, Kirk Verner, John Leming, and Mark Kirkby.
Photo credit: Michael McGowan.

Airspeed at the 1995 world championships walking to the plane for a competition jump. From left to right: Mark, Jack, Dan, Kirk; not pictured, John Leming.
Photo credit: Tim Wagner.

Arizona Airspeed 1996 8-way World Cup Champions.
Photo credit: Michael McGowan.

Arizona Airspeed, 1997 World Champions.
Photo credit: Michael McGowan.

A very challenging 52-way formation at the P3 Power Play at Skydive Perris, 2010.
Photo credit: Craig O'Brien.

Square One 200-way 2010.
Photo credit: Craig O'Brien.

Dan and Chloe Layne, 1995.

Dan and Landen Jack, 2000.

Mother Mimi and Dan.

Dan, Kristi, Chloe, and Landen, 2011.
Photo credit: KC Photography.

Dan under canopy, 1993.
Photo credit: Mary Pat Avery.

discomfort was like ecstasy in comparison. All they had done was reopen the old incision from the exploratory surgery that was done just after the crash, so it wasn't anything new. All in all, this was the best I'd felt in months.

Before I could be released from the hospital, this time they were going to be certain that all systems were a go and confirmation of that was me taking a dump—excuse me, having a bowel movement. The more active I was, the sooner this was likely to happen; the more pain medicine I took, the longer it would be delayed. That wasn't going to be a problem. After my experience at the other hospital, I loved pain and preferred being a complete masochist rather than have one more shot. From the moment I got up in the morning, I was doing laps up and down the hallway, pushing the IV tube stand along with me and using it as a cane.

During a marathon session, to my surprise, Airmoves suddenly appeared, marching down the hall carrying a TV and VCR. I was glad to see them but pissed. I asked what the hell they were doing here, they needed to be at the drop zone training. They told me to shut up.

It was great to see them and get to hang out with my buddies. We watched a video of all the training jumps they had done so far, complete with enthusiastic play-by-play analysis. It was hilarious, so much fun. It was clear from watching the video that they were flying all heart, gas pedal floored, and going for it for all they were worth. All discipline and proper technique tossed to the wind. They didn't want to be bothered with it. Even on the video I could see how much fun they were having. But I could also see they definitely needed a coach, and they knew it too. I had to get out of the hospital and back to the drop zone as soon as possible.

34
Finally, Back to Training

FROM HERE ON in, it was smooth sailing. We got back to business dealing with all the normal challenges of team training, of which there are many. Nothing dramatic compared to the obstacles we'd been dealing with and definitely nothing that would slow us down.

The team was jumping every day. All of our equipment was destroyed in the crash, but by now Rigging Innovations and our other equipment sponsors had provided us new gear. We had people packing for us and keeping the team in the air. I would often ride to altitude with them to review the video and bring up anything that needed to be paid attention to on the next jump.

You could tell watching Tom and Troy walk in from a jump that they were hurting. But they kept it to themselves and never asked to stop jumping before I called it for the day.

We would meet in the morning before jumping to begin the day playing a gentle game of basketball or go for a slow bike ride. At the end of the day we headed to the gym. Jump by jump and day by day, we were making steady progress again. But the nationals was coming up fast. If only we had more time.

We caught word of an announcement from the United States Parachute Association. Due to administrative difficulties, the location for the nationals was changed from Skydance Skydiving in Davis,

California, to Skydive Arizona. With the location change, the date was also moved from September to October. Yes! That was the extra time we needed. Finally, something fell into place for us; it had been a long time since that had happened.

Obviously the extra time and training would be an advantage for every team, but it was essential for us. When the original dates of the nationals arrived, we weren't quite ready. But after that last month had passed, we were kicking ass. And there was one more thing. It put us past the ten-week mark.

I was riding in the plane again with the team, still thinking about what Dr. Dennis had told me. "If everything heals at record pace, if everything fuses perfectly together, then the area where the surgery was done will be strong enough after ten weeks. You won't break it again there."

That day was exactly ten weeks to the day after the neck surgery. I had been keeping track.

I felt good. I'd been training hard, eating well, gaining weight, and getting stronger every day. I didn't quite have the pit bull neck I wanted yet, but it wasn't that of a Chihuahua either. A month earlier, with Dr. Dennis's permission, I had gotten rid of the hard neck brace and was only wearing the soft collar. Based only on how I felt, with no consideration given to the history of the past six months, I figured I'd be okay to jump.

Every time I had ridden along previously, I wore a pilot "bail out" parachute rig. That old expression, "Why would anyone want to jump out of a perfectly good airplane?" was obviously crap, so we never knew when we might need one.

But in preparation for today, just in case I decided to jump, I had pulled an old parachute system of mine from the closet and dusted it off. One I knew was guaranteed to open slowly (or "snivel," in skydiving terms) and minimize the opening shock. I brought a pair of goggles along in the plane that day as well. I had taken all the necessary steps to be ready to jump, if I wanted to. But it wasn't decision time yet.

No one on the team knew what I was thinking about, and I certainly hadn't told Kristi. After the neck surgery they had never even considered there was any chance of me jumping before the nationals, even with the dates being moved back a month. Only I had logged that "ten week" comment into my weakened, or now possibly just more selective, memory.

There I was, in the airplane at 12,500 feet. A few minutes before exit I joined Airmoves for the "team count." As they did their final visualization, I quietly tightened up my harness and took the goggles out. I still hadn't decided if I was going to jump or not, but when that door opened, I was going to be ready to if I wanted. Just like always, as decision time was approaching, the fear was building.

It had been a while since Doomsday Dan had anything to say, but he jumped up screaming then. "Why would you want to jump? What are you trying to prove?"

"Oh I get it, you think you're a tough guy. Well you may just find out."

"If you're going to jump again, at least wait a few more months."

"You're an idiot, and it's really f——ing stupid."

I hate excuses, especially when they make such good sense. As scared as I was, the logic was working.

The green light came on and the team started climbing out. As he was reaching out the door, Troy looked back at me with a confident competitor's nod. It was just at the moment I was putting my goggles on. In that instant he had a curious expression on his face, but the instant was quickly gone as he moved to his exit position outside the plane.

Doomsday Dan had more to say. "Don't do it, Danny. Just sit back down, relax, and enjoy the plane ride. Don't do it. There is nothing to be gained and everything to be lost." More common sense.

The team gave the exit count and flew off the plane looking like champions. I watched them as they started going through the formation sequence. I wanted to follow them, but when decision time came, I couldn't do it. I was too scared. The decision made, I sat back down for the airplane ride to the ground. It was the right thing to do, the smart thing to do, but the instant the decision was made, I regretted it.

Out of nowhere, the Lover of Life Dan woke up and yelled, "Go!" Without thinking, I took it as an order and shot out the door. The instant my body hit the wind, the fear was gone, defeated by pure excitement and exhilaration. I had never felt so good in my life. I was home, I was flying, I was free as a bird and living my childhood dream for the first time all over again.

I located the team maybe 800 feet below, put my arms behind my back, rolled over on my head, and dove down at them. I could hear the wind pick up as I accelerated, now about 50 mph faster than they were going and approaching fast. They were cranking through the formation sequence as I arrived and threw my arms out to flare and stop.

It was like a car wreck on the freeway when one at a time they saw me. Kirk was first. He stopped dead in this tracks and looked across to see who it was. He burst out laughing, realizing it was me, with an expression that said, "You crazy SOB." When he did, Mikey turned and ran right into him with Tom and Troy close behind. They pointed at me and cracked up. Tom was the only one who looked concerned. We built a "star" formation and laughed and played until we saw 4,000 feet on an altimeter. The guys waved, saluted, or high-fived as they shot away and instantly put enough distance between us all so that we had adequate airspace to safely deploy our parachutes.

Deploy our parachutes? Uh-oh, I forgot about this part, opening shock. I guess there's no way around it now. No matter how hard the opening shock may be, it won't do as much damage as not having any opening shock at all. I spread out my arms and legs, cupped all the air I could with my torso, trying to slow my free-fall speed down as much as possible. The slower the free fall is, the softer the opening. I even opened my mouth, trying to inflate my cheeks and nostrils—anything I could do. I heard the wind decelerating a little.

As I deployed my parachute, I grabbed my neck and braced myself. The pilot chute pulled the deployment bag with my parachute in it off my back. The lines' stows started coming out of the Tube Stoes. The last stow held the bag shut; as it came out, the nylon from my parachute caught air, slowed down, and stood me straight up. I squeezed my soft neck collar with both my hands to give it added support, bracing myself for the worst. The canopy started spreading out ever so slowly and gently sniveled until it was completely inflated. It was so slow that a normal jumper would have been scared it was malfunctioning, but for me it was perfect. It worked just as planned.

I went from being scared that I might snap my spine and gripping my neck for all I was worth, to being safe, secure, and completely undamaged by the opening. Being under canopy was like floating in the comfort of heaven.

I held the steering toggles halfway down for nearly the entire flight. It reduces the angle of attack and slows down the descent. I wanted to stay up as long as I could. Coming in to land, I put the toggles all the way up and let it go into full flight again. Then I pulled them back down and flared the canopy for a tiptoe landing.

The other jumpers on the drop zone that day came running out to meet us. We were ready.

35

1992 U.S. Nationals—Game On

THE ROAD CRUISE to the nationals again provided me time to think, and my mind traveled back to the year we'd had. I missed James so much. This would have been the competition we had talked about since he was a boy. When I left Ohio, I told him not to lose sight of our dream, that someday we'd have our chance to be on a team together and go for the gold. I remembered my disbelief when Pat and Mel made me the offer to start a team at Perris and that dream finally came true. This first thing I did was call James, bursting with excitement even before he picked up the phone.

I remembered when James and Troy first showed up in Perris, and had to laugh just thinking about it.

Getting to know James the man and finding out we were even closer as teammates than as mentor and protégé.

Seeing the team improve and excel at a rate better than I had ever hoped. I was sure that Airmoves was going to be the best team the sport had ever seen at this national championships.

And then it was over. James was gone.

What would I have done? How would I have handled all of this if James hadn't visited me and told me that he was okay, that it was okay, that we'd see each other again someday? I couldn't even imagine.

That experience with James was as real to me as any physical experience I've ever had in my life, my memory of it more vivid than most. I will always thank him for coming to me, and preparing me to get control of the situation and to better understand life itself.

This experience provided all the evidence I needed to know that there really is more to "life" than what we experience in this physical world during this lifetime. I didn't pretend to think I knew what "more" was, but I knew there was something.

Knowing this didn't lessen the value of this physical world for me. It actually enhanced it and enabled me to focus on what is truly important. It helped me realize that the superficial things we often value far too much are in themselves worthless. It became very clear to me that one thing life certainly was about was finding things we truly love, challenging ourselves to be the best we can possibly be at them, and sharing our passion and love of life with anyone who cared to be a part of it. It is in this journey that we will discover who we really are, what we are capable of, and choose who we want to be.

What lessons were there for me now? How would I choose to use this knowledge and enlightened sense of spirituality?

I turned into the entrance road to Skydive Arizona and passed a sign saying "Welcome to the 1992 U.S. National Skydiving Championships." I looked up and saw the Golden Knights' black and gold parachutes open overhead. I remembered Woody getting hurt and our chance for winning the gold in 1987 vanishing, the Fource losing in the last two rounds in 1989, and then blowing a good lead in 1991.

The hell with that spiritual enlightenment, I was there to win.

The competitor in me won out over the advanced soul. Once I was on site at the nationals, it was all about the meet. I'm sure James wouldn't have had it any other way. We got right down to business. Airmoves arrived at the nationals with almost 250 training jumps under our belts. The guys were flying great. On most jumps they were able to match and possibly even beat the top teams. But there were particular jumps involving very complex sequences that were weak. These were jumps referred to as "slot switchers." On slot switchers two of the team ended up switching places, so after completing the 5-point formation sequence they would be in a different position for the second time through the sequence. Basically, they had to remember ten formations instead of five and be skilled at two slots. These types of jumps required training and experience they just didn't have. The short season simply didn't allow the time needed to dedicate to them.

With the team's minimal training and relative lack of personal experience, these jumps became our weakness. We would certainly lose the rounds on a jump that a slot switcher was drawn. If we lost all of these rounds, we would lose the meet. Our only chance of victory was if all the top teams had poor showings, and that was no strategy for winning.

We were on site for the nationals with two training days left before the meet was scheduled to begin.

There simply wasn't time to improve our performance on these complex jumps. Furthermore, it would have been unproductive to spend our last practice jumps focusing only on our weak areas when our strengths needed all the reinforcement they could get.

We were playing to win. We had fought our way past every obstacle that stood in our path, and we weren't about to let this one stop us.

In lieu of more training, the only other way to gain an advantage on these complex jumps would be having a more experienced person in the air, a very experienced person that had trained on these types of jumps in the past. We needed me.

Could I jump? What is the risk, and is it worth it? If I did, would our jumps improve enough to increase the likelihood of winning?

I had made a few jumps after the first one back, even a couple of 4-ways. The 4-way jumps were much more aggressive, much more physically challenging, than the first one. But they were okay; no bad pain, no close calls. I could jump.

I had never completely given up hope of being able to jump at the nationals if I was needed. My old parachute had come through as expected, with the gentle openings and easy landings. By wearing the soft neck brace in the air, I should be able to limit how far my neck would compress or extend if I was hit in the head in free fall. I was certain, if I jumped in competition at all, that I was going to strain my neck to some degree. But the same was true for Troy's hip and Tom's back. The metal plate and reconstructed vertebrae were not going to break. I was not at any greater risk of paralysis than anyone else on the team. In my mind, the risk was minimal, and if there would be a competitive edge gained by my jumping at the meet, it would be worth it. (I can convince myself of anything if properly motivated.)

The team spoke about it, and together we decided the only way to find out would be to put me in for a few and see. I made four practice jumps with the team the day before the meet. All were the complicated type that had given us trouble. My experience was the benefit we were looking for; the jumps rocked. The decision was made that I would substitute into whichever position made the most sense on any particular jump that had the highly technical sequences.

Was there really any chance we could win? Yes, as small and unlikely as it may have been, there was definitely a chance. But only if we continued to make every decision with that goal in mind, as we always had. So that's what we did.

Tom Piras was coaching Jack's team, and to no one's surprise, he started right in trying to screw with and psych out my teammates, just as I had warned them he would. Oddly enough, it didn't bother me. That he thought it necessary and put as much effort into it as he did was somewhat of a compliment. It showed me he was nervous, and I liked seeing him nervous. I was quite entertained by it and even asked him how that was going for him, working on my teammates and all. He didn't try to hide his intentions in the least and came right out with it. "Not very well, you've got some tough boys there." We both laughed. For the first time in the nine years we'd been competing against each other, this was the nicest conversation we'd ever had. It almost seemed like we were old friends surrounded by all these young whippersnappers.

I was on the ground for the first round. As a coach I had found out how difficult it was to turn my team loose for the meet. As I saw it, my job was to do all I could to help my team discover and define what their *true best performance* really was, push it to the highest level possible, and show them how to perform at that level under the pressure of competition. But like the director of a play watching the opening night performance, once they left the ground, there was nothing more I could do. I had to sit back and wait, fingers crossed.

I'm not good at waiting, and I don't know how to cross my fingers. I couldn't sit still and started pacing back and forth across the drop zone. I had never been this nervous at a meet when I was jumping. But when I was jumping, I was in control. I recognized that at the heart of all, this nervous energy was a feeling of helplessness and fear: wishing for something good to happen in a place I now had no control. Nervousness, helplessness, fear, wishing—those couldn't be good things. I thought I'd better settle down. I found a quiet place, sat with eyes closed, and visualized the jump as if I was there.

I could see it perfectly and even felt the confident energy and attitude I loved so much about those best meet jumps. I hoped they were in the plane doing exactly the same, and knew if they climbed out the door after visualizing like this and feeling like I was, they'd be unstoppable. I remembered being in the plane at competitions before and how one teammate's confidence or fear could be infectious. How someone could be nervous and one glance of carefree confidence from a teammate could instantly change his attitude. I hoped they could feel what I felt now and tried to send that feeling to them.

By this point in my life I firmly believed in the power of visualization and a person's ability to change themselves through thoughts and beliefs, and by doing so becoming empowered to change the world around them. I had heard of others who believed that through visualization alone, we could directly influence the world around us. Now that's Jedi-like.

As Airmoves was only minutes from exiting the plane, I visualized the team count as if I was there with them. When the plane was overhead and I knew it was time to exit, I visualized climbing out the door as if I was filling a slot. My visualization skills had become so good while sitting on the couch all night for the last few months that I could see it all perfectly, every detail. I exited the plane with them and went through the entire jump. I actually felt how I knew they'd feel in the heat of the meet. At four thousand feet, when the thirty-five seconds was up and it was break-off time, I jumped up on my feet out of breath, certain that they had just done the great jump I had watched in my head.

I have no idea if this did the team the least bit of good. But it was the only contribution I could make, and I didn't want to sit idle if there was even a remote possibility of making any contribution at all.

I met Airmoves as they landed. They were coming down from the jump and off a high. Relieved that the first round of the meet was a good one and that it was behind them. After round one, the scoreboard showed us 1 point ahead of Deland Vertical Speed and 1 point behind the army's Golden Knights.

At that moment I had nearly forgotten about all the events of the last year. It was just like old times, a three-way race again between Deland, the army, and my new team, Perris Airmoves.

The contest resembled previous nationals. Like fighters in the ring trading punches, all three teams landed shots and won different rounds.

As planned, I stepped in on all the slot switchers. I was the skydiving equivalent of being the quarterback on one play and the wide receiver on the next. I weighed in at 135 pounds, still about 25 pounds under my fighting weight. To make sure I fell at the same speed as the team, I wore an additional 12 pounds in a weight belt. That plus the extra weight from the old parachute rig I was using put me about even.

At this point, it was just a little over the ten-week mark. The scar in my abdomen was beginning to allow me to stretch back out to a good free-fall body position. I had hardly jumped at all and the physical training I had done, though it was as much as I could do, was minimal. But what I lacked in physical preparation, I made up for with all the visualization. I didn't feel like I had been away from the sky at all. I felt "current" and ready, almost as if I had made four thousand jumps in the last few months, because in my head I had.

As it turned out, the visualization proved to be worth more than the actual training ever could have been. No amount of practice jumps could have ever given me the same degree of repetition and experience in all the different positions. In the airplane I was able to see the jumps in my head perfectly and, because of that, felt confident and ready to do any job required of me.

When visualizing in the plane, I had every reason to expect we'd have a great jump and my confidence was high.

The decision for me to jump turned about to be a good strategic call. We stayed in the race during those jumps too.

Perris had many teams at the nationals that year and many other jumpers that came just to be there and support the home teams. We were surrounded by friends pushing us, cheering for us, and wanting so much for us to succeed. Kristi was there with me, as she had been every step of the way.

Close meets are like emotional roller coasters. You're up, you're down, you win a round, you lose a round. No matter if the last jump was a good one or a bad one, you have to forget it. It is immediately history and nothing can change it. You have to put all you have into the next one. All you can do is to keep fighting, and Airmoves did. One round at a time, the team stayed strong, and I was so proud to be a part of it.

That year our team experienced absolute emotional extremes. Before the crash, we had a team of friends that shared a dream. We had the opportunity to make our dreams come true, and it was happening. Our team had excelled at an unheard-of pace, achieving performance levels in less time than any skydiving team before us. Success was in our hands.

Then, due to something out of our control, it was all taken away. We lost time, equipment, our health, and the life of a friend and teammate that we loved like our own brother. But we still had our dream, if we wanted it badly enough.

It's been said that the true worth of our pursuit of victory is defined by the obstacles we must overcome to achieve it. During this year with *Airmoves,* the idea of living life to its fullest brought on a whole new meaning. The questions, "How badly do you really want it?" and "Are you willing to do whatever it is going to take?" were challenged like they had never been before. The depth of our desire, passion, and commitment reached levels we could not previously have even imagined. We learned more about ourselves, each other, and life itself through overcoming these obstacles than in any other experience we had ever encountered.

This was the most worthy victory I had ever achieved and one that to me will forever stand alone. But we didn't win the meet. Deland Vertical Speed won the gold, the Golden Knights finished second, and Perris Airmoves came in third.

At the awards ceremony we may have received the loudest, longest standing ovation ever witnessed at any skydiving event. At the front of it and cheering louder than anyone was Tom Piras.

36
Moving On

AND JUST LIKE that, it was over. I don't know if we ever get used to having such a huge goal, pouring our hearts and souls into it for months, or years, and in a moment it's done. I experienced the same thing to a lesser degree in theater. We'd hear about which play was chosen, think about which role we most wanted, prepare for the audition, get our part, practice on our own, rehearse, rehearse, rehearse; finally it was opening night, we'd do a few shows, and it's done, finished.

The actual show or competitions themselves were only a minute fraction of the time we invested in the effort. Yet we put all the value of that effort on the "show" and often judge the total worth of the experience and ourselves based on that alone. When that's over, we feel empty. I thought it would have been different if we had won. It must be different for winners.

All of the Airmoves teammates, myself included, were physically and emotionally exhausted. For months we had been running on excitement and adrenaline produced by being committed to such a clear purpose. We needed a rest. Kristi and I went back to California. She returned to work and school. Troy returned to Colorado, Mikey to his studies, Kirk to his drop zone in Illinois, Tom to California, and Richard went back to Australia.

Had we won, we would have immediately been planning out the next training year in preparation for the 1993 world meet. But without that specific goal, we were all in limbo and the following world meet wasn't until 1995. We spoke briefly about keeping the team together, but before any of us signed on for another year, we needed time to be absolutely sure we were ready to live up to that commitment again. We understood more than ever what would be expected of us and knew it was huge.

I had made it through the meet okay, but without the competition staring us in the face, there was no urgency to jump, so I promised my body to give it the break it had been begging for. I would definitely not be jumping for at least a few months. We gave everyone until after the New Year to think about it.

It was never her intention or desire, but by default Kristi had gotten used to us living together after the accident. We had moved out of Kenny's house over the summer and into our own apartment. But she was still uncomfortable about the idea of living together without a real commitment to our relationship, and the only way that commitment could be defined was by marriage. I didn't want to lose her but didn't want to get married either, so I tried to prolong the decision and keep things as they were for as long as possible. Conveniently, right about that time a team from Australia contacted me. They were aiming to win their national championships and asked me to coach them in Australia for a few weeks leading up to and during the meet being held over the holidays just prior to New Year. I needed the work and it bought me a bit more time with Kristi, so I took the job.

While in Australia, I was tracked down and received two shocking phone calls. The first was regarding my old nemesis and new friend Tom Piras. Tom, the most recognized skydiver in the world, the man who more than anyone almost single-handedly transformed the competitive sport of formation skydiving, had died jumping.

He was working in Panama with some novice jumpers. One of them had gotten far below Tom in free fall and deployed their parachute right under him. Still in free fall, Tom had hit the canopy and was knocked out. He was wearing an AAD, and an automatic activation device that works on rapid pressure changes and is designed to deploy your reserve parachute if you are below one thousand feet and still in free fall. Tom hadn't turned it on, unbelievably. It was a dark day for skydiving and it brought 1992, a dark year, to a close.

According to the statistics, compared to what would be considered other "high risk" activities, skydiving is relatively safe. But if you are in the sport, you hear about every incident. Kristi had heard enough of it and had become increasingly worried. She had already started jumping much less and was hoping, especially if we were going to get married, that I would quit altogether.

I had assured her that fatal accidents don't happen to skydivers like me. I am one of a smaller group of jumpers with so much experience and who jump so frequently that we are always on top of every situation we might encounter. It might happen to other jumpers, but not me or anyone in this group. As an example of other jumpers in that group, I had always mentioned Tom. So much for that theory.

While still trying to accept that reality, I received a call from Jack Jefferies. The world meet was ten months away, and Jack was putting together the final plans for Deland Vertical Speed's assault on the French. After comparing their two teams, man for man, he came to the conclusion that he didn't think he could win. He was prepared to make some changes to the team and was asking Kirk and me to move to Deland to join him on Vertical Speed and compete with him against the French at the 1993 world championships.

What a surprise and what an offer. Finally, after all these years of trying and failing to actually win the U.S. team selection meet, I'd be on the U.S. 4-way team, proudly wearing red, white, and blue and representing the USA at the world championships. But I didn't want to make a decision too quickly. Not at least until I had a chance to think it through and talk with Airmoves.

It wasn't long after Jack and I hung up that Kirk called me. As expected, he had said yes to Jack's offer as quickly as he did mine when I asked him to join Airmoves. He was pushing me hard to do the same, and he was saying all the right things. "With you, me, and Jack on a team, we'll kill 'em. We'll have the best team ever."

Airmoves met after the New Year to discuss our plans. Troy announced he was stepping out. It had been the time of his life, everything he had expected and way more than he had counted on. But he had other dreams he wanted to pursue. Richard was also moving on. That left only Tom and myself.

Perris had become like home and the drop zone group like family. After all we'd been through the last year, I didn't want to leave. And I didn't know if Kristi was going to have much interest in following me around the country chasing after "the team of the year." Not without a bigger commitment from me, like a ring. Staying in Perris and starting a new Airmoves team was a definite option, and if I did, I already knew who I'd want to pick up.

Even with all the trauma of 1992, my net was still wide open, and two younger competitors from Perris had dove headfirst right into it. Mark Kirkby and John Hamilton had jumped on a team the year before with members of the Gumbies and had finished in fourth place, right behind Airmoves. I had coached their team all year and had gotten to know them fairly well. They were both amazing fliers with huge potential and high ambitions to excel in 4-way. I was certain we could grab them both for the team. I thought with this team we'd have the potential to ultimately have a chance at beating the French and winning the world meet. But we wouldn't even have a chance to try until 1995 at the earliest.

If I moved to Florida, we'd have Jack, Kirk, and myself on the same team and we'd be going to the world meet this year. But I was concerned about the potential of the fourth member, who happened to be the team sponsor. When I watched the video of Vertical Speed's jumps at the '92 nationals, he did well, good enough to beat us, but didn't look like a natural to me. All the guys on the French team were so damn good. We'd have to have four flyers that were just as good to have any shot at beating them. Even with Jack, Kirk, and me on the team, I still didn't think we'd be able to win. And I wanted to win.

Mark and John said yes before I even finished the question. Sean Capogreco joined us as the cameraman, and the new Perris Airmoves got to training.

37
Till Death Do Us Part

I HOPED MY DECISION to stay in California would have been proof enough to Kristi of my commitment to our relationship. She didn't see it that way. She knew if I had thought my team with Jack and Kirk could win, I'd have moved to Florida whether she wanted to come or not and hoped she'd be waiting for me when I returned.

After cohabitating for over a year with no statement of commitment made other than constantly voicing my love for her, she had had enough. As far as she was concerned, it was all talk. The living arrangement I thought was perfect was history. Once again, my old van became my home. Lying alone in my van at night gave me plenty of time to think. I missed Kristi, wanted to be there with her, and hoped I could somehow become everything for her that she had been for me. I didn't want to be single. Not for more than a week anyway. What was it about marriage I was so scared of? What was it about losing her I was so scared of?

My grandparents and parents were shining examples of living the commitment defined by the phrase, "Till death do us part." They were devoted to each other through thick and thin, richer and poorer, and in sickness and in health. The depth of my commitment to my teams wasn't even on the same scale. Teams were temporary. Marriages are supposed to be forever. After my experience with James, I thought there may actually be something to this concept of a "soul mate." If there was ever a woman who I thought could possibly be my soul mate, it had to be Kristi.

But what if things went bad between us? "There is no problem so big that it cannot be run away from."

Another quote from *Illusions* I thought had to be reserved for only the absolute worst-case scenarios.

But what if it was great? What if we really were soul mates? What if, like my parents and grandparents before me, through our undying love and devotion we worked through thick and thin, overcame every obstacle we faced, and built the kind of deep, loving relationship that can only be achieved through the test of time? Kristi and I had become so much closer over the past year. We learned more about ourselves and each other than what could have been possible had the year been without such enormous difficulties. What an incredible relationship we might build if we shared our lives together, if we raised a family together. If this wasn't possible with Kristi, I doubted it would be with anyone. If Kristi and I didn't get married, I would probably be giving up on ever having this in my life.

I went to bed that night planning to get up the next morning, drive to Kristi's apartment, and ask her to marry me. I could still back out because in my mind, the actual proposal would be decision time.

But once I proposed and she said yes, there would be no turning back. If I did this, I needed to be 150 percent committed to building that lifelong relationship and couldn't let any obstacle stop me. I couldn't aim for a dream this big and only be in halfway. It was all or nothing.

As always, as decision time was approaching, the fear was mounting. Thoughts of everything I had to lose were haunting me, and my eternal optimism must have clocked out. Doomsday Dan was back. "Are you out of your mind?"

"You've got a great thing going right now. Why would you want to ruin it?"

"You're going to lose your freedom."

"Your relationship is going to change for the worse."

"What if through thick and thin, richer and poorer, in sickness and in health turn out to be thin, poor, and sick?"

"Odds are fifty-fifty at best?" He never had as much to say as he did now. And where was Lover of Life Dan? Apparently off to the side, searching for a good argument and failing to find one.

I arrived at Kristi's still with all this noise in my head. But I'm a stubborn SOB, and I had learned, once I set my sights on a goal, to ignore the fear and keep moving forward until decision time.

I knocked on the door. Kristi answered and said good morning. I returned the polite greeting. She stood quietly, waiting to hear why I was there. Doomsday Dan screamed like the chickenshit he is. I stared at her, visualizing the couple I hoped we could become, the partners we would grow into, a happy little old pair looking back on their lives with pride and joy at what they had done and shared together. The Lover of Life Dan finally spoke up now. He didn't yell, "Go!" or order me at all. He calmly and quietly said, "Do it, Dan."

I listened, bent down on one knee, and proposed. She said yes so quickly that it kind of worried me. How could she be so sure? There had to be something not right about any woman who wanted to marry me.

Now that Kristi had said yes, I was so nervous I didn't think I could do it. I could tell that the anticipation of getting married was going to be ten times more intimidating than thinking about the opening night of a play or round one of the meet.

I added one condition to my proposal. I told Kristi we had to do it right then, before I chickened out. I wanted to go to Las Vegas, get married before anything in our relationship could change, and be back to the drop zone like nothing had happened. And that's what we did.

We got off the plane in Vegas, grabbed the first cab, and told the driver we were there to get married. He knew exactly where to take us—the Silver Bell Wedding Chapel. I'm pretty sure he was on commission there.

Reverend King, obviously an Elvis impersonator at night, was the first to welcome us and said he could conduct the service. He asked if we had any religious preference. I thought that was kind of odd and doubted that religiously devout people flew to Vegas to get married very often, but figured if I had a choice, I may as well request a Jewish service. Hopefully that would make my parents and grandparents feel better about it whenever it was that I decided to tell them I was married. Reverend King dug through a suitcase and came out with a yarmulke. He put it on his head then flipped through his manual for a sermon of sorts that would be Jewish enough.

An hour later we were on the plane home. Other than committing my soul to Kristi until death do *us* part and not having to sleep in my van anymore, nothing had changed. I needed to let the idea of being married settle, so we didn't tell anyone for a few months. Instead of a honeymoon, I was back to team training at the drop zone the next day.

38
Arizona Airspeed

AT THE 1993 U.S. nationals, Deland Vertical Speed and Perris Airmoves were in a class by themselves, the Golden Knights couldn't keep up. But either I had been wrong or all the natural ability I saw in our team wasn't enough because Deland averaged 18 and won. We averaged 17 and lost, again.

A month later, at the 1993 world championships, Jack and Kirk's team was beaten by the French as the French team averaged 19 points per jump and captured their fourth consecutive world championships.

At the close of that world meet I was speaking with Philippe Schorno, the captain of the French team who had been there since its inception and for all four world championship victories. We had first met and become friends back in 1986 when Fusion went to Deland and trained alongside their team, and we had stayed close throughout all these years. As friendly as we were, starting from the first day we met, I'd been dying to take on Philippe and beat the crap out of his oversponsored team in competition. He had been ready and waiting for me to show up for the fight, but I still had yet to make it to the world meet.

Philippe told me this was his last world meet, he was retiring from competition. I begged him not to quit and joked that he was running scared, leaving before I had my shot at him. I told him that for years it had been my dream to defeat and dethrone him at the world championships. He looked directly into my eyes and spoke with the most quiet, smug French accent when he said, "You will die with that dream."

I just about died right there. That was the best line I had ever heard any competitor say in my life. Wished I had said it myself and immediately logged it in my mind in case I was ever half the champion he was and had the chance to say the same to another punk like myself. We smiled and laughed, then I shook the champ's hand and bought him a beer. I guess I just had to accept the simple fact that I couldn't have all my dreams. But that wouldn't stop me from going for all I could.

After his third straight world meet defeat, Jack had had it. He's a competitor. He likes to win and was sick and tired of getting beaten by the French. I, on the other hand, was sick and tired of being beaten by someone who kept being beaten by the French. I would have at least felt a little better if I was losing to the world champions.

Since I had first moved West and started the Fource and then Airmoves, a definite regional rivalry had developed between the East Coast and West Coast, between Jack and me. Besides regional loyalty, there was also a distinct difference in training technique, philosophy, flying style, and attitude. You could see this across teams from the United States and even from around the world. Most competitors could tell at a glance where a team had trained. The phrase "You do it West Coast (or East)" was commonly used to describe them.

Kirk had jumped in both the camps and was the only person who had been on a team with both Jack and me. Throughout his year training for the '93 world meet, Kirk never let go of the idea Jack started when I was in Australia, for the three of us to jump together on the same team.

It was clear to Kirk, and he had the evidence to back it up, that by continuing to operate from the two separate East/West camps, the United States would never produce a team that could beat the

French. The French team was too strong, the athletes too talented, and the project too well funded. We knew of no way to match the financial support they received, and to train a rookie team up to their level in one year would be all but impossible. Jack and I had both tried and failed.

Our best chance of winning was to try and match them on the strength and talent of the athletes, but the only way to do that was by putting together one team made up of the best competitors from across the country, East and West.

Kirk approached both me and Jack with the idea to join forces. He wanted to start a team with the three of us and pick up the best fourth person we could find and the finest cameraman around.

I didn't know if I had two more years of this in me. After the last two years, I felt like I was a thirty-two-year-old man walking around inside an eighty-five-year-old body. I had made it through a complete decade competing in formation skydiving, had done over nine thousand skydives, broke the hell out of myself both physically and financially, and wasn't quite sure how many more years I was going to be able to pull this off for. At this point I simply accepted the pain in my neck, the limited flexibility in my upper body, and daily anti-inflammatories as standard.

But damn it, I still hadn't won yet. I wanted to win just once, just to see what it was like. I knew I had better do it now.

I really wasn't sure what to expect from being on a team with Jack. For the five years prior we had been archrivals, going head-to-head at every meet. It might be difficult to join forces with someone who for half a decade had been the main obstacle between me and my goal. After that long, it had become almost as much about seeing him lose as it was about me winning. We were from two different schools and had two completely different ways of doing things. We were both accustomed to being the leader on our teams and doing it our way. Were we going to be able to make it work?

Kirk assured us we would be the perfect teammates, the ideal combination, a match made in heaven. But Jack and I knew better.

Over the years we had observed each other in training and competition and watched how the other behaved and treated people around them. We hadn't always liked what we thought we saw. Most people who knew us both told us we were nothing alike, two totally different people in every way, opposites. But what we never for a second questioned was the other's passion for the sport and desire to win. If we knew one thing, it was that both of us had absolutely proven our commitment to excellence and to the pursuit of victory. Every year we had done all we could to win and had come up short. This was the last card either of us had to play. So we played it.

Jack wanted to have tryouts for the fourth position. I told him there was no need. "Mark Kirkby is the man for the job, no question about it." I assured him that Mark had been trying out with me for the last two years, and if we wanted to win, we needed him on the team. But Jack had never jumped with Mark, so for his own peace of mind he insisted on the tryouts. In my effort to be a team player and to get us started off on the right foot, I went along. We held tryouts (token tryouts, as far as I was concerned) and in no time a unanimous decision was made. Mark was in. (I love it when I'm right.)

John Leming, a childhood friend of Kirk's whom he had been jumping with since high school, and the funniest man I've ever met in my life, became our cameraman.

We were hoping to be able to bring a drop zone sponsor on board and put a proposal together that stated what the team was looking for and what the team could offer to them. Jack and I were the busiest coaches in the country, and we'd have many national and international teams coming to train wherever we were located. In addition to that, we planned to hold other events that should bring a significant amount of additional business to our sponsor's facility. In exchange for that, we were asking the drop zone to cover the cost of our jumps, pack jobs, and pay our videoman. This wouldn't come close to matching the French team's financial support, but it would be enough that as long as we lived cheap, we'd be able to train like we needed to.

We presented our proposal to three drop zones. Neither Deland nor Perris went for it. Larry Hill and Skydive Arizona quickly stepped up, and he was back in the game. Larry and I had remained very good friends after I had left Arizona to go to California. He welcomed me back, especially since I was bringing with me the team he always wanted, the one that could help his drop zone to become the biggest training center in the world. And just as when we first met five years earlier, Larry, like the rest of the team, still wanted to hang a world championship gold medal on his wall.

Kristi understood I had to go. In 1993 she was able to return to school after being interrupted by having to take care of me. She didn't want to move to the desert and put her degree on hold again, so she stayed in California while I moved to Skydive Arizona in the town of Eloy, located halfway between Phoenix and Tucson. Like Coolidge, it is still in the middle of nowhere, but with the luxuries that come with being closer to a freeway, like having a really nice truck stop only fifteen minutes away.

We had half of Perris Airmoves and half of Deland Vertical Speed. Being far better at skydiving than we were at branding, we went with the easy name, Arizona Airspeed.

With this team lineup, we were going to take the sport where all of us had only imagined. The 20-point average had been to skydiving what the four-minute mile was to runners. The French had gotten close at the 1993 world meet but still came up short. We were determined to be the team to do it, and we'd have to do the best 4-way anyone had ever seen to make it happen.

In January of 1994, the team moved into trailers and we were all living side by side on the drop zone. Kristi was coming to visit every few weeks. I would have also traveled back to California more often, but Gramps wasn't doing well. He and Grandma had moved closer to my folks in Columbus and I was trying to fly back to hang out with him whenever I could.

It became clear from the start of training that the differences between Jack and me went beyond our differences as competitors.

We were from different families and backgrounds as well, and had a different outlook on just about everything. We annoyed each other. What he thought was funny, I thought was hurtful. What I thought was fun, he thought was boring. Honest communication to me was sugarcoating to him. We approached nearly everything from two opposite points of view.

The only thing we shared was an absolute passion and total commitment toward reaching the same goal. And that was all we needed. We didn't have to love each other or to become best friends. We just needed to work together. Fortunately, we were more committed to our goal than we were to our egos. If nothing else, even when we disagreed, we never had to be concerned about each other's priorities. We knew the other would always put first what he thought was in the best interest of the team. As it turned out, not only did our differences not matter, they were an advantage.

We knew from the start that neither the East nor the West Coast method had worked well enough to win, so we made no attempt at forcing the training plans we had each developed down the throat of the other. Instead, we came up with a strategy for surgically figuring out the best of both and looking for new ways neither of us had previously considered. We threw out all limitations we had accepted before and decided to believe that Airspeed was capable of doing what we thought was impossible on previous teams. We realized that in the process of developing new and improved techniques, we would have to make a lot of mistakes, and that making those mistakes was a necessary part of the process and a part that would be much better accomplished sooner rather than later.

Neither Jack nor I cared if we were right as long as the team figured out what was right. We made a plan for how to best access, understand, and choose between the different techniques and styles that each of us believed in, between "Jack's way" and "Dan's way," "East Coast" and "West Coast." We knew we had to isolate each particular training item and look at it on its own merit.

We decided that it would work best if one of us led the first training camp and shared everything they had to offer. When that person was finished, the other would take the lead at the next camp and do the same. At the end of that time we would have all the information we needed and from there would be able to formulate a complete training plan that utilized the best of both.

Of course, by this time I thought I already knew it all. Every year I had tried to steal all the secrets I could from Jack, the Golden Knights, and the French team's training methodology. I put to use what I liked and discarded what I didn't. But I had also recognized that in previous competitions between our two teams, I was 0 for 4, and based on that statistic alone, there must have been something I was missing.

Sure, there were many excuses to blame losing on. I could've made the case that it was never my fault: "I did all I could do to lead my teams to victory," "Someone else got hurt," "Someone else's brain locked," "Someone else took the wrong grip," "The plane crashed."

But the fact was that when we arrived at the meets, Fusion, the Fource, and Airmoves all could have won, and didn't, and I was the only common denominator. I didn't know what I had done wrong, but I must have done, or not done, something. Hopefully on Airspeed I'd be able to find out what. To learn all I could, and with respect to the many times over national champion, I suggested Jack take lead on the first camp.

Airspeed was quickly able to combine all the strategies and techniques that our separate teams had used against each other to create a hybrid made from all the best parts of both. It didn't stop there.

Even with the open minds that Jack and I tried to approach things with, we were both too set in our ways. With as many years of experience as we had, there were some things we both agreed were limitations, impossibilities, ideas that separately we had proven couldn't work. This was our limitation, and luckily Mark and Kirk would have nothing to do with it. They were as skilled in the air as either of us, but they had a much-fresher, less-tainted outlook on what could be done.

Nothing was impossible, only things that had been tested by teams that couldn't do them. Mark and Kirk came up with ideas Jack and I had never thought of and others we had decided were impossible years earlier. The final Airspeed strategy included ideas that had never been previously done or even imagined.

We pushed ourselves, our team, and our sport further and faster than ever before. And we shared everything we learned and how to do it with any team that wanted to listen. No longer would teams have to "steal" training videos and information. There were no more secrets. We wanted the entire sport to be able to benefit from what we were learning and doing.

Other competitors were shocked when we sent our videos out and gave tips to any team that asked for them. Doing this not only felt great in terms of sportsmanship, it also built our confidence. Fear would have been the only reason to withhold the knowledge we had. Sharing it showed us and everyone else that we were fearless. Could this information be used against us by another team? Sure, but if anyone was going to beat us, we wanted to say we showed them how.

The 20-point average was our target. We knew we would need to break that barrier before we'd be able to win the world meet.

We trained hard. Each day would start out with a four-mile run or the cardio equivalent, followed by a thirty-minute stretching session, six hours of serious skydiving, and finishing with an hour at the gym. We researched and found ways to increase flexibility, reaction time, improve visualization skills, "burst power," balance, and team synchronicity. With guidance from sports psychologist Dr. Bob Moore, we developed specific plans for dive preparation, dive review, personal critiques, open communication, and goal setting. We were constantly aiming for our personal and team best, reevaluating what that true best really was, pushing it further, and analyzing what we did to reproduce it. Even at this new heightened level, the process of reaching my peak performance was the same as what I had learned in theater and confirmed at my first nationals with Fusion.

We used the phrase "on the line" to describe being in that perfect mental state that led us to our best performance. When we were *on the line*, we were flying as aggressively as possible while still calm enough to maintain total control of the jump. "Under the line" referred to when we were being too passive or cautious. "Over the line" was when we were being too reckless, and flying more aggressively than the team could control. The better trained a team is, the more narrow the line becomes. You want to push it as far as you can, stopping just short of crossing the line and holding on to it right there.

Our best changed, but the skill of performing at our best stayed the same. When we were on the line, we were at our best. We trusted our instincts and we naturally performed up to our current full potential.

As cameraman, John was in a unique position to read the team's mood and attitude. He was close enough to be able to see and feel whatever was really happening with us but also had an outside view of the big picture. His sense of humor was as fine a coaching tool as I've ever witnessed. When we were getting too cocky, he knew just how to cut us down before we started thinking too much of ourselves. When we were getting down and our confidence waned, he knew just how to push us further so we had no choice but to bounce back. And almost always so we ended up nearly falling over laughing at ourselves, each other, or him. No matter what the skydiving community thought of us, with John's help, we never started taking ourselves too seriously.

As individuals, we made no awkward extra effort to try and get along. We had a wide-open line of communication and could freely share our thoughts, decide together on a direction, point out each other's mistakes, and never, ever, no matter how fragile or insulted we felt, was any of us allowed to respond to criticism in a defensive manner.

We knew that we needed each other to succeed and were counting on each other to come through. And we did. We worked well together and communicated so clearly with one another that getting along was easy. Even Jack and I started to appreciate, admire, or laugh at the differences in each other. We learned more from each other as competitors and human beings than we ever could have from someone who was just like ourselves. We all became and still are great friends.

Airspeed won the 1994 national championships and was selected as the U.S. 4-way team for the 1995 world championships. From there we traveled to the world cup (an unofficial world championship, held biannually in between official world championships) and won the gold with a 19.9 average. But it was the world championship and a 20-plus average we were after. That was still to come.

39

The Ultimate Power of the Human Spirit

KRISTI AND I didn't like being apart, so in March she moved in with me in the trailer and looked at transferring to a school in Arizona. Kristi was going to be turning thirty-four that year. We were both from very close families and knew that if we wanted to have a family of our own someday, we shouldn't wait too long.

In April we found out Kristi was pregnant. Oh boy, I didn't think it was going to happen that fast.

I took Kristi to the doctor for an ultrasound. We were going to have a little girl. My heart dropped out of my chest. A baby girl; we were going to have a daughter. My baby, my angel. I couldn't wait to hold her. As we were walking out of the doctor's office, we passed a mother and her maybe fifteen-year-old daughter. She was buying her birth control pills. Well, I tried not to think that far ahead.

On December 28, 1994, I took Kristi to the doctor a few days before her due date for a scheduled visit. When the doctor checked the baby's heartbeat, it was erratic. She immediately took Kristi in for an emergency C-section, and within an hour I was holding our daughter Chloe Layne, named after James, in my arms. Chloe was the most lovely, precious human being I'd ever laid eyes on. During the pregnancy, Kristi and I had been as ridiculous and silly as any young pregnant couple could be. We had been talking to her, singing to her, and loving her so much for months. But there aren't words to describe the incredible love that I felt when I actually met our little girl for the first time and got to hold her in my arms. I still had not become a person who prays often, but, again, I found myself thanking God for the miracle she was.

With team training, working as a coach, and a wife with a newborn baby living in a trailer on an airport in the desert, I couldn't travel back to Ohio to see Gramps for a while, but we spoke on the phone often. I would give him a full report of everything Chloe was doing. She was as cute and plump as a baby could be. We couldn't wait until I would have a chance to bring her to meet him.

During my prior trips to see him, Gramps and I would spend most of the day just hanging out and talking. Though we never dwelled on it, we didn't hide from the conversation of life and his mortality. I told him about my experience with James and hoped it might bring him some degree of comfort. He didn't know what to make of it. His health continued to deteriorate and he was in and out of the hospital often. I wanted to bring Chloe to see him, but I hated to travel to Ohio in January with a new baby.

We made plans for my family and brother's and sister's to all go to Columbus in April to celebrate the holiday of Passover. We could only hope Gramps would make it that long. Soon after we made plans for this family reunion, Gramps was back in the hospital. It didn't look good, and the doctors couldn't say how long they thought he had—days, maybe weeks. We had heard that before and each time Gramps had come back. But even someone as strong as my grandfather could only win that battle so many times.

When we spoke on the phone, I flat out told Gramps he couldn't go anywhere until he met Chloe. For her own sake and mine, it was important to me to see him hold Chloe in his arms just once, just like he did me. The same way that James had ordered me to "get control of the situation," I told Gramps he "better still be there when we arrive." I made him promise me he would be, and he did.

Gramps was out of the hospital a week later and stayed out for the next few months. In April, just as planned, Kristi, Chloe, and I headed to Ohio to meet up with my entire family. I called Mom from the Sky Harbor Airport in Phoenix to tell her we were on our way. She told me they had just taken Gramps back to the hospital.

As soon as we landed, I took Chloe straight there to see him. I didn't think it possible, but he was even thinner now. He was lying back, unconscious, when we walked in the room. His mouth was wide open. He barely looked alive. But when he saw that we were there, his eyes lit up and were as bright as ever.

We raised Gramps's bed so that he was almost straight up, and I put Chloe in his arms. He was so physically weak by now, his arms so thin and face so gaunt. But the look of pure love and joy he had holding his great-granddaughter was incredible. He said, "She's so beautiful." I guarded Chloe while he held her for a few minutes, tickled her belly, and made silly sounds and faces at her. While she was still in his arms, he looked back at me with an extraordinary expression of almost silly pride and said, "Told you I'd still be here." He had won. Out of his sheer will to live, he had beaten death again. Like a competition, there was a date and time clock on his contest. And one more time he kicked death's ass. He kept his promise. His was the most unbelievable victory I have ever seen.

My entire family was there with him. A man like my grandfather definitely doesn't die alone. I got to sit with him by myself for a little while that night. He was too weak to speak much, so I did most of the talking. I thanked him for being there now to see Chloe and for me my entire life. I admitted that I didn't know for sure what happens when someone dies, but with all my heart I truly believed that there were more places to go, more things to do, more fun to have. I told him I thought it was going to be okay and somewhere, somehow, I was sure we'd see each other again. I didn't know if he could hear me, but I believed deep in my heart that everything I was saying was true. I hugged, kissed him, and left the room. Two days later he was gone.

40
World Champs

AFTER FOUR TEAMS, twenty teammates, ten thousand jumps, fifteen years of skydiving, and twelve years of competing, I was finally wearing red, white, and blue and representing the USA at the 1995 world skydiving championships as a member of our national 4-way team. I couldn't have been more proud.

The two years' training with Airspeed had been incredible. I had learned more and given more to the team in those years than I had ever done before. No matter what happened at this meet, the journey with Airspeed would have been worth it.

But there was only one reason that we were there, one thing that had drawn this team together. One goal that motivated us to work harder and push ourselves further, to run four miles every day before the sun came up, to do one more jump, one more push up, one more sit up, to stretch until it hurt, and visualize until the pictures were as clear in our heads as they were when seen through our eyes. We were there to win—to be world champions.

The competition was being held in Gap, France, home of the French team. It couldn't have been better. Not only were we going to clobber these guys, we were going to do it on their home turf. At times I found it no less than bizarre the way I felt in competition. The members of the French team were good friends and colleagues of ours. When the meet was over, win or lose, we would sit down together and celebrate the brotherhood of skydiving competitors and talk about the fantastic competition we were sure to have. But when the bell rings, the plane door opens, and the pilot yells, "Go," I want to tear them apart. Friends, family, and skydivers from around the globe were waving American flags and cheering us on. Standing in front of them was my beautiful wife and in her arms our nine-month-old daisy, Chloe Layne.

Chloe was downright—what comes after chubby?—fat. She was so fat she was too round to crawl and had been trying for weeks to skip crawling and just pull herself up to her feet. She was able to hold her balance after we had stood her up, but that wasn't good enough for her. She wanted to stand up on her own, and she had been trying to do it for weeks. Every morning we would find her with a look of frustration and determination as she reached up to the top bar in her crib, trying to pull herself up. It looked like it was going to take longer arms and more heavy weight lifting for her to be able to do it. But she kept trying, refusing to give up.

The meet was a battle. As expected, the French team was as tough as ever and we were going to have to be at the top of our game. *I knew that all I had to do was trust that if I relaxed and just let it happen, I would perform to the top of my abilities.*

Sounded good in theory, but this wasn't a high school play, or my first year at the nationals; this was the world meet, and we were the U.S. team! My heart pounded so hard it felt like it was going to burst out of my chest and rip open my jumpsuit.

I trusted my plan and tried to do it as I practiced, but it had never been this hard. Now, more than ever, it was about calming myself down and staying cool. On every jump I reminded myself I could do it, that I had practiced the moves hundreds of times and visualized them thousands. I told myself, "Just relax. You've practiced enough. Wait for the pilot's exit command and climb out. It will be fine. Stay calm and climb out, just climb out."

I'd take one more deep breath, climb out the door, and let it happen. The instant we left the plane and the wind of free fall hit my face, the fear was gone, like some kind of magic spell came over me. It seemed to happen automatically, instinctively. I wasn't thinking or trying at all. Almost as if I was just along for the ride as I watched my body, mind, and soul do what they had practiced doing. If I started thinking too much about it, I got in their way, so I just let it happen.

At least that's what I did on most of the jumps. But on other ones the fear would win out and I'd start thinking too much. I paid the price for it with a less-than-stellar performance. But regardless of how the prior jump went, I would go back up and try to stick to the plan every time.

We had to put it all out there, every jump. Nothing less than our best would do. I could see the fire in my teammates' eyes as we got ready to exit. Going up on the last round we had a lead, but not enough to be comfortable. On that jump, the fear slightly won out. The jump was okay, but it was short of our best. At four thousand feet, as we tracked away from each other and deployed our parachutes, I hoped, almost prayed, the jump would be good enough to hold on to our lead.

As we were flying in to land, we could see hundreds of people waving American flags, running out to the landing area to greet us. We could hear them chanting, "U-S-A! U-S-A!" The jump must have been good enough. Champagne was sprayed in our faces before our feet even touched the ground. The five of us huddled up in a tight circle, arms around each other, with our friends and fans gathered around us screaming and cheering. We didn't have much to say, just smiled, stared, laughed, and almost cried. Everyone around broke into our huddle and hugged, kissed, high-fived us, and raised us up on their shoulders. We were the first team to break the 20-point average mark, posting a 20.7.

A little while later, we walked up onto the podium, and in front of all our peers, friends, and fans, we were presented with world championship gold medals hung around our necks. We stood proudly with our hands over our hearts as they played the national anthem. When it finished, a deafening cheer broke out. We looked at each other with complete satisfaction. We had done it. We had won.

A huge party commenced and lasted for hours into the night.

I woke up the next morning and couldn't wait to jump out of bed and look in the mirror to see the new man I was, the winner I had become. I ran into the bathroom, flipped on the light switch, and with great pride took a good look at myself, expecting to see a bigger, stronger, faster, smarter, taller, and better man than I ever was before.

To my dismay, I was just the same as before.

Between the five members of our team we'd spent thirty years working toward this goal. We were in the best physical shape of our lives. We had trained to be mentally and emotionally tough, and we were. We had overcome all obstacles and pushed ourselves to be the best we could be and reached a level in the sport that no team had ever achieved before. We were unquestionably the best team in the world, and the best team there ever was. We were definitely winners. So why didn't I feel any different after actually winning the meet?

The answer suddenly became clear. Everything that defined us as winners happened long before the meet. The commitment, dedication, passion, perseverance, and drive, the qualities that overcame all obstacles and led us to victory are not awarded as prizes that come with a gold medal. It was in the pursuit of our dream that we had chosen to practice and continually strengthened these qualities in life and training. They were who we were, who we had chosen to be, and trained to become. We had brought them with us to the meet.

We didn't feel any different after winning the meet because it was in the pursuit of our goal that we had become winners long before the meet had ever started. Being a winner was not defined by the victory alone or, for that matter, the victory at all.

Only then did I realize all the decisions I had made in my life that had made me feel like a winner at the time had also actually trained me to become a winner. Every time I had the courage to make the hard decisions to

- jump off the high diving board at six years old, pretending to fly;
- walk out onstage when my cue came in a play;
- talk my fingers into letting go of the wing strut so I could drop away from the plane and begin my first jump;
- sacrifice doing the things I enjoyed so that I could put 100 percent of my time and energy into studying;
- leave Ohio in pursuit of my dream and trust that the world would allow the things that were out of my control to work out as they should;
- take control of the situation at the hospital by believing we could win even when it seemed impossible;
- have faith that the incredible moment I experienced at Apache Lake was real;
- follow the team out of the plane, despite my fears, on my first jump back; and,
- live by my dad's rules.

These were all decisions made in pursuit of a dream. A dream of reaching for excellence and toward becoming the best I could be as a person and in an activity I loved. At those moments of decision time, I felt strong, confident, powerful, faithful. Winning this actual gold medal now was nothing in comparison. I guess it wasn't about winning after all. It was about playing to win.

"If only I had known back then what I know now."

It was probably better that I didn't. What choices would I have made if I had?

I walked back out to check on Chloe. There she was, with the same look of frustration and determination, reaching for all she was worth to get a grip of the top bar in her crib. This time she stretched her arm up just a little higher, pointed her fingers a little farther, her arm almost seemed to get longer. Finally, she had a grip with her right hand. With a more confident little face now, she reached for the stars with her left hand, ever so high, stretching up—she got it. She gritted her gums, growled, and grunted, Kristi and I watching on the edge of our seats. Chloe pulled with both hands for all she was worth. A little higher, a little higher, aaannnnd SHE'S UP! Kristi and I erupted in applause, cheering and looking to see if there was any champagne left to spray in celebration. She stood straight up and looked at us with the cutest expression of pride and accomplishment. Chloe had been playing to win, and she won. I hoped she would never forget and hung my gold medal around her neck to remind her.

Epilogue

AFTER WINNING THE world meet, my mission was complete and dream reached. Chloe was almost a year old by then, and I couldn't ask Kristi to continue living in a trailer with a baby on a drop zone in the middle of nowhere. It was time to get a real job so I could support my family. I expected to be done with skydiving.

But even I couldn't believe it when I still hadn't had enough. I had always thought the 20-point average would be as fast as a team could go, but having accomplished that, it was obvious we still had the potential to go much further.

I now had as much coaching work as I could possibly fit on the schedule. Much of this was coaching national teams from around the world, but I was also working with less-serious teams of recreational jumpers that weren't out to win but who loved the sport and wanted to improve as much as they could.

Several of the members of those teams were also professional people with their own businesses. They saw a direct link between the concepts I was teaching them for reaching their peak performance and team building in skydiving to their own work, and some hired me to speak and do seminars with their staff and employees.

Kristi and I finally moved out of the trailer on the drop zone and into a house.

As Arizona Airspeed, Jack, Mark, Kirk, John, *I*, and our second cameraman Steve Nowak went on to win the U.S. national championships of 4-way formation skydiving every year from 1994 to 1999, as well as the world cups, World Games,[1] and world championships from 1994 to 1997.

In 1996 we decided to expand the team and attempt to win the U.S. national and world championships of 8-way formation skydiving as well. Craig Girard, Gary Beyer, John Eagle, Alan Metni, John Hamilton, and George Jicha joined Airspeed to complete the 8-way lineup. No single team had ever been able to accomplish winning both events at the same world championship.

Arizona Airspeed won both events at the 1996 world cup, but lost in 8-way to the U.S. Army Golden Knights at the 1996 U.S. nationals, meaning we would be representing the USA only in 4-way. Finally, in 1998, we won both events at the U.S. nationals and became the 4-way and 8-way teams that represented the USA in both events at the world championships in Australia. At that competition we won the 8-way but lost in 4-way to the French.

Our son Landen was born in 1999, and I decided after the world championships that year to retire from full-time team training. Since then Arizona Airspeed has continued on and has represented the USA in either the 4- or 8-way event every year and has won most of those world championships. In total since its inception, there have been over thirty-three members of Airspeed, and twenty-five of those thirty-three have become world champions. Since 1999, I have still at times had the opportunity to serve as the team's alternate and the privilege to jump with the Airspeed 8-way team at the 2007, 2008, 2009, and 2010 U.S. nationals of 8-way (which all but 2010 I am proud to say we won).

In 2003 I returned to California and became a partner with Melanie and Pat Conatser in running the Perris Valley Skydiving Center. I have

[1] The World Games is an Olympic trial event where sports are competed in that are being considered for future Olympics. Skydiving has still not been included as an Olympic sport.

continued coaching many teams including Synchronicity, Airkix, and Storm, the 2004, 2006, and 2008 women's 4-way world champion teams.

While coaching the Russian national 8-way team, the team's sponsor told me that they'd worked with several coaches before me but never had anyone taught them the things I was teaching them. He asked me to write a book about "how to win the world meet." I told him this would only be about 10 percent skydiving. The real meat of what it takes to win the world skydiving championships is the same as excelling in any other activity or endeavor.

The same ideas that helped me to be the best I could be at skydiving also worked for acting, writing, public speaking, sales, and any type of business performance. How to push your performance to your full potential and consistently perform at that level is a trained skill and the same skill regardless of the particular activity you're involved with.

Part 2 of this book, "How to Win," lays out the key points and proven tools and techniques that can be used in everyday life, for anyone trying to reach their full potential in their activity of choice and to follow their dreams and make them come true.

PART II
PLAYING TO WIN

Clarification: For the purpose of conversation, it is simpler for me to refer to "teams" in terms of athletic or skydiving teams and "goals" as sporting competitions. However, the ideas I address are in no way limited to sports and certainly not only to skydiving. Everyone who goes after a dream is a competitor, and their goal is the win. Anyone who chooses to work together with others toward the pursuit of a common goal is part of a team at some level. These concepts easily transfer to individuals or groups pursuing excellence in business, the arts, or any field they are drawn to. Athletic or skydiving terms no more imply that these ideas are limited to sports than saying "he" or "she" suggests a particular gender in this book. The word "training," used throughout, refers to the process of pursuing your goal, including practice, preparation, rehearsing, working out, cultivation of your skill, etc.

1

The Goal of Winning

"**WINNING" MEANS DIFFERENT** things to different people. To me, winning means having a dream, establishing a specific, ambitious goal, pursuing it with a passion, and achieving it.

There doesn't need to be an external prize or recognition awarded for the achievement for it to qualify as a victory. It just needs to be something that is important to you, that you set your sights on, devote your efforts toward, and accomplish. Winning to you may be losing weight, graduating from college, saving money, recovering after an injury, quitting drinking, getting the next higher belt in martial arts, starting a successful business, increasing your sales, having a great marriage, or seeing if you can break your own record for holding your breath underwater or standing on your head. If it's important enough to you that you're willing to work for it, then it is a worthwhile victory.

Your dream may be one that is greatly admired by others or one that no one even knows about. It doesn't matter. The value is something only you can measure for yourself. No one else gets a vote. It can be learning to play tennis, or winning at Wimbledon. It can be learning to play an instrument or being hired as a member of a professional symphony. It can be as small as finishing a big Lego and standing up in a crib. Or as big as fighting off death long enough to hold your newborn granddaughter in your arms.

Pursuing a dream often involves improving at an activity you love. To be better than you are, the best you can be, or even the best there is. Everyone who has the courage to pursue a dream is by definition a competitor. You're always competing against yourself, sometimes against other people, sometimes as part of a team, at other times solo. Too often people let the actual "victory" they are after define them as winners. Using that as the one and only measure of your success is very inaccurate. The final score or the best time may determine who won a contest, but in no way does that alone define who is a winner and who is not in the bigger picture.

Titles are temporary.

I was a world skydiving champion and now I'm not. Does that mean I used to be a winner but now I'm a loser?

If your goal is to lose one hundred pounds and you do it, you're a winner. But if you only drop ninety pounds or two years later you gain back a pound, you're still a winner.

It is always possible that you won't win. Even if we train hard, train smart, and reach a performance level no one in our field has ever achieved before, we still may lose the "meet." There may be injuries, personal tragedies, circumstances beyond our control, or simply an opponent more skilled than ourselves. Does that mean we lost? We may have lost the "meet" but won in the process.

Becoming a winner is an ongoing process that involves making the decision to pursue your dream, waking up every day to face the obstacles that pursuit will inevitably present, keeping your eyes on your goal, and not backing off for anything. It will almost certainly require you to step out of your comfort zone, work hard, experience days and weeks of pain, frustration, and personal and financial sacrifice while enjoying mere moments of incredible joy, pride, and fulfillment.

All this will happen long before the day of the "meet." And unlike a title, money, or fame, what you gain in this process cannot be taken away from you. It is yours forever and yours to use toward any other goals you may have in life.

It's Not About Winning, It's About the Journey

I have poured my heart and soul into training for the U.S. National Skydiving Championships only to go to the competition and lose by 1 point. Of course, this was very disappointing. In fact, finishing within a few points of being a winner was more frustrating than losing by 10 points and not even being in range of winning the gold medal. But once a little time had gone by and I could examine the experience with an unemotional mind, it was clear that it was well worth the journey even though we "lost" the meet.

Pushing to win, playing to win, doing all you can do in pursuit of the dream of victory, is the magic that winners are made of and what defines the winning spirit. A meaningful journey only exists within the passionate pursuit of an ambitious goal, the goal of "winning."

I know of many great competitors who never won. But I don't know of any great competitors that didn't have the goal of "winning."

But the best chance of ultimately winning, however you define it, is also to take your attention off of the specific "victory" you are after and focus it on the pursuit. These will be the goals you can define, target, and sink your teeth into every day.

It is easy to commit to the final goal. To say, "I want to be a world champion." It is entirely different to say, "I am committed to doing the work it takes and making whatever sacrifices necessary to overcome all obstacles that cross my path in my pursuit of becoming a world champion." Many people have committed to the goal, only to find out that they weren't up to the challenges required to attain it.

On the road to achieving any ambitious goal, there will be times when we question our capabilities, our sanity, and our desire. During these times the goal will seem out of reach, even impossible. Our belief that we are capable of winning will be questioned and sometimes lost. This is when individuals and teams that are focusing only on the final goal will often give up.

Those of us who are committed to the *pursuit* of that goal will power through these hard times. The final goal may temporarily seem unattainable. But by facing, attacking, and overcoming each individual challenge along the way, we will recognize real progress toward that ultimate goal. Each day will be a victory in its own small way. And those small victories will eventually add up to success.

2
You Have to Believe

EVERY SUCCESSFUL PERSON is a dreamer. But every dreamer is not successful.

Pursuing an ambitious goal in any field comes down to asking ourselves two questions:

1. Do I believe it's possible to succeed?
2. Do I want it badly enough to do what it's going to take to make it happen?

When I took over the Greene County Skydiving Center, I was certain it was possible to succeed and knew what I had to do to make it happen. Once it became apparent I had signed a bad contract, I determined there was no longer any chance of being successful, so I gave up and turned my efforts elsewhere. *I wanted it badly enough but didn't believe it was possible for me to succeed.*

In competition skydiving, I wanted to win, loved training and competing with the team, and would do whatever it took to achieve that victory. But after winning for several years, my desire for another gold medal wasn't as strong anymore. I was still capable but didn't want it badly enough, so I moved on to other challenges. *It was possible for me to succeed, but I no longer wanted it badly enough to do what it was going to take to make it happen.*

Before you decide to pursue your dream, be sure and ask yourself the same two questions:

Do I believe that it's possible for me to succeed?

Simply put, if you truly don't believe there is any way you could possibly accomplish your goal, then you probably can't. (Let's not waste any more time on that.)

Do I want it badly enough to do what it's going to take to make it happen?

The depth of your desire will usually be the primary factor in determining your true capabilities. Don't underestimate them. One-hundred-pound mothers have picked up cars because their children were trapped under them. Hostages have escaped capture when no one would have thought they had a chance. There are hundreds of miraculous stories like these. They happen every day. It is amazing what we human beings are capable of doing if we want it badly enough.

In most cases it is possible for us to succeed if we want it badly enough to do what it's going to take to make it happen. So you better know what it's going to take.

As a teenager, I sometimes thought about being a Navy Seal. How cool it would be to be the baddest of the bad, able to stand up to anyone, take charge of any situation, and withstand anything? Those guys are some tough dudes. In my fantasy world, I thought I could do it. Then I got the facts straight and realized how they actually train and better understood what they may be called to do. Once I got it straight, my respect and admiration for this elite branch of the military went up tenfold. Part of why I admired them so much was because I no longer thought I had it in me to do what it was going to take to become one.

Was it possible for me to become a Navy Seal? Yes.

Did I want it badly enough to do what it was going to take to make it happen? No, I'm nowhere near tough enough for that.

Like most other teenagers, I used to think it would be great to be a millionaire. It has to be good to be rich. How hard can it really be? There are lots of idiots out there who have gotten rich. Why couldn't I do it? Did I want to put all my efforts toward figuring out how to make lots of money and then pursuing a path where that was my main goal in life? Not really.

Had I made getting rich my goal, would it have been possible? Yes.

Did I want it badly enough to do what it was going to take to make it happen? No.

Make sure you have it straight. Winning something always sounds good, but know what you're getting yourself into. What do you have to do to make it happen? What are the necessary sacrifices? How is the commitment defined? How hard is the work? How much time will it take? What are the risks? What are the costs? If, after thinking this through as completely as you can, the answer to "Do I want it badly enough to do what it's going to take to make it happen?" is "Yes, I want to go for it," then it would be a crime against yourself not to.

3

Make the Decision

NOW IT'S DECISION time. This first required step is usually the hardest. People make excuses and avoid making the decision to follow their dreams for entire lifetimes. It's easy to keep saying no. There is always a reason to do it later, or not at all. But once you've thought it through completely and are certain you want to go for it, nothing feels better than to finally make that call, that promise to yourself to open the door to the chance of achieving a dream. Once you've made the decision, even before you've taken any action, you will start feeling the pride you've earned through the courage you've shown. You'll be flying.

Decision time isn't the final decision. It's the first of many. It sets you in motion toward your goal, but a million more decisions will have to follow, some seemingly insignificant, others monumental. With each decision, no matter how small, you continue to build momentum toward reaching your goal. Keep making the right decisions, and soon there will be no stopping you.

Building Momentum One Decision at a Time

You're "rolling" now. You have set things in motion, and once that momentum is established, it actually takes energy in the form of negative decisions to stop it. (Newton's law of motion.) Here is an example of how this works.

Since my lung spontaneously collapsed when I was nineteen, I have tried to be disciplined about always maintaining a good workout routine. Even after almost thirty years of this, I have yet to enjoy going to the gym and still have to force myself to do it. Now that I'm not competing full-time anymore, working out is no longer part of my "work" schedule, so I have to find other times to get it done.

I have other goals in my life that require my time and effort as well, specifically work and family. I can't go to the gym during my work hours, and I don't want to go to the gym after work because that is family time. The only available time I have left would be early in the morning, early enough that I can be home in time to get the kids up, see them off to school, and be to work on time.

I have set my goal and figured out a plan for what I need to do to achieve it. Now it is all about making one decision at a time that will lead me down that path. After a series of positive decisions, I will cross the threshold where enough momentum is established that I am committed to moving forward and retreat will no longer be an option for me.

But first, it is all about the first decision. What is that first step I have to take that will set me in motion toward achieving my goal of staying in shape?

First decision: Get my ass out of bed at four thirty in the morning! When my alarm goes off at 4:30 AM, there is only one thing I have to do. Get up. Don't think about anything else. Don't think about what I'll do when I get to the gym, how long it's going to take, or how good it feels to lie in bed. Sit up. Throw the covers off and get off the mattress. That's all. That's the initial decision. I'm out of bed. The first action has been taken.

Next decision: Get my clothes on! I leave my gym clothes right next to the bed so I won't have to look for them. Don't think about anything else. Just put my clothes on. Done.

Next decision: Get out the door! Don't stop to comb my hair and straighten my clothes. It's four thirty in the morning. The other nut-cases at the gym before the sun comes up aren't going to care what I look like and I shouldn't either. Just get out the door.

Next decision: Get in the car and drive away! Get away from the house, farther from the bed. The more space I can put between myself and the mattress, the less likely it is I'll change my mind.

It is essential to continue to take that next small step forward, no matter how small it is. With each step, each decision, you build momentum and it becomes easier to continue moving forward and harder to retreat.

I could have easily gone back to sleep after my alarm went off. We've all done it so many times they invented the snooze button and made it standard equipment on every alarm clock. If I was still in bed, lying down, all I would have had to do was choose the one negative decision to close my eyes.

But once I had sat up and thrown the covers off, returning to bed wouldn't have been as easy as just closing my eyes. I could have made the same negative decision to retreat, but it would have required a greater action. I would have had to lie back down and pull the covers back up.

Once I had gotten out of bed and gotten dressed, returning to bed would have taken even more. Once I was out of the house and actually driving to the gym, I had crossed the threshold. It was easier to keep moving forward than to go back. Each little step is critical. With each step forward, we are that much closer to our goal and that much less likely to turn and run back to our comfort zone. Once you cross this threshold, you won't be able to live with yourself if you turn around.

4

Overcoming Obstacles

IT IS ALMOST humorous that overcoming obstacles is seen as an issue that needs its own detailed analysis and discussion. But some people who choose to pursue their dream seem surprised when an obstacle appears in their path, as if they expected it to be a walk in the park.

You are striving to achieve an ambitious goal. It is only ambitious because there are so many obstacles. Obstacles are what create the challenge, and the challenge is what makes it worthwhile. Pursuing an ambitious goal is nothing but obstacles.

From the moment you decide to reach for your dream, obstacles of all shapes and sizes start lining up for the fight. And they rarely fight fair. They gang up on you from every angle—emotional, physical, financial—they can and take full advantage of any weakness. Committing to the pursuit of an ambitious goal is promising to meet each one of these obstacles head-on. You'll need to be ready for them.

No matter the size or severity of an obstacle, overcoming it comes down to the same two things:

- Is it still possible to reach our goal?
- Do we still want it badly enough to do whatever it's going to take to make it happen?

For people who stop believing it's possible to achieve their goals, or aren't committed enough to the pursuit of those goals, even the smallest obstacles will be enough to stop them dead in their tracks. They become discouraged by the slightest setback and realize that they don't want it as badly as they thought they did. They may even begin to hope that insurmountable obstacles arise that will give them justified reasons to quit or to fail.

But for people who believe their dream is possible and are truly committed to the pursuit of it, obstacles that at first seem insurmountable only serve to inspire and motivate them even more. They decided from the beginning that they will rise to any occasion, at any time, with whatever it is going to take to overcome any obstacles that get in their way. They are prepared and even look forward to the challenges.

Fear: The First Obstacle

Fear: "anxiety caused by the possibility of danger or pain."

The emotion of fear is our single, most powerful survival instinct. Fear's purpose is to respond to imminent danger by giving us a mega shot of adrenaline that instantly provides a seemingly endless supply of additional speed, power, and stamina with which we can either defend ourselves or run like hell.

But except for situations when our lives depend on it, fear is a very unproductive emotion.

Fear of losing stands in the way of winning. Fear of making mistakes stands in the way of achieving our peak performance. Fearing what other people might think of us only makes us think less of ourselves. Hating to lose or make mistakes or hating other people's false impressions of us can often be very productive. Fearing them never is.

This fear is also unsubstantiated. There is no possibility of real danger created by making mistakes, losing, or other people's poor opinions. These fears are created by ourselves; they are self-inflicted. We don't have to entertain them.

We cannot significantly improve at anything unless we are willing to explore our potential beyond our accepted comfort zone. The top performers in sport, business, and the arts are in a constant state of innovation, experimentation, and discovery as they try to raise their performance to new heights. This brings excitement, uncertainty, passion, and reward to their daily lives. This also by definition demands that they are willing to risk making mistakes.

It is impossible to reach new heights and push your skills to new levels without making mistakes in the process, lots of mistakes. So hurry up and get on with it. The sooner you make these mistakes and learn from them, the better.

Fear for your life if you need to, but don't waste your life fearing things that can't harm you. And don't waste your time either. There are *real* obstacles that need to be addressed and overcome in order for you to achieve your goal.

Three Other Obstacles: The Expected, What-Ifs, the Unexpected

Obstacles are anything that stands in the way of accomplishing your goals. Regardless of what it is you are trying to achieve, you will need to develop a specific strategy to most effectively and efficiently overcome them. When organizing that strategy, break the obstacles down into three categories.

The expected obstacles are those that are guaranteed. They are known antagonists.

- You don't yet have the technical expertise and skills you need.
- You're not strong enough.
- You're not fast enough.
- You're underfunded.
- You're overfunded and often take the opportunities your financial support provides for granted.

- You're overly emotional and take setbacks too personally.
- You're not disciplined enough.
- You're inexperienced.
- You're too experienced and set in your ways.

If you take the time to examine your strengths and weaknesses and honestly evaluate them, the *expected obstacles* will be obvious before you even begin. Create a plan and strategy that addresses each one. *All* of these can be overcome through good planning, hard work, and smart training.

Other expected obstacles that many people choose to ignore are the fears and emotions that we inflict upon ourselves and our teammates. To some degree or another, everyone will have to face fears of making mistakes, concerns of what other people think of them, or judging themselves based only on the final outcome instead of how they approach the journey.

Expect to confront these obstacles, so prepare for them by clearly stating your goals, purpose, and expectations of yourself and your teammates. Define the type of person, team, and teammates that you want to be. Commit to treating yourself and each other with respect and support. Establish open lines of communication that provide the opportunity to build confidence instead of fear and doubt.

What-if obstacles are those that could happen. They are not guaranteed like the expected obstacles, but they are within the realm of possibilities.

Use a bit of foresight to anticipate what obstacles might arise, and how you plan to handle them if and when they do. All of this is best addressed prior to the start of your training. In addition, after training begins, and when you recognize the possibility for more "what-if" obstacles, make plans for them before they materialize.

Examples of *what-if* obstacles and possible agreed-upon responses that a skydiving team should expect (these are applicable to many other team goals too):

- What if we lose our funding?
  Beg, borrow, and steal. Fill out every credit card application you can get your hands on. Find the money now. Figure out how to pay it off later.
- What if we have bad weather and can't skydive?
  Travel to other locations with better weather, or spend additional time training in a vertical wind tunnel.
- What if for some reason we lose a necessary teammate?
  Have a list of potential alternates. If at all possible, include your alternates in the team's plan as a regular part of training so if and when you need them, they are ready to step in.
- What if a teammate has a difficult personal issue that must be dealt with?
  Give your teammate your full support. Be there to help them through this difficult time.
- What if a teammate has personal conflicts like a family tragedy?
  Don't quit. There are some personal situations that must take priority over training. Rework your timeline and goal setting so that you or your teammate can take care of things. Everyone on the team will become a better teammate knowing that the team will be there to support her if she needs it. In the meantime, bring in the alternate, reschedule the camp, or extend other camps to make up for the lost time.
- What if our competition is far ahead of us and the strategy we planned won't be enough to make us competitive with them?
  If your goal is to "win the meet," then you must increase your training or find other ways of improving the effectiveness of your scheduled training within the time you have.

If not addressed before they actually happen, what-if obstacles can cause you to panic. You rush to make a decision that isn't well thought out or take so long to choose a course of action that you create another obstacle by limiting the time frame you have to work within. Without prior planning, all these things seem to be beyond your control. You could feel lost, fragile, and overwhelmed.

Had these issues been addressed before you began, you would have already had a well-conceived plan and response. You would immediately shoot into action as soon as the obstacle presented itself. With a clear plan, you will be ready to handle anything that is thrown at you. You will welcome the challenge. The anxiety is minimized and the likelihood for success greatly increased.

Unexpected obstacles are the ones that you can't really predict and are very difficult to plan for. Unexpected obstacles are those that involve tragic circumstances. These experiences are generally traumatic and beyond our imagination. Consequently, they are beyond our ability to anticipate how we will choose to respond.

But in terms of accomplishing our goal, even an obstacle of epic proportion is still just another obstacle. Whether we overcome it or not will still come down to the same two questions:

Is it still possible to succeed?
Do we want it badly enough to do whatever it's going to take?

The plane crash Perris Airmoves suffered was obviously unexpected and much more tragic and severe than any obstacle we had previously experienced. The team was finished. We had lost one teammate, and all the others were severely injured. It was no longer possible to succeed. The team and local skydiving community had accepted this before I woke up from the coma. This was the reality I woke up to.

Fortunately, my head injury was so severe that I wasn't thinking straight. What I did still understand and knew to ask were these same two questions. If the answers were yes and we chose to go for it, it was going to be one *unexpected obstacle* after another.

The loss of James was devastating. Nothing could be done to bring him back.

But did we have to give up on our team? We'd been doing so well and having such an incredible experience. We were truly living our

WE CAN'T DO IT	WE CAN DO IT
The doctors said that with my injuries, I could never jump again.	Doctors always protect themselves and tell you your limitations. I was very weak and damaged but fully functional. I could walk, talk, think, and move all my body parts. The doctors were wrong.
We lost a very valuable teammate. James was the best flyer on the team. He had that pure, childlike passion, which is such a valuable asset. He helped us to keep our sense of humor during the most trying times in training. How could a teammate that brought so much to the team be replaced?	James couldn't be replaced. But there were other experienced competitors that could fill the slot. We brought in Mikey Traad, my old friend and former teammate from the Fource, to jump in the position James had flown.
I would have the halo brace on for another two months. The absolute soonest we could begin jumping was in three months. That wouldn't be enough time to train before the meet.	If that's all the time we have, then that will have to be time enough. Every goal has time constraints built into it.
We don't have gear. All of our parachute equipment was destroyed in the crash.	We can have new equipment made. The manufacturers will help us out and rush it through.
Even if we get new equipment and train as much as possible in the time we have, there is no chance we can win. We are too far behind. It is no longer possible to succeed. Right around this time we received a "message" from James. Troy and James lived and worked together. Troy was going through the painful process of gathering all of James's things when he found a sentence James had carved in his worktable. It read: "The hardest part of winning is just showing up."	The timing of this discovery was bizarre. But it was exactly something James would have said had he been standing there. We definitely couldn't win if we didn't show up at the meet. If we do show up, anything is possible. We are a great team. Just making it to the meet will be an incredible accomplishment that will translate into the fighting spirit we will need to win. It is still possible to succeed.

dream and taking on all challenges with fierce passion and desire. This was the true pursuit of excellence, and it was an incredible way to live. After having experienced such a fulfilling life, I wasn't willing to accept anything less if I didn't have to. *But aiming for this dream meant aiming to win.* Was it still possible to succeed?

I gathered the remaining members of the team. We were all in different stages of recovering. I had a plan. I wanted to train as hard as we could and go to the nationals playing to win.

They thought I was out of my mind. Obviously the head injury was even more severe than they had perceived. They brought up reasons why we couldn't do it. I searched for a way we could.

There are always excuses. Don't ask yourself if it's going to be easy. Ask if it's possible.

Do the circumstances exist that make it even remotely possible to succeed? Do we want it badly enough? Do we realize what it is going to take to succeed, and are we willing to do it?

Airmoves was. Absolutely.

Throughout the continued pursuit of our goal, both before and after the crash, we moved forward, motivated by the idea that it was possible to succeed, to win. As long as it was even remotely possible to win, we found a way and were willing to do whatever it was going to take to make it happen. Had we ever assessed the situation and come to the conclusion that it was impossible, that there was no possible set of circumstances that could take place that would give us even the slightest chance of winning, we would have stopped and put our energies toward something else.

We always believed we could win and were willing to do whatever it was going to take to make it happen.

You Can Apply This to the Pursuit of Any Goal

Imagine you wanted to start your own business. You know what you want to do. You can then look at the three types of obstacles and plan your reactions should you encounter them. The key is to ask if it's possible for your venture to succeed.

Do the circumstances exist that make it even remotely possible to succeed?

Do you want it badly enough?

Do you realize what it is going to take to succeed and are you willing to do it?

Then brainstorm your *expected obstacles* (getting the bank loan, finding your channels to market, sourcing your product, distribution, inventory, etc.).

Next, look at the *what-ifs*. What if I start up and another player enters the market with the same offer? What if the market prices drop by *x* percent, can I make money? What if the competition closes ranks and gangs up against me? What if I don't reach my sales income as forecast, etc? Many large businesses would see this as necessary contingency planning.

When it comes to the *unexpected obstacles*, it's not possible to plan for them now, by definition. If we could, they would just become further *what-ifs*. So now is the time to ask yourself, "How ready am I to take on the challenge of launching my new business? When I come across something I wasn't expecting, am I prepared to ask, is it still possible to succeed? Am I really sure I want it badly enough to do whatever it's going to take?" If you can answer, "Yes!" then you are ready to launch your business with the best possible start. That in itself is no guarantee of success. But it will help you get the start and build the momentum you need.

5
The Team

MOST PEOPLE WHO have the courage to pursue their dreams are strong, highly motivated, self-sufficient individuals. You may not perceive yourself this way, but by making the decision to go after your dream, you have already taken the first step toward proving it to be true. The decision alone is evidence that you are more confident and willing to step out on your own than you may have previously given yourself credit for.

This is very important, because the fact is that no one can do it for you. It is your goal, and if you want to accomplish it, it is you and only you that can make it happen.

Going for it alone has the potential of being a powerful character-building experience. It may very well be the most effective way to strengthen your independence, self-reliance, and self-confidence.

However, going solo when you don't need to is rarely the smartest and most efficient strategy toward reaching your goal. *If you knew everything you needed to know about how best to accomplish your goal, you would have already achieved it.* Don't be too arrogant, too afraid, or too shy to ask for help.

Any ambitious goal is going to take significant time, commitment, and sacrifice. Even in a solo endeavor, the smartest course of action will almost always include bringing in advisors, trainers, or other individuals in positions of support. To some degree or another, you are putting together a team.

Being part of a team presents the opportunity for many character-building experiences as well. As a member of a team, you have an opportunity to learn the valuable skill of how to communicate with others clearly, honestly, and effectively. On a team you will have the chance to recognize how your attitude, emotions, and behavior affect the people around you. With this understanding, you will be able to learn how to conduct yourself in a manner that leads to the most positive results in any situation. You will learn how to understand what the team and your teammates need from you and will have the opportunity to come through for them and experience the tremendous pride and fulfillment you get from being a great teammate. As a member of a team, you will learn to trust and appreciate other people and you will experience the incredible feeling of being trusted and appreciated by them.

Unless you plan to live as a hermit, the lessons presented to you by being part of a team will be an enormous benefit to you in everything you do for the rest of your life.

What Is a Team?

In the deepest sense of the word, a *team* is a group of individuals who are committed to the pursuit of a common goal and who need each other to achieve it (my definition, I didn't like *Webster*'s).

The degree that you *need* your teammates will define what type of team you have. In college, my classmates and professors were more of a support team. We each had different specific goals. Our goals were independent of one another but came together well, so that in pursuit of our individual goals, we were also in a position to help and support each other.

It was a better experience because we had each other, and a more efficient path to reaching our goals. When the "game" was on and we were taking the final exams, it was a solo event, every man for himself. At that point there was nothing that the support team could do for us.

Most teams fall under the category of support teams. You support each other, provide knowledge and tools for each other, and gain from the others' victories. But you don't *need* each other to the extent a competition sports team does. You are not on the same actual "playing field" together at the same time, so you don't have to trust each other to the same degree. You don't absolutely "need" one another to succeed. If someone isn't pulling their weight, the more motivated team members can pick up their slack, replace them, or just remove them from the team completely.

A 4-way formation skydiving team is an example of a team based on "need." Like many others, it requires a specific number of players, five to be exact. Everyone has to pull his own weight. When the "game" is on, you are tested as a team. Your personal success is completely dependent on your teammates' commitment to the team, as theirs is on you. Your performance in competition rides on their performance as much as your own. You can't win unless they win. If they lose, you lose.

When people can't achieve their goals on their own, they need teammates who are committed to the same goals. This common need, a need that cannot be realized by a solo effort, is what forces teams to form and what glues them together.

Over the last couple of decades, the concept of *team building* has come into the forefront of sports, business, and relationship development. Highly trained advisors and consultants describe team building in very complex terms, almost as a foreign concept that we need to research and explore in order to fully understand.

Teamwork. Team bonding. Team dynamics. Team communication. Could it really be that complicated? Throughout history, we've seen great teams in many different fields display exemplary teamwork. Ancient hunter-gatherer cultures had to hunt as teams to survive, and they didn't even have the benefit of team-building seminars. For them, the success of the team was a life-or-death matter.

When you truly need something, that need will define all of your actions. Nothing else exists. That need is your single priority. You stay unquestionably focused and determined until your need is filled. If you cannot get what you need on your own, you must find other people that need the same thing you do. That is why teams form.

Life was so simple when basic survival needs were all mankind had to be concerned about. Fortunately, for most people who are reading this, your survival needs are met. Your goals in life are not about what you need, but what you *want*. Whether you are successful or not will depend on how badly you want it. Do you need it or not? Are you going to quit when it gets difficult or work through any issues that arise until you have won?

Life is more exciting when you are so passionate about your goal that your desire borders on need. You want it so badly that sometimes you can't sleep at night. It is on your mind all the time. You will do whatever it takes to make it happen. You may not want a team. But if you can't accomplish that goal on your own, then you have no choice.

Assembling Your Team

High-performance, top-notch teams usually start as one person, obsessed with his or her dream. That's probably you. The ultimate goal you are reaching for is still so far out on the horizon that it seems like a fantasy. You cannot accomplish it on your own. You need a team. You need teammates who share your dream, whom you will be able to depend on and trust, who will stick it out when the going gets tough. This is a lot to ask and even more to demand of someone. Where will you find these teammates? How will you know if they are the right ones?

There is a long list of qualities that define great teammates. Some of these are experience, skill, knowledge, technical expertise, ability to communicate, good sense of humor, drive, compassion, ability to focus, open-mindedness, self-confidence, and emotional toughness, just to name a few.

These are all essential, but the fact is that you won't know if individuals, including yourself, possess any of these qualities until you are deep into your team training. There will always be people who talk a good game. It is easy to act confident, have a fun personality when you are not being pushed or tested. Wait until the struggles, challenges, and demands of training set in, and then we'll see who's laughing.

Be certain to first demand from yourself the qualities that you are looking for in others. Be the great teammate that you are looking for.

Look for these traits in people you are considering, but understand that true confirmation of these qualities in your teammates will not come until after the team is in action. Make your best guesses, your best predictions; but even if you are looking at individuals you think you know well, until it is proven in training, there will still be some risk involved.

Passion, Potential, Desire

There are three particular qualities which are essential for anyone to become a great teammate: passion, potential, and desire.

Passion: At the core of each team member's motivation should be an intense emotional excitement toward the activity itself. First and foremost, they should love to "play the game" and the personal challenges it presents.

Potential: Each team member must have the potential to achieve the performance level the team's goal requires of them within the time frame established.

Desire: Each team member must want to achieve the team's stated goal badly enough to do the work required and make the sacrifices necessary for them to reach their full potential.

When you first start looking for teammates, throw out a big net. A net designed to catch anyone who shares your passion and dream.

The first time, you will come up with all the obvious people. Individuals who already know what they are after and are trying to be found. They say all the right things: "I want this more than anything," "I'll do whatever it's going to take," "I've been looking for a team like this for years." Everything they say may be true. But saying it alone doesn't make it so. If they wanted it so badly and had been trying to find a team for so long, why hadn't they caught you in their net? The truth is, they may have just done so, but they may also be full of crap. Keep throwing your net out and see who else gets caught in it. The best possible teammates are not always the loudest and most obvious ones. I'm glad Fang and Woody knew that; otherwise they never would have found me.

When I showed up at the Greene County Sport Parachute Center that first morning, I thought I was a pretty good flyer, but I had never jumped with anyone as good as Woody and Fang. When I compared myself to them, it quickly became apparent that I wasn't even close to as good as I thought I was. Actually, I stunk.

I demonstrated few, if any, of the ideal traits we look for in teammates.

Experience – *None.*
Skill – *Nope.*
Knowledge – Not hardly.
Technical expertise – Don't be funny.
Fun personality, good sense of humor – I'd certainly be giving them a lot to laugh at.
Compassion – I hoped they'd have some for me.
Ability to focus – I was eighteen, it was doubtful.
Drive, open-mindedness, self-confidence, emotional toughness, ability to communicate – Who knows?
Potential – Maybe.
Passion and desire – *Absolutely.*

Fortunately for me, when scanning for teammates, Woody and Fang used a really big net that didn't let any possibility slip by. They saw potential in me that I didn't even know I had. When it came to my passion and desire, they could tell that if nothing else, I loved skydiving, I loved flying, and I desperately wanted to find out just how good I could be at it. They thought it a good bet that I would be willing to put in the work that would be necessary to reach that potential.

Potential and desire go hand in hand. One isn't worth much without the other. *Most people have more potential than they realize and less desire than they think they do.* They are capable of doing more than they give themselves credit for, but don't want it as badly as they thought they did when they find out how much work and sacrifice is going to be required.

There are those individuals that at first glance you can tell are naturals. They clearly display the potential and leave no question that they could be great someday. But often it has come so easy to them that they have become strangers to hard work. They may have the potential to be great, but they may never reach that potential. No matter how naturally gifted someone is, those gifts will never replace hard work, emotional toughness, perseverance, and a deep desire to win.

On the other hand, I know of skydivers who looked more awkward and uncomfortable in the air when they first joined teams, not "naturals" at all. All indications suggested their ultimate potential limited them at best to becoming competent recreational jumpers, certainly not world-class competitors.

But through their efforts and persistence, and to everyone's surprise, they far surpassed their perceived potential and became national champions and world meet medal holders.

This is not limited to physical athletic potential. Rarely do individuals come to your team already packaged with the necessary qualities, abilities, and skills in other areas such as technical knowledge, communication, self-confidence, open-mindedness, and focus. These are just as essential to any team as the physical qualities are to a sports team. And like the physical qualities, these also can and will be learned if an individual wants it badly enough.

The Value of Different Personalities and Perspectives

If I had to create a model for the "ideal team," it would consist of a group of very different people from different backgrounds. It would include individuals that bring a variety of skills, perspectives, experiences, and personalities to the team.

When forming teams, we look for individuals with the different skills the team needs. The specific technical skills required are obvious. A business requires specialists from different fields like accounting, advertising, graphic design, PR, and manufacturing. A football team needs front linemen, a quarterback, receivers, defensive ends, and so on.

But outside of these types of particular skills, when it comes to qualities such as varying personalities, perspectives, experience levels, age, background, and sense of humor, there is a tendency to look for people as much like ourselves as possible. Commonalities like these may help to get a team off to a smooth and easy start. But ultimately, the team will benefit greatly from a variety of personal qualities as much as it requires a variety of technical skills.

Veterans and rookies. A balance of youth and experience is a great value to any team. Though it is common to have some friction between these two types of teammates, they very often bring to the team exactly what the other needs.

Arizona Airspeed's success was largely a result of having two veterans and three newer competitors. The younger teammates bring new fire and energy to the team. They are absolutely convinced that they can and will win and can't even imagine that anything will stand in their way.

Their expectations of themselves and the team are high, but often unrealistic, their efforts sometimes misguided. They pour out their hearts and souls but don't see the immediate results they were expecting. In the face of certain setbacks, their unbridled enthusiasm may soon become hampered by discouragement and doubt. They become very frustrated and don't realize that even on the best team, frustration is part of the game.

The more seasoned teammate has the experience to help the younger team members direct their energies and put their focus in the right areas. They can offer more realistic expectations, keep things in perspective, and minimize frustration.

On the other hand, without the influence of their younger teammates, the veterans may become somewhat complacent. They don't recognize if they have lost that competitive fire until they see the same fire in their younger teammates' eyes. The enthusiasm the younger teammates bring to the team serves to remind the more experienced teammate of how they used to be, how they used to feel. And in doing so, it rejuvenates that fire and passion in them.

The veterans have been there before. They know what systems work but are likely to be somewhat set in their ways. The rookies bring new ideas and the confidence to try them, ideas that might have been prejudged or never even considered if not for the blind ambition and confidence of the younger team members.

In addition, as long as you don't mind the terms "punk" and "dinosaur," these relationships can provide fuel for some of the best harassment-based humor a team has to work with. The inner competition between these teammates, and the laughs that go along with it, will provide never-ending fun and entertainment.

A hard-ass and a comedian. On the best teams I have seen there has usually been a hard-ass, someone that demands each teammate to be disciplined and pushes everyone every step of the way. This is often thought of as a needed personality, but left on its own it can cause too much tension and stress within the team. It is important the team be disciplined and focused, but at times it is just as important that the team doesn't take itself too seriously. We must be able to maintain our sense of humor and the ability to laugh at ourselves and each other. Every hard-ass needs a comedian. But you can't make a joke out of everything. Every comedian needs a hard-ass.

Different approaches to training (planning) and communicating. There are two general common teammate personality types: those that are loose and playful, and those that tend to be more serious and uptight. Either one of these on its own may have a negative impact on the team. But together, they keep the team in check, always providing whatever positive influence is needed given what the moment calls for.

In competition, there are often times when a team needs to loosen up and relax. Other situations, more frequently in training, demand the team to tighten up and get down to business. For a team to stay cool and maintain that laser-tight focus under all circumstances, they need both. The combination of these personalities helps the team to be emotionally balanced instead of overly emotional.

Being part of a team that is trying to achieve great things provides an amazing opportunity for personal growth. *We will be faced with many obstacles, one of the strongest being negative psychological barriers we impose on ourselves.* As teammates, we must help and support each other to overcome obstacles like self-doubt and concern of how other people perceive us. That support could come in the form of compassion, toughness, or humor. We may be in need of a hug, a joke, or a good kick in the ass. If a team is made of all like individuals, then we only have access to one type of support, one perspective of how best to handle any given situation. And one perspective, no matter which one it is, won't be enough to succeed and grow.

Friends as Teammates

It is a rare individual who decides, "I want to be the best in the world and I'll do whatever it takes to reach that goal." You are lucky to find anyone that shares that passion and drive. It's a gift to find someone as obsessed with the same goal as yours, who is also a close friend that you care deeply for.

You are likely to create great friends by being on a team together. But you'll be lucky if you can find great friends with whom you should be on a team.

An equal level of commitment toward a common goal is what ties teammates together and builds unlikely friendships. Sharply different levels of commitment between teammates can destroy friendships just as easily.

Though preferable, being close friends is not a prerequisite for being good teammates. An amazing thing happens when you have a group of people who share a passion for a particular goal and need each other to achieve it. Being equally committed to that goal, and working together in pursuit of it despite your differences, will often create new friends, "friends" in the deepest sense of the word. You can't help but develop a great appreciation for someone whom you share a dream with, whom you rely on to help make that dream come true, and who comes through for you.

Personal Goals vs. Team Goals: Selfless or Selfish?

Most of us who decide to pursue excellence in any field do so initially from a purely selfish motivation. I want to win. I want to be a winner. I want to be a world champion. It is all about our own personal goals and rewards. But if our selfish desire toward personal success requires a team, a profound evolution can often take place.

For *me* to achieve my personal goal, I *need* a team.

For *me* to achieve my goals, the team has to achieve its goals.

For the team to achieve its goals, my teammates must achieve their personal goals.

So, for *me* to become the winner that I want to be, it is also required of me to become the teammate my teammates need me to be. Though originally spawned from selfish motivation, I am now forced to learn to be supportive, compassionate, honest, and understanding. If I don't develop these attributes, my teammates will fail, my team will fail, and I will fail.

In the process of providing the emotional support and encouragement my teammates need, I witness positive results in each of them and the team's performance as a whole. They are all feeling much better about themselves and their confidence is growing. The team is achieving better results and having more fun in the process.

Suddenly I realize that it makes me feel great to be able to provide the support that strengthens my teammates and the team. Not only is it personally fulfilling, but the team needs this from me if we are to win. There is immense personal gratification in being a teammate who can make this kind of difference for my teammates and the team. I feel wonderful about myself that I am able to help my teammates to be stronger, more confident, and better competitors—the teammates I need them to be.

This support goes both ways. Unbeknownst to me, of course, being the full-of-myself, overconfident person I am, I have needed and received the same support from my teammates, and they have been just as fulfilled providing it to me. This experience can change someone from being a selfish punk to a reliable, supportive human being that truly cares about the people around him.

Selfish, or selfless? Both. On a true high-performance team, the individual goals of the teammates are so directly tied to the success of the team that you cannot separate the two. What is best for the teammates is best for the team, is best for you.

The pursuit of victory, of becoming a winner, always provides the opportunity to become a better human being. Don't miss out on it.

Motivation

It is very powerful for all the members of a team to share the same reason and motivation for being on the team, but even that, though far preferable, *is* not absolutely essential.

One teammate might be in it for the pure love of the game. Another one primarily for the praise they will receive once they have become a "winner." To be honest, for most people it is a combination of both.

It is possible for a team to succeed even if the teammates have completely different reasons as to why they want to achieve the goal. But for the team they are building together now, at this time, they need to agree on the same team goal and be fully committed to the goal they've set.

As long as their reasons and personal goals are not in direct opposition to each other, then it is possible for them to be achieved together. It is imperative, however, that each teammate *needs* for the team to achieve its goal in order for them to achieve theirs. The personal goals have to be a result of, and dependent upon, the team's goals.

Joining an Existing Team

It is great to be in a position where you are able to choose the people you want on your team. Most of us do that with our partners in life. There are other situations where you join preexisting teams and usually have little or no say of who your teammates are. This could be the case in many jobs and positions you may be hired into, or even families you marry into.

Most often in these situations, your teammates have the potential to do a good job and make a positive contribution to the team. They were probably hired based on that alone. But whether they have a passion for the activity or a deep desire to "win" and achieve the team's goals is more often in question.

It is not uncommon to find teammates who approach work the same way that I had first approached college, asking themselves, "What is the least I can do that will still be enough to get by?" Or for the more motivated ones, asking themselves the same question I originally had when beginning to compete in 4-way: "What is the least we can do that may position us to where there is some chance that it is possible to win?"

Neither of these questions opens the door for particularly inspiring answers. These are questions asked by people who have accepted mediocrity as their goal and don't expect or think their team is capable of any more than that.

Most of the time, if you ask them, they will tell you that they are personally capable of more but that they can only be as good as their team is, and others in the team, or the structure of the team, are holding them back. It's a good excuse, but not necessarily true. Your job may not be something you are as passionate about as I am at skydiving. But as I discovered in my last year of college, having something you are driven to excel at is an incredibly rewarding experience, regardless of how much you love the activity itself.

Most people would want to operate at work like a high-performance team but think this is something reserved only for the best sports teams. They don't believe it's possible to achieve this because they have never been a part of one. They can't even imagine that their work team could be a high-performance team, and no one is stepping up to prove it otherwise. Be that person to step up.

High-performance teams aren't created overnight. It takes time and commitment. You need to prove to yourselves and each other that working together in this way is far more personally rewarding than intentionally accepting and aiming for mediocrity. Start planting the seeds of success right from the beginning.

Be the person to recognize and point out the team's common goals and what it means for your team to "win."

Define your own personal goals. Pinpoint the specific areas in which you need to improve and what you want to accomplish that will help the team to reach its goals.

Ask people for help if you need it and give your teammates the chance to experience, through helping you, how great it feels to contribute to the team's effort.

Find one teammate and work together to achieve a goal you share. There is certain to be something; find it. Without at first becoming completely dependent upon them, let them feel what it feels like to be trusted, to have teammates counting on you, to be working together toward a common goal.

You may not have picked the team, but that doesn't mean you can't mold it into the ideal team you want it to be.

Mediocrity is something people accept, not something they aspire to. As individuals realize they don't have to accept it, they will aspire to do more and to be more. The team you are trying to build is the team most people will want to be a part of. Your motivation will become contagious.

Lead by example and don't let those who are determined to perform poorly drag you and the team down. Don't waste your time trying to force your inspiration on everyone else. But be inspired nonetheless.

Make one good decision at a time. Stick to what you know is right, and continue to operate as the teammate that you would want to have. Little by little, you will start to build momentum. At some point you will pull your team across the threshold of becoming a high-performance team. There will be no turning back.

Trust

Mutual trust is an essential element of all great teams. Specifically, you must be able to unconditionally trust that the actions and words of your teammates are motivated by what they think is best for the team.

You may disagree with and not even understand certain behaviors, attitudes, and decisions. But if this level of trust is built into the foundation of your team, you will always know that at the core of each teammate's conduct is what they feel is in the team's best interest. And that's all you need to know. This deep-rooted trust is what holds teams together during hard times or when dealing with difficult relationships and heated debates.

Trusting our teammates, and being trusted by them, is incredibly motivating, even inspiring. We all know the value we give to people we truly trust. We are well aware of what it feels like to count on people and to be counted on by them. Once given that trust, we will always want to demonstrate that we are worthy of it in everything we do. It encourages us to communicate freely and openly and to do all we can to become the teammate that the team needs us to be.

A mood of distrust has the exact opposite effect. We are suspicious, even paranoid, of our teammates' intent, and they look upon us in the same light. The most honorable conduct is seen as being motivated for the wrong reasons. In a team environment like this, we end up walking on eggshells because we fear what the others may think if we say or do the wrong thing.

Trust is an essential quality of high-performance teams in every field. But trust is not something that we tend to just give away. Think of the people in your life who have your complete, undying trust. These are usually family members or very close friends. People who have earned your trust by proving they deserved it many times over years of shared experiences.

It's hard to trust. It costs time and risks disappointment. We all know the pain of having someone that we truly believed in break that trust.

Therein lies the problem when forming a new team or joining an existing one. If it is true that (1) the definition of a great team includes a deep sense of mutual trust, and (2) trust is something that takes a long time and shared experiences to earn, then it is impossible to assemble a *new, great team.* The team can't be great without trusting each other. And they can't truly trust each other until they have shared many experiences together and proven they deserve that trust. This could take a very long time, longer than the time the team has before needing to reach its objective.

If you want your new team to be a great team, you will need to get past this problem.

The only way to do this is by giving that trust to your teammates without first requiring that they earn it.

The first response most people have to this idea is that they would never do that. You may prepay for goods and services, but not trust.

A teammate is someone you are counting on, someone you need, someone you can't achieve your goals without. You would never just hand over your dreams to someone who hadn't proven they deserved that trust.

But that's not true. The deepest, most intense trust that one human being can ever give to another is given without having previously been earned. I'm referring to the trust between a newborn baby and its parents.

Moments after our first child Chloe was born, it hit me: "Wow. I'm someone's dad."

Kristi and I had the good fortune to have come from warm, loving families and had been a part of some great teams. But never before had we experienced anything that compared to this level of unconditional trust.

Chloe needed us. She counted on us for everything: warmth, shelter, love, food, affection, protection, and knowledge. She needed us to hold her when she cried and comfort her when she was scared. No one else cared as much as we did that she accomplished the goal of growing up in a healthy and loving environment. Her goal was our goal. We were teammates.

A baby has no reason not to trust the people who brought her into the world. Why would we have "assembled that team" if we weren't worthy of that trust? She hadn't yet learned it could be otherwise.

We had never proven to our children prior to having them that we were worthy of the level of trust they gave us. They gave that trust first. After being given that trust, we then felt obligated, inspired, and committed to live up to it. The trust was given before it was earned.

The responsibility of having been given this kind of trust was intense. We decided right then that we would never let her down. We considered how every decision, action, and choice of words would affect her, always striving to be the best examples we could be. We thought about how we treated other people, ourselves, and each other. We consciously made sure that we were demonstrating the qualities we wanted her to learn.

The trust that is asked and required of parents is far greater than anything that could possibly be asked of a teammate in sports, the arts, business, or any other field.

If we want our new team to be a great team, we must also be willing to give our teammates that same trust. Why would we have assembled or joined this team if we didn't think they were going to be worthy of it? Expect that they are, and trust them to be.

Ultimately, we will all have to prove that we are deserving of each other's trust every day through our choices and actions. If a teammate is not deserving of this trust, it will usually be revealed very quickly. But by giving this trust first, we enable our *new* team to become a *great* team in the shortest time possible.

Everyone on the team is in the position of both trusting and being trusted. Knowing what we are counting on from our teammates, and they from us, builds a strong sense of personal responsibility and accountability into the culture of the team. We don't want to be let down by our teammates, and we are certainly not going to let them down.

If in the initial formation of the team we require each teammate to *prove* they can be trusted before we truly trust them, we are building suspicion and distrust into the culture of the team. In the best-case scenario, we are still able to establish the trust necessary to become a great team, but in a much longer time frame. In the worst-case scenario, the air of suspicion and distrust poisons the team before it has a chance to become the team it is capable of *becoming*.

Team Rule

If you are confident that everyone is committed and dedicated to the pursuit of the team's goals, then *give* them this trust that is an essential quality of all great teams. By doing so, you will provide the shortest road possible for the team to reach its full potential and accomplish its goals.

Whether as a parent or a teammate, being given this trust is an honor, a privilege, and an enormous responsibility. Don't accept it unless you plan to prove you deserve it.

Communication Plans

Once the team agrees on the goal, you must evaluate the team's starting point and the performance level you are aiming for. Through early brainstorming sessions, and later more focused planning meetings, create a training strategy that is a step-by-step map of how to get from where you are to where you want to be.

You require much from your teammates, including, but in no way limited to, their skills, experience, judgment, encouragement, perspective, motivation, and input. You will get little of any of this if your team does not have a *communication plan* designed specifically for the purpose of giving each member the tools and information they need to become the best they can be in their role. The team's success is counting on it.

The communication plan needs to provide opportunities for the exchange of constructive input or criticism that will give team members the information they need to excel while at the same time extinguishing the natural defensiveness that so often comes from receiving constructive criticism. It is possible for this to happen on its own without a communication plan as such. But I wouldn't count on it. More often, the results are just the opposite.

For our purposes now, consider that the team's primary goal has been established and a team captain has been selected. At this point the team needs to develop a communication plan that will involve meetings held for the purpose of *goal setting* and *debriefing*.

The **goal setting** meeting should follow a format similar to this:

- The team's short-term team goals will be made clear and reiterated by the team captain.

- Each individual will have certain tasks that need to be completed and areas of improvement that require her immediate attention. Her personal goal becomes to accomplish these tasks and to make specific, measurable improvements in these areas.
- One at a time, each individual will state to the team exactly what her short-term goals are and specific plans for how she intends to accomplish these goals.
- Teammates then have the opportunity to provide input to help that individual achieve her goals. These goals could be ones that other teammates have had for themselves in the past, and they may have valuable input to share. But they shouldn't choose to offer any input unless they are certain that the input they offer is a proven method that is likely to be an improvement on the individual's plan. No guessing, only solid suggestions.
- The individual can then choose to use or file the input she has received.
- These specific goals will be reviewed in the debriefing meeting.

Each person walks away from this meeting with very specific goals and plans for how to accomplish them. They have all received support from their teammates and know whom to look to if they need additional guidance along the way. This helps each individual to focus his attention and effort in the most productive direction. He knows that the team is counting on him to get the work done, and he is motivated to do it because he has developed a plan he is confident will lead to success.

The debriefing meeting plan would be similar. The purpose of this meeting is to evaluate whether goals have been met. If the goals have been met, it is important to define what parts of the plan designed to accomplish these goals worked. With this information, you can repeat the same proven strategies in future planning. Debriefing the positive, successful aspects of your endeavors is easy. The conversation and exchange of ideas is generally welcome, complimentary, and pleasant.

If the goals were not met, it is important to figure out why and what needs to be done to reach them. Debriefing the negative, unsuccessful aspects of your endeavors can be much more difficult.

Recognizing errors and accomplishing stated goals requires input from teammates. This is a large part of why you have teammates in the first place. But no one wants to stand up in front of his team and admit that his goals have not been met, and no one looks forward to taking responsibility for failing to reach them. It is not uncommon to feel personally insulted when receiving input from teammates even when that input is offered with all the best intentions and aimed to help us in our efforts.

Giving constructive input to your teammates is often as hard as receiving it.

It is in this exchange of what was intended as constructive criticism that the least productive characteristic of normal human behavior shows its ugly face. I am referring to the natural emotional reaction of *defensiveness*. Defensiveness can become an unsurpassable roadblock to reaching your goals.

A very clear debriefing plan with specific rules is necessary if a team is going to have open, honest, and productive communication that is unhindered by individual defensiveness.

DEBRIEFING PLAN GOALS

- Maintain a positive attitude. Remember that you are receiving input from your teammates. Individuals you trust to always have the team's best intentions in mind. Everything being discussed is intended to help you accomplish your goals. Your goals *are* the team goals.
- Be responsible for your own and each other's learning.
- Maintain a line of open and honest communication.
- Recognize positive aspects and use them to build on.
- Recognize mistakes and decide on specific plans that will lead to solutions.

NOT ALLOWED IN DEBRIEFINGS

- Defensive responses.
- Saying "It's not my fault" or "I couldn't do anything about it."

DEBRIEFING PLAN RULES

- One individual speaks at a time.
- Take personal responsibility for the success or shortcomings of accomplishing your goals.
- State your goals and report on your success.
- Define what parts of your plan are working.
- Report on your efforts that have been unsuccessful.
- Recognize your errors and define the plan for fixing them.
- The floor is now open for input. Generally speaking, when the person debriefing has reported in honestly and has made well-thought-out plans for fixing any problems, there is little input anyone feels compelled to offer. *But if there are errors that aren't being recognized or a teammate is certain that she has input that will help the individual accomplish his goals, it is her responsibility to speak up.*

When giving input, you must be certain that what you are saying will be valuable in helping the individual accomplish his goal. This is essential. If teammates start throwing in every idea that crosses their minds, the person being debriefed won't stand a chance of filtering through it all to find the jewels of pertinent information. The filter gets clogged, and the receptors shut down. But if he knows that the only input permitted is that which has been well thought out, and the person offering it is absolutely certain it could be of help, then he will absorb and consider the information carefully. Save the loose, untested ideas for the brainstorming session. They will only serve to cloud, confuse, and lengthen a debriefing.

When receiving input from teammates, don't allow yourself to operate from defensive feelings. Listen to what they say. Remember that these are your teammates, and with this input they are trying to help achieve goals that you all share.

Accept this information without discussion or debate. It is up to you to decide if this input is worth applying. If you think that the information provided is not applicable, then carry on as you had planned. If the errors continue to resurface, then you should consider the input again in the future.

A communication plan like this builds the framework for honest and direct conversation while removing the temptation for pointing blame and defensiveness. The process is efficient and the particular goals are identified, targeted, and generally achieved with a minimal amount of time and effort.

Transforming Defensiveness into Accountability and Confidence

Reporting in at your debriefing after any less-than-a-flawless effort can be difficult. No one likes to admit weakness, and the thought of letting down teammates is crushing.

When reporting in for a debriefing, each individual has a very important choice to make. This single decision, more than any other, can have an incredibly positive influence on the respect and trust the team develops in its culture. Or it can be poison.

The decision is how you will answer this question. Will I take full personal responsibility for my mistakes and for not achieving my goals, or will I look for reasons and excuses as to why I failed?

This choice, one way or the other, will immediately start a chain reaction of feelings and events that will define the attitude and culture of your team.

It's not my fault. We have all worked with people that whine, complain, and point blame in any direction they can as long as it points away from themselves. These are behaviors rooted in fear and are evidence that the individual is emotionally fragile. The mere thought of a problem being their fault is enough to terrify them. Rather than taking the bull by the horns, they try to protect their self-esteem by shielding themselves from responsibility.

It is difficult to communicate with teammates who refuse to take ownership of problems that are clearly theirs to own. They have convinced themselves that the problems are not their fault, so they are not open to receiving input. But their teammates have a lot of input to give.

One common reaction is *conflict avoidance*. When avoiding conflict, all productive communication shuts down and the chain reaction begins.

- The teammates have input that is not being received, so they stop giving it.
- Problems are not addressed because team members are avoiding confrontation they fear will further hurt an already-fragile teammate.
- Problems are recognized but never fixed because they are never addressed.
- The teammate in question realizes that they are being treated with kid gloves and becomes even more insecure and defensive.
- Talk amongst the ranks begins behind his back.
- When the gossip begins, other teammates become less secure and more paranoid that they may be the next target.
- Ultimately, this becomes a poison that infects the entire team. Trust, honesty, and productive communication all break down.

Another negative reaction is *fear-induced motivation*. We become angry and intolerant of the individual. The tone becomes brutal. You'd rather just punch him and get it over with. You should let your anger lead you only after exhausting all other possibilities of support and guidance that have the potential to lead to a much more productive result.

When other teammates see this anger, they in turn begin to fear making mistakes themselves. Fear of making mistakes is the biggest mistake of all. In our fear of making mistakes, we try to always stay well within our comfort zone. *By definition, choosing to stay in our comfort zone is the same thing as choosing not to improve, experiment, or explore new ideas.* Whether intentional or not, the team has established the goal of maintaining the status quo. They will never be the best they can be. They will never win.

Both the common responses of conflict avoidance and fear-induced motivation lead the team on a course of self-destruction. These paths are exhausting and provide little if any chance for positive, lasting results. Both easily could have been avoided if there was a concrete goal setting and debriefing plan in place.

Accepting personal responsibility. An amazing thing happens when you bite the bullet and, for better or for worse, take personal responsibility for your behavior, attitude, and mistakes. It is so refreshing to have someone step up and flat out say, "I tried this, it didn't work. Here is how I am going to fix it." That is a person you know you can trust, one that you can count on to get the job done. The immediate respect you gain from your teammates when you take ownership and responsibility for errors is very powerful.

All it takes is one person to set this tone of personal accountability, and instantly everyone else on the team feels obligated to live up to it. The confidence it demonstrates when someone stands up and takes responsibility for errors, and for guaranteeing they are dealt with, inspires others to do the same. No one who follows in the debriefing would ever present a whining "It's not my fault" excuse after watching the team respond to a courageous teammate who has identified and attacked the problems. Ultimately, and sooner than you might think, this personal accountability becomes part of the culture of the team. With that comes the trust and respect that every team strives for.

The Fear of Making Mistakes

It is essential that teams create an environment that not only allows individuals to make mistakes but goes even further and at times encourages and requires them to. For each single great discovery, you will usually make hundreds of errors.

A good coach will often be able to predict the mistakes you are likely to make, when you are going to make them, and why. But to fully understand a situation that frequently leads to a particular error, you will *need* to actually make the error yourself. *Making mistakes* needs *to be a welcomed and strategized part of the process of excelling at anything. Learn to love it. Realize that each time you make a mistake, you are one step closer to learning the skill that will prevent that same mistake in the future.*

It is essential that your teammates understand that making mistakes is a fundamental part of the learning process. Don't assume they do. It needs to be clearly stated and frequently repeated if your team is to break down this innate fear that most of us have spent so many years developing.

If your strategy toward achieving excellence in your field involves improving individual or team skills, it will generally break down into two stages of training:

1. Defining your current best performance level and aiming to repeat it. (To turn "your best" into your average.)
2. Pushing yourself or the team to reach for a new and higher level of performance. (Making "your best" better. More specifics on these in the upcoming chapters.)

During the stage of training when your team is trying to push your best to new heights, you are instructed to reach past your perceived limitations. Mistakes are not only accepted, they are essential. If you are not making mistakes, you are not pushing yourself far enough. By making this goal clear and understood, much of the pressure for perfection is greatly diminished.

6

Training for Peak Performance

Becoming a Natural by Learning to Trust Your Instincts

A *natural*: "an individual who instinctively performs to the best of his or her abilities under any conditions while making it look easy" (my definition again).

In many ways, becoming a natural in his or her field is everyone's goal. We have all marveled at how some athletes can "read the play" and intuitively handle rapidly changing conditions. Even when under intense pressure, they instinctively respond to the situation and do whatever is necessary to "make the play." And they do it while staying calm and making it look easy in the process.

When I was working as a cook, I saw the same ability in some waiters and waitresses. They had to handle very different and ever-changing conditions on their "playing field" as well. At some times they had to deal with incredibly rude and disrespectful individuals. At others they would need to figure out how to make the best of the situation when food came out of the kitchen late or the customer hated it.

Like the athlete, the best waiters and waitresses would instinctively adjust their approach and strategy and would immediately find a way to handle whatever they were dealt with. They were able to take full control of the situation and steer in the direction that led to the best results regardless of the conditions. When we knew we were going to have a tough table, the best waitresses or waiters would often be asked if they would "take the ball," and they enjoyed "stepping up to the plate" when no one else wanted to.

It's a good thing I was in the back cooking, because if I had to deal with the same people, I may have blown up and lost my job when the best waitstaff had them eating out of the palm of their hands and leaving them huge tips.

I've seen the same abilities demonstrated on every conceivable playing field. This is a common trait shared by the best of teachers, attorneys, policemen, and countless others. It is more frequently recognized among athletes because of the public stage they play on, but it is no less true amongst the best of the best in any field. How do they do it? Are they really "naturals"? Is it truly the birthright of a very select few?

Learning to Trust Your Instincts

Most people who excel in any field have trained their skills to the point that they have instinctive muscle memory. What is exceptional about these individuals is that they have also trained the *skill of trusting their instincts.*

It is true for individuals striving to reach their peak performance in any field. Dancers, musicians, writers, artists, pilots, actors, and public speakers will tell you the same thing. They perform at their best when they just relax, stay calm, rely on their training, trust their instincts, and "let it happen."

On the other hand, there are also many people with amazing technical skills, but who aren't able to consistently perform to the full potential of those skills. Their minds are too busy with other thoughts that don't concern the task of the moment. They don't have the confidence to stay calm and trust that their instincts will lead them to their best performance if they just let them.

We are all born with the innate inclination to trust our instincts. As babies and even toddlers, we had little other than our instincts when determining a course of action. A "gut" feeling would tell us to do something, and we would follow it.

Fortunately, as we grow up, we have many new experiences and gain a lot of new information. Unfortunately, we start to pay less attention to our gut feelings, intuition, and instincts, and instead are led by fears of making mistakes, worrying about other people's perceptions of us, and concern for the final outcome rather than the task at hand. All of these are contrary to operating on instinct.

We operate on instinct when our minds are calm, undistracted, and purely focused in the moment. It is an incredible yet very natural experience. Our senses pick up and make us aware of everything that is happening around us. We see, hear, and feel what we are confronted with and instinctively respond to it without analysis, or at times without even conscious thought.

Many of us have experienced unique moments in various activities when we stopped thinking and were going on automatic. These moments often happen when something suddenly forces us to operate on instinct without giving us a chance to think or do otherwise. The result is often a level of performance we didn't even know we were capable of.

Nearly everyone who drives a car has had an experience like this. There you were, calmly cruising down the road, enjoying a good song, when another driver suddenly pulled out in front of you and slammed on the brakes. In the fraction of a second that you had to respond, you hit the brakes, looked in your mirrors, looked to the sides, hit the gas, turned to avoid the collision while not causing another one. You took evasive action in a matter of seconds. You never trained for, or practiced, the particular maneuver that was required of you. But the situation demanded that you respond without hesitation. You handled it and didn't even realize how terrified you were until it was over. You don't even know how you did it. You were forced to trust your instincts because you didn't have time to think or do anything else. Your instincts came through for you and they always will.

Our instincts are only as good as we have trained them to be. If you had come across the same situation during your first time behind the wheel of a car, you would have been less likely to respond as well. An experienced taxi driver would have handled it better. A NASCAR driver, better still.

We will perform at our best, whatever level that best is, when we trust our instincts to take us there. If we are trying to excel in any activity, we should be constantly training our skills and developing our instincts with the goal of becoming a "natural." To do this, we must start practicing the "skill" of trusting our instincts while our abilities and skills are still early in their development.

Training to Trust Your Instincts

Few concepts are less understood than that of trusting our instincts. We all get the idea. But isn't it something that just happens by chance? Something only exceptionally talented individuals can do? And what exactly are our instincts anyway? Is it really possible to actually *train* to trust them?

Deep inside us all, the innate ability exists to trust our instincts. Given the fact that it exists, it is also possible to train the "skill" of trusting our instincts.

To become a natural who can instinctively perform at the best of your abilities without obvious thought or effort, you must do two things:

1. Train your skills to the point that they become instinctive muscle memory. (This is not limited to physical skills used by athletes. The same is true for social, communication, mental, and emotional skills that are required in so many other fields.)
2. Retrain the actual instinct to trust your instincts that you had as a small child.

Some people may be genetically built to more easily accommodate the skills necessary for certain sports or activities, but we are not born with specific instincts for them. These types of skills are acquired. Only after much repetition and extensive visualization do such skills become instinctive and happen automatically as muscle memory.

When our minds are calm, undistracted by outside thoughts, and focused only on the task at hand, trusting our instincts and performing at our best happens automatically. In that moment, nothing else in the world exists except the next "move" we need to make. We aren't aware of physical pain and don't feel fear or anxiety. The only thing in our world is this basket, this pass, this joke, this comment, this expression, this stroke, this dance step, this chord, or the free-fall formation that is required from us at that moment. When we stop "trying to think" how we do a move and just do it, we are allowing our instincts to take over.

I am pretty good at typing. But if asked to write down where the letters are on a keyboard, I couldn't tell you. My fingers know where they are, but I don't. If I think of what I want to write, not "how to" write it, and trust my fingers to hit the correct keys, they usually do.

For the purposes of this conversation, please accept these two definitions:

Instinct – A move or a skill that you have trained to the point that it has become muscle memory and happens automatically without the need for conscious thought. (Putting one foot in front of the other when you are walking.)

Trusting your instincts – Trusting your mind and body to do the move or skill it knows by muscle memory on its own, without conscious input from you. (You don't think about how to walk, you just walk.)

For simplicity's purposes, please allow me to approach this conversation in terms of sports. But understand that the skills an athlete trains in are no different *from* the skill of responding to difficult customers and students that waitresses and teachers must learn and practice.

In formation skydiving we can most efficiently train our individual flying skills in a vertical wind tunnel, incredible machines that are basically free-fall simulators. In the same way a golfer spends a great deal of time slowly and smoothly working out the body mechanics of a perfect swing, a dancer methodically practices new dance moves, an actor rehearses expressions in a mirror, or a lawyer practices approaching the jury, in a wind tunnel skydivers can practice the exact physical input necessary for aggressive, precise body flying moves.

With enough practice, we all eventually learn the technical skill. It's not perfect, but we understand how it is done. We do it slowly because we have to think through every part of the move in order to coordinate all the participating body parts so that they work together as one.

At this time the skill is not yet trained to the point of muscle memory. We are capable of performing the move, but to do it correctly, our bodies require many reminders from us in the process. With enough repetition and visualization, our body begins to develop some degree of muscle memory. The muscle memory allows us to think less because our body knows more. The more of a move our body knows as muscle memory, the fewer reminders it needs from us during the move. *If we relax and trust our instincts, we will naturally allow our body to do what it knows how to do, while only giving it the additional information it needs.*

The ultimate extension of this is when we have executed and visualized it so many times that the entire move happens with minimal thought or none at all. We recognize the need to make a specific move, and it happens automatically, instinctively. This is true, whether learning to play a sport or an instrument, fly a plane, drive a car, or type on a keyboard. It's all the same.

It is a long road from the time when we first learn a particular move and must think through each part of the exact physical input necessary to the time when that perfect move happens automatically with little or no thought at all.

This raises the question, If during our learning progression the amount of conscious reminders we need changes, then how do we know how much we need to think about it at any given moment?

We don't want to be mentally lazy and not think enough. But we also don't want *to* overthink. Everybody understands how crippling thinking too much or overanalyzing can be. *Overanalyzing is the opposite of trusting your instincts.*

We know what *not* to do, but we don't know what *to do*. If we don't know the answer to learning how to trust our instincts, who does?

Our bodies do. If our minds are calm, focused, and distraction-free, it happens easily. Here is how it works:

- The more muscle memory our body has, the fewer conscious reminders it needs from us.
- If we let it, our body will automatically perform the amount of a move it currently knows as muscle memory without additional conscious reminders from us.
- If your body knows 40 percent of a particular move by muscle memory, it only needs the other 60 percent reminded from you. Our body will know how much of the move it has trained as muscle memory and will "ask" us for the other 60 percent.
- If we are calm and focused in the moment, we will "hear" our bodies ask for this information and we will instinctively answer with the information it needs and only the information it needs.

There is an internal conversation going on between our mind and our body. We cannot "try" to make this conversation happen any more than we can "try" to walk or make our body do anything it already knows how to do. This internal conversation will happen instinctively if we let it. (Most often during this process, the part of a move you have to remind your body how to do is the beginning of a move. Once you get it started correctly, your body will often finish the job on its own.)

When we stop trying to tell our bodies what to do and allow them to do what we have trained them to do, we will be trusting our instincts. When we do, our bodies will come through for us.

Trusting our instincts is not limited to sports. In every walk of life, regardless of how well trained our instincts are, we will usually do our best by trusting them. Recent brain-scanning technology has shown that the brain unconsciously makes rational decisions, quickly analyzing the data it gets, and reaches a decision sometimes seconds before our conscious minds "think up" that same decision. Actions that feel like random choices or instinctive responses are often logical thought processes using available information carried out in the unconscious mind. Many successful businesspeople say their best decisions are the ones they make using "gut feelings" or instinct.

How Overanalyzing Cripples Our Performance

If we are wrapped up in external concerns and distractions, our instincts are not able to take over. Usually out of fear, we don't trust that our bodies or minds will do what we've trained them to. In addition to the 60 percent it needs, we also try to force on it the 40 percent it already knows. Now instead of operating at 100, we have overloaded it at 140 percent. This is more than a natural internal conversation. It becomes noisy and distracting as opposed to calming and focused. Our instincts are blocked by too much thought, worry, and analysis.

We end up poorly executing skills *that* we had already trained to be muscle memory and that we were previously doing well. We analyze our performance in a desperate attempt to figure out what we're doing wrong. Being the dedicated people we are, we start trying even harder to fix the problem. But the actual problem was trying too hard and thinking too much in the first place.

In trying so hard, we have obviously decided that everything we are aiming to achieve must be very difficult. The more difficult we think it is, the harder we try. The harder we try, the worse we do.

The most unfortunate thing here is that this "analysis paralysis" only happens to people who truly care and are giving a 110 percent effort to make it happen. It is usually caring so much that causes them to go down this path in the first place.

To become a natural, you must have the confidence to try by not trying. To care by not caring.

Consistently performing at our best is easy. We have to work hard in training and bring our skills to a high level. We have to visualize extensively (see page 299) and do many repetitions in order for those skills to become instincts. There are no shortcuts. We have to be disciplined in training ourselves to trust our instincts. But once we have done the hard work, we just relax, calm our minds, trust our instincts, and let it happen.

If you want to have this relaxed confidence when you are called upon to perform at your best, you must have practiced it in training. You will have proven to yourself in practice that it works, and you will be calm and confident the day of the meet, the meeting, the big day. You will know without any doubt that as long as you calm your mind, rid yourself of all distractions, and focus on the task at hand, your absolute best performance will emerge on its own.

This may sound as if I am describing some mystical experience that brings to mind "Feel the force, Luke." And that is exactly what I'm saying.

The Optimum Performance State: Flying "On the Line"

There are many definitions for the mental state we are in when we perform at the top of our game. It has been referred to as "flow," "the zone," "on the line," or the "ideal performance state." It is a place where our minds are calm, undistracted, and focused in the moment. When we let our instincts take over. It happens almost effortlessly for us when we allow it to.

Slalom skiers achieve their fastest times when they are on the line. They can only go down a hill as fast as they can control. If they try to go faster, they will be less efficient in their handling of the course and lose time or fall and be out of the race.

On the other hand, if they are led by the fear of falling, their priority becomes to not fall rather than to go as fast as they can control. This approach will prevent them from pushing themselves to the fastest speed of which they are truly capable.

It is important to start training this ideal mental state, whatever you want to call it, right from the beginning.

There is one thing that is absolutely essential to understand: the ability to perform at your best is a trained skill. Though your "best" performance level will progress with training and time, the skill to perform at that best is the same skill for a novice as it is for a pro. The skill to perform at your best will remain the same skill even as your "best" advances.

It is a rare individual that is perfectly balanced. In our daily lives and activities, most of us tend to be either on the more aggressive or more passive side. This is not simply a learned and acquired behavior. Infants come out of the womb with a tendency toward one or the other. It is truly a part of who we are. We are born this way.

Our best performance happens when we are right on the line or in the zone. If our instincts are to be overly passive or overly aggressive, then trusting our instincts will not lead to our best performance. We will tend to favor one side of the line or the other. We need to retrain ourselves to be instinctively on the line. Though it may be difficult to change "who we are," it is not impossible. We are certainly able to change who we are in the limited context of performing in our chosen field.

When we review and evaluate our performance, it is not enough to ask whether it was technically correct. We want to dial in our natural state so that we train it to be right on the line. The questions we need to ask are "Was that my best?" "Was I on the line?" "Did I have more in me?" "Could I have been more aggressive?" "Was I too aggressive?" "Do I need to calm down more?"

In order to be right on the line, you must give yourself conscious reminders during your preparation, visualization, and during the actual performance. If you are someone that tends to be too passive, you will need to remind yourself to "Go," "Push it," or "Gun it." If you are someone who tends to be too aggressive, it will be more along the lines of "Stay calm," "Stay cool," or "One at a time."

Your abilities change, but the skill of performing up to the full potential of your abilities doesn't change. You must learn this skill at the beginning of your training and continue to practice it as your skills progress. Anytime you are required to perform at the best of your abilities, it will just be another step in this process.

How to Put Yourself "On the Line"

In skydiving and other high-speed precision sports (HSP sports), there are two diametrically opposed qualities. By definition, high speed implies high adrenaline. When you are racing down a ski slope, around an auto track, on a motocross trail, or through the sky, your heart pounds and the adrenaline flows.

But to stay on the line, maintain control, and maneuver your specific "course" at the highest speed possible, your mind must be calm. Things are happening at an incredibly fast pace. Within fractions of a second you need to be able to recognize adversities that require you to alter your plan, or advantages that allow you to push yourself harder. You must instinctively make the decision that produces the best results. There is no time for extended analysis or deliberations.

As you increase your speed, you squeeze the same amount of information into a shorter amount of time. For this amount of information to be instantly absorbed, processed, and for the correct decision to be made, you need to be calm, *very calm*, in an almost meditative state. The faster you go, the calmer you must become.

The common error for many HSP sport athletes is that they don't establish the necessary level of calm. Our adrenaline is pumping and we love it. We come out of the gate, kick it into high gear, and try to hold on. In formation skydiving, this may work for a few seconds or, if you are really lucky, for an entire jump. But you'll never get through the meet without blowing up.

To put yourself right on the line and perform to the best of your abilities in competition, you need to have a proven process that you have practiced and had success with in training. This process must be specifically designed for your particular field of interest. The skydiving teams I have coached have had great success using the four Cs approach. The principles are fairly universal and can easily be customized to produce your peak performance in nearly any endeavor.

The Four Cs: Calm–Communication–Control–Confidence

Calm

Being on the line begins with a very calm mind.

Sit back, slow down, and relax your breathing. Don't give any thought to the technical aspects of the performance. Trust that if you are calm and focused purely in the moment, your body and mind will know what to do. Visualize only the feeling of being right on the line. Remember the effortlessness when you trust your instincts and allow your best to happen. Remind yourself that it is going to be easy. When you are calm, focused, and free of all distractions, it will happen automatically, as you have trained it to.

Communication

Eye contact and awareness establishes a heightened degree of communication. It enables you to actually see what your teammates are thinking and feeling and to instinctively make instant decisions together. If you recognize that a teammate is over the line, you can calm him down with just a glance. If you realize a teammate is scared and being too cautious, you can pump him up just as quickly.

With this level of communication and awareness, nothing is going to get by you.

The members of a band, a sports team, a dance company, a military unit, or a team of doctors and nurses all must have this level of communication and awareness. If you enter your "playing field" with a calm mind and focus on establishing communication with the people you are working with, your awareness of everything around you will increase and you will be able to read the play, whatever that means at any given moment.

Control

You are aware of everything that is happening. Your "team's" communication enables you to "talk" and make decisions together instantly. You recognize any obstacles and can instantly decide and communicate how to fix them. You recognize when you are on your game and can decide together to proceed with confidence. You can easily adjust to handle any unexpected problem, or take advantage of any opportunities. This communication establishes a level of control that allows the team to adapt instantly to any situation, often without any verbal communication.

Confidence

It is this control that justifies you having complete confidence in yourself and the team. With control established and recognized, you must then choose to be confident. That is when a skydiving team must choose to fly fast and hard. This is a very conscious decision that is made in a fraction of a second. Recognize the team has control and then choose to move with as much confidence as you can continue to control. With proper training, you will establish this control and immediately and instinctively respond with pure confidence. But it won't happen on its own. Like any other instinct, it requires extensive repetition. Whenever the team demonstrates control, you must answer by choosing confidence. With enough practice, the team will nearly always be under control, and confidence will become your natural state.

A Skydiving Example: Perris Airkix

It was a month before the 2006 world meet. Perris Airkix, the women's 4-way formation skydiving team from the United Kingdom, had been very disciplined about training this program to the letter. At this point, they were putting the finishing touches on their performance in preparation for the meet. All the individual pieces of the puzzle were strong. But it just wasn't all coming together like it should've been. Their average had been stuck between 16 and 17 for too long.

It looked to me that they were getting nervous as the meet was approaching and that they were trying harder than ever to improve. They were trying too hard. I decided to run an experiment. I asked them to calm themselves down further than they had ever done, in fact, to nearly sedate themselves. I told them that it was an experiment, they needn't question the idea. Just do it and see what happens.

With the deeper level of calm successfully established, everything else they had trained for happened for them naturally. They turned all their attention to calming themselves down, and the rest of the four C process happened automatically, without them thinking about it. They were moving at full speed and with total control immediately out the door and maintained that calmness and speed for the entire jump. The team recognized any mistakes, dealt with them, and returned to the same pace.

It was so easy for them that when they came in to review the jumps, they didn't think they had done anything special. They were shocked to find out that they had added 2 1/2 points and achieved a 19-point average. They couldn't believe it. They won the world meet a few weeks later with the same 19 average. It was easy then too.

7

The Power of Visualization

VISUALIZATION IS THE ability to create clear, detailed, and accurate images in your mind of something that you want to reproduce as physical reality. In essence, quality visualization is much like a very well-trained imagination. The images created by people who have practiced this skill are complete, precise, and specific. We see the image, feel the physical sensations, and even experience the emotion so vividly that it almost seems as if we are actually doing it.

Developing your instincts, building muscle memory, requires doing tons of repetition. A great deal of experience and research has proven that people with highly advanced visualization skills can create through visualization the same experience in their minds as that of the actual physical activity. Our minds don't recognize much difference between full sensory visualization and actual physical training. Time spent practicing our skills through visualization can be as beneficial as the real thing and allows for far more repetitions than we could ever do in actual practice alone. Through visualization, we can train our instincts and build muscle memory in far shorter time.

I cannot possibly stress enough the importance of *positive visualization*. Every sports psychology and peak-performance book contains extensive chapters on its benefits and value. This holds true in all areas of life far beyond sports.

Regardless of your skill level, I guarantee you this. If you can easily create a clear, detailed, and accurate image in your mind of you or your team performing your best, it will often become reality. As you visualize this in preparation of your "competition," your confidence will soar. There it is right in front of you, as if you just did it perfectly one hundred times. Quality visualization registers on your consciousness just as actual experience does. So does poor visualization. Learn to see it right, and you will do it right.

To maximize your learning and the opportunity for doing extensive repetitions of skills, you should give your visualization training as much priority as you do physical training.

How to Visualize

- Find a quiet place where you can be without distractions. Relax, calm your mind, and slow down before you begin.
- Have a clear picture that you want to start with. For instance, if you are an ice skater, it would be a benefit to have an actual photo of yourself at the moment when you are preparing to attempt a particular action. Having this picture will help you to recreate the same image in your mind. It will then be easier to visualize a frame-by-frame execution of this move because you have a vivid image to start from.
- It is also very useful to have previously watched moving images of yourself, or other people performing the move you want to visualize. Watching a DVD of yourself or others executing the same skills will put a blueprint in your mind of the pictures that you want to paint.
- Take the time you need to produce the correct picture in your mind. Start with something simple. Like mastering any skill, the more complex it is, the more difficult it is to learn to do or visualize correctly. This can be frustrating. Be patient. If the picture in your head gets scrambled, stop, erase it, calm down, and start again. Don't try to force it.

- As you begin to visualize a particular action, try it first in slow motion. As with training physical skills, your initial visualization training will require you to think through each part of a particular move as you create the image of that move in your mind.
- Once you are able to really see the correct technical move in your mind, repeat the process again and again.
- With repetitions and practice, your mind, like your body, will start to learn the particular skill on its own. It will develop its own mental muscle memory. Soon you will be able to think less because your mind will be familiar with the picture and will create it effortlessly.
- After training the ability to visualize particular images, you will be able to create these images in your mind with minimal preparation. You won't need to find a quiet place or take time to slow down and relax. You will be able to flip the switch and clearly visualize what you have practiced in any place and at any time you choose.

Turning new skills and habits into instinct can only be done through repetition. There are no shortcuts. Quality visualization allows you the opportunity to dramatically increase the amount of repetitions you can do. It gives you the chance to practice the perfect move or gesture a hundred times in only a few minutes. If your visualization skills are well trained, this practice you do in your head can be just as valuable as actual training time.

To get the most benefit, do the visualization training alongside the physical training. Work on visualizing the same skills in the evening that you are practicing during the day. As your visualization skills improve, so will your actual performance. As your performance skills improve, so does your visualization. By working your visualization skills in parallel with your physical training, you will reach your performance goals in far less time.

Learning to visualize requires the same commitment as learning physical skills. The benefits are every bit as valuable. Some would even argue that, at times, the skill of creating vivid, full-sensory, positive images in your mind can be just as powerful as training the physical skills themselves.

Quality Visualization Can Greatly Accelerate Your Learning

I had been competing in 4-way formation skydiving for twelve years, and my visualization skills were excellent. I could close my eyes and see myself and the rest of the team in perfect detail. I could see my moves done correctly as well as the technically perfect choreography of the entire team. I could see the jump from above (the judging video angle), from my own eyes, and even from any teammates' point of view. I was able to run it in slow motion or fast speed with the same precision. I didn't need to slow down and relax. I could immediately create the images at any moment even while involved in other activities. I didn't even need to close my eyes. I could see the correct pictures as if they were superimposed over what I was actually looking at. All of my senses were active. I could feel the jump in my muscles and my mind would anticipate one move ahead. I was aware of my breathing and the mental calmness the sport requires. My visualization even had the confident, competitive attitude I wanted to exhibit on the skydives. For all practical purposes, I was doing the jumps. It felt the same in nearly every way.

The funny thing was that I took all of this completely for granted. I had no idea how good my visualization skills actually were or how crucial they had become to my performance. I had practiced them frequently and thoroughly, but mostly by accident. It was fun and seemed like the right thing to do. I hadn't had a specific visualization training plan.

My team, Arizona Airspeed, won the national and world championships in the 4-way formation skydiving event two years in row.

In addition to continuing with 4-way, we decided to also enter the 8-way event.

In 8-way the rules are the same and it requires mostly the same individual flying skills. The real difference is the actual pictures that we see. The 8-way formations are twice as big as 4-way formations. To see an entire 8-way formation, we must look much farther and greatly expand our awareness. During the transitions from one formation to another, there is twice as much going on and people are moving twice as far. All in all, when you add it up, 8-way was exponentially busier and noisier than 4-way. All of this activity made it very difficult to create the same clear images in my head that I had in 4-way. But since I took for granted how good my visualization skills were in 4-way, I also discounted how weak they were in 8-way.

As a 4-way competitor, I was fast, precise, and confident in my abilities. I deserved to be; we had just won two consecutive national and world championships. I was sure this would carry over to 8-way. I was wrong.

When we started training 8-way, I basically stunk. I was making mistakes that could only come from a novice competitor. My flying was soft and my anticipation dull. During the video reviews of the jumps, I was embarrassed. What had happened to me? Had I lost it? Should I have quit while I was ahead? I punished myself with self-doubt.

The next day we were in the airplane on the way up for an 8-way jump. I was visualizing the jump as I always do on the ride to altitude when it hit me. I wasn't seeing anything. There weren't even eight people on the screen in my mind. There was just me, fumbling through a mass of bodies. I couldn't even see what the formation looked like. I suddenly realized that I had no visualization skills at all for 8-way.

If I couldn't see, or even imagine, what a good jump was going to look like, the odds weren't very good that I was actually going to contribute to making it happen. And if I did, it would be due to nothing but pure luck. I certainly couldn't make much of a contribution to a good effort if I didn't know what one looked like.

Our team took two weeks off. During that time, I spent two hours (eight fifteen-minute sessions) a day dedicated to visualization training. I didn't have to learn the skill of visualizing, I had extensive experience already. I just had to apply that skill to a different event.

I looked at videos and photographs of the formations that were taken from above and then practiced creating the same still photos in my head. I switched the "camera angle" to my point of view and practiced creating the image that I would see while in the same formation. Once I was able to see these still photos in my mind, I added movement and began working on producing the picture of what the team looked like when transitioning from one formation to another. I had to slow it way down so that I had time to paint the picture in my mind.

At first it was difficult and took quite a bit of time for each picture. But once I had accurately created the picture the first time, it became much easier. With frequent, consistent training, the skill of producing the 8-way images in my mind was quickly learned.

On our first jump back after the break, we were on the ride to altitude and I visualized the jump we were about to do. I could see everything perfectly. I knew exactly how the jump was supposed to go, what I had to do to make it go that way. I could see every detail of every person during every transition to every formation. It had a calming effect on me. The images were so clear that it felt like I had done them hundreds of times before. *I knew from experience that if I could visualize the jump this clearly, all I had to do was calm myself down and let it happen. The rest would be automatic. My confidence soared.*

We exited the airplane, and the jump went just as planned, just as I had seen it in my head. It was amazing. *I had visualized a performance level in 8-way before actually ever performing up to that level.*

During our two weeks off, my athletic potential didn't change. I was the same athlete with the same skills and abilities. I already had the potential to be a good 8-way competitor. The visualization training helped me to reach my full potential in a fraction of the time it would have taken otherwise. Through visualization training I reached the same performance level that would probably have taken hundreds of jumps to achieve. And I did it in two weeks instead of two months. It happened in my head first, and my physical reality followed in line.

In essence, the extensive visualization training I had done basically replaced the need for any significant physical training. I don't recommend this as a training plan, but it does demonstrate how powerful quality visualization can be. Don't underestimate it. Be sure to give visualization training a valuable place in your training program.

Visualization Skills Are a Huge Benefit Beyond Sports

Visualization skills can be learned by everyone and applied to an amazingly wide range of everyday events. All it takes is a little bit of imagination, or better yet, a fantastic imagination. By using visualization to train your instincts and the four Cs to prepare you to trust your instincts, you will be able to consistently reach your peak performance at anything.

It will work for you if you're a salesperson making that sales pitch. By visualizing yourself at the presentation, you become familiar with the event before it happens. When doing this, you would visualize giving the presentation as perfectly as you would want it to go. See it from the audience's view, as well as from your personal view. You will be able to feel the calmness and take control of the "field" as part of the visualization too, adding to the total sense of being there.

Through studying and practice you have learned your trade and developed your skills. But that isn't always enough to give you the confidence you deserve. That only comes with having had positive experiences. And visualization will give you as many great experiences as you want and need. Then on "competition" day, with a quick preparatory visualization, you will be 100 percent on the line, in the zone.

"GO FAST!"

A couple of minutes prior to exiting on a practice or competition skydive AirMoves would bring our hands in for the "team count". As the team's Captain I would use this opportunity for some last minute tips. "Take your time, go slow, don't rush. See all the targets of each of the moves. Keep it calm." James was such a natural, with such confidence that he knew what he was going to do and how he was going to do it.

But Troy had been successful at everything he'd done by working his butt off. And if I told him to "Keep it calm, don't rush, see all the targets" he was going to try as hard as he could to do just that. If it didn't work he'd try harder, the text book definition of "trying too hard" and "over analyzing". And James could see it.

James climbed out of the plane first as we prepared to exit. Troy followed him. As they both took their position James looked back at Troy and with a big smile on his face yelled, "Just go fast!" It made Troy laugh, smile and relax. As we flew off the plane Troy was calm, confident, trusting his instincts and having a blast, exactly where I wanted him to be. And not because of anything I told him. "GO FAST!" became the team theme. It eliminated the over thinking, put our attitudes where we wanted them and infused us with playful, calm confidence, a winning recipe for sure.

Still living by our code even after his competition days were over Troy formed the company "GO FAST!" He knew if the GO FAST attitude worked in skydiving it would work for any goal that required you to be at the top of your game.

8

The Goal of Personal and Team Best

WE ARE NOT always competing against other people, but we should always be competing against ourselves. Each day, whether in the morning or evening, tired, sick, or wishing we were somewhere else, we should be challenging ourselves to deliver our personal and team's best performance. If we are disciplined enough to demand this from ourselves in practice, we will be ready to deliver our best performance whenever it is required from us in "competition" (whatever our field defines that to be).

That personal and team best, even above winning, should be our primary goal. Few things are more rewarding than training hard all year long for the big "meet," raising our abilities to a level we had only dreamt of, and actually delivering our best performance in competition.

As the clock runs out on a formation skydiving competition jump, we know immediately if we just did our best. We don't yet know the score, but we absolutely know if we just "tore up" that jump. When tracking away (breaking apart) from my team at the end of a great jump like that, I knew we had done our best and I'd dare any other team to try to match it. Sometimes they did. Sometimes they beat us.

If you do your best in competition but are beaten by a better team, you still walk away proud of your performance. You may be disappointed by the outcome; it's always preferable to win. But if you do the best you can, you can't help but be happy with your performance.

There were also a few meets when my team fell short of delivering our best performance. The jumps were okay, nothing terrible, but we didn't track off with a "Beat that!" feeling.

Our performance was average. But we won. We didn't quite do our best, but we were the best.

We were victorious in our battle against the competition, but the victory was less rewarding than it could have been. We came up short in the battle against ourselves, the personal challenge to do our best at the meet.

Looking back on it now, doing our best was more fulfilling than being the best.

But doing either one on its own is no comparison to doing both, especially when the race is tight and the heat is on. For competitors, there is no greater moment than doing your best when you have to, and having your best be the best.

The Skill of Performing Your Best

Though often perceived as a mystical talent that only the most exceptional and gifted people possess, the truth is that our ability to deliver our best performance in competition is a trained skill in and of itself. Remember:

- The mental and emotional process you use to perform at your best level is much the same process, regardless of the activity you're involved in.
- You can practice this process when doing the activity you are most passionate about or when just enjoying something you do more recreationally.

- This process is the same for beginners and experts. Your best is your best at any level, and the skill of performing your best doesn't change as your best changes.
- Trusting your instincts will always lead you to your best performance.
- Your instincts will only lead you to the best performance that you have trained them for and expect from them, a level of performance that you have proven you are capable of and have clearly defined, visualized, and are confident that you can and will deliver.

If you want to be your best when you get to the meet, you need to begin practicing this skill from the beginning of your training and try to use it in everything in which you participate.

The mistake many people make is that they don't learn the skill of performing at their best from the beginning. They wait until their best is at a level they are proud to display (usually just before the big meet) and then "hope" it actually happens. There is no hope in competition. You make it happen or you don't.

To be able to deliver our best when it counts, we need to have three things:

1. Knowledge of exactly what our true best is
2. A clear understanding of what we need to do to deliver that best performance
3. Confidence built on sound evidence that we can and will deliver our best performance anytime we choose to

Defining Your Best

The first step in developing the skill of performing at our best is figuring out what our "true best" really is.

All of us have a certain "safe performance" level. This is the level that we normally aim for, a degree of speed, aggression, and confidence where we are sure we will not make any big mistakes. Although we usually perform competently and consistently here, it is certainly less than our best, and aiming to perform here will restrict us from ever reaching our best.

But while operating from that safe performance level, there are those times when suddenly and seemingly, out of nowhere, we perform better than ever. We are smoother, faster, sharper. Where did it come from? It was almost like magic.

These unexpected magical moments happen maybe 5 to 15 percent of the time and are usually brushed off as having just been luck. But the reality is that these were our true best. There is no magic and there is certainly no luck. We performed at a new level. That was our best, and if we did it once, we can do it every time. We just need to understand what makes those moments happen. With that knowledge, we can structure a training plan specifically designed so that we can learn to create our own magic anytime we want.

Turning Your Best into Your Average

The next step of performing our best is turning this new best that we have just defined into our average.

As a general rule, we spend more time in training trying to fix what's broken rather than in reinforcing what's working. We so despise and fear our weak performances that we devote a great amount of effort to analyzing the many ways there are to do something wrong. This strategy leaves us with a long list of things *not to* do.

Fearfully trying to avoid mistakes is no strategy for learning to confidently repeat our best performance. The answer to tapping into our peak performance lies within our best performances, not our weaker ones. Get to work on repeating your best instead of avoiding your worst. This strategy leaves us with a very short list of things *to do* instead of a long list of things to avoid.

Analyze those best "moves." What were you physically and mentally doing different that time? Where was your attention? Where were you looking? What were you thinking? How was your anticipation? What was your mood? Were you carefree like a child or perhaps a little angry?

We've all had times when we were "just on" one day. *Get this straight. We are never "just on"!* Angels and fairies don't look down from the heavens and sprinkle magic dust on us. If you're "on," it's because you did or thought something that put you on. Or perhaps didn't do or didn't think about something that would put you "off." But take responsibility and credit for it. One way or another, you made it happen, and if you ever want to make it happen again, you better figure out how you did it.

Ask every question you can think of. How did you sleep the night before? What did you have for breakfast? Did you visualize before going to bed? Did you visualize when you woke up? After asking enough questions, you'll find the answers that you need and will be able to create a process that sets you up to perform at your best. It may require a little experimentation, and you may have to try some things and see how they work for you. But over the course of time you will find out what works best for you and your team that prepares you to perform at the top of your game whenever you choose to. Remove the element of luck from the equation. Take full responsibility. Only you can make it happen.

Now that you have recognized, analyzed, and defined exactly what your current true best is, you must commit to that and only that being your performance target.

You know exactly what your best is and what to do to make it happen.

Don't attempt to do any better. Don't accept any less.

Do it every time, one step at a time.

Document Your Best

As soon as you define this new true best, start to collect as much evidence of your best performances as possible. Write it all down. If it is any type of performance activity and something you can video or record, then you should make a copy of all of those magic moments and put them onto a "best of" DVD or CD. This should include any and all moments of excellence. Every outstanding part, no matter how brief, is still outstanding. At first your "best of" footage will probably come in the form of shortcuts of three- to ten-second intervals.

This is the footage you want to watch. Nothing is more powerful than watching yourself perform at your best. Besides providing a source of accurate data for your technical analysis, it instills belief and confidence. This is not a fantasy; the evidence is right in front of you. Your confidence is real and well deserved. You must completely absorb yourself into that 15 percent of your best performance. If you don't make a sound effort to do so, your attention will be distracted by the 85 percent of less than your true best.

When first reviewing any footage of your performance, examine all the original data or footage. Analyze the areas that need improvement and decide how to fix them. From then on, focus only on your true best. Watch yourself doing your best moves and watch it a lot. Before long, you'll forget what the bad moves looked like. You won't be able to even imagine them anymore, and you don't fear what you can't imagine. There is only your best. Believe in it, expect to do it; you deserve to.

By focusing on your best and watching your "best of" footage, you have given yourself the tools you need to build your visualization skills. With these pictures carved in your mind, use your visualization training to get repetition upon repetition until the mental muscle memory is so well built in that you don't even have to think about "how to" do your best moves anymore. You just do it.

If you are disciplined about this process, you will find that in a short time your best that was happening 15 percent of the time is now happening 30 percent of the time. Continue on the plan. You will soon see it 50 percent of the time. Continue on the plan. Soon it will happen 85 percent of the time. You'll realize that you are performing at that level naturally, effortlessly. This is no longer your best, it's your average!

Suddenly, again out of nowhere, you notice that a new best has emerged. Faster, sharper, smoother performances that you are doing the other 15 percent of the time. This is your new true best. Recognize it, define it, analyze it, start a new "best of" DVD, and begin the whole process again.

Making Your Best Better

The process just described, of turning your best into your average, and allowing a new best to emerge on its own, will work if you stick to the plan. You will see steady and consistent improvement.

But for everyone there will be times when you feel like you are not making any progress, like you've hit a plateau and can't get past it. That new best just isn't emerging as expected. It may even seem at times like you are stepping backward.

This is usually when it's time to up the ante. You can't wait any longer for that new best to emerge on its own. It's time to push yourself and reach for new heights that you have never even seen a glimpse of. It's time to go for it with a bit of reckless abandon and see what happens. Keep the pedal to the floor and find out how far you can push it. It's going to be a lot of fun.

At this stage, you will lose a lot of consistency. The quality of your work, and your "scores," will almost certainly go down. The frequency and magnitude of your errors will dramatically increase. It will be important to maintain your sense of humor because you're going to need to be able to laugh about it.

But, you will absolutely discover a new best. In the midst of this madness, there will again be spectacular moments. They may not happen 15 percent of the time. But they will happen. Recognize them, define them, analyze them, and establish them as your official new "best." Start a new "best of" DVD and begin again the process of turning this new best into your average.

This stage of your training serves another purpose. It provides the opportunity for you to completely disregard scores and results. Not only that, but you have been ordered to make mistakes, lots of mistakes, big mistakes. If you are not making mistakes, then you are not applying yourself to the task at hand. During this stage, it is your job to just go for it, have fun, and see what happens.

The chance to truly experience this carefree attitude is invaluable. Having actually trained this attitude, you will be able to tap into it when you experience performance anxiety. Fears of results are self-imposed. Only you can replace those fears with more playful thoughts of having fun and going for it. You will be more successful at replacing those fears with positive thoughts if you have actually trained the positive thoughts. This stage of the training is the opportunity to do just that.

Performing Your Best or Pushing Your Best—Not Both

You must be very clear during each part of your training: Are you working on the skill of performing at your best and turning your best into your average, *or* are you pushing your best to new heights? You cannot do both at the same time.

As individuals working to excel at anything, we are never satisfied. Our best is never good enough, and we can always see room for improvement. As soon as our best even minimally begins to evolve into our average, we immediately want to push further. Pushing too soon can have negative consequences.

The process of performing at your best involves the following:

- Aiming for a best-performance level that you have clearly defined, previously performed at, and are familiar with

- Trusting your instincts to take you to this predetermined best
- Building consistency because you know what your target looks like and how to reach it
- Building confidence in delivering your best performance because the process for accomplishing that goal has proven itself again and again in training

The process of pushing our best involves the following:

- Aiming for a performance level that you have not clearly defined or previously performed at and which you are certainly not familiar with
- Not trusting your instincts to take you there because you have trained your instincts to take you to, not past, your best
- Building inconsistency because you don't know what exactly your target looks like or how to reach it
- A risk to your confidence because pushing to new heights is fraught with an increase in the number and magnitude of mistakes

These processes are polar opposites. Decide every day whether you are aiming to perform at your best or trying to push your best to new heights. *Don't allow yourself to make the mistake of doing one when you are actually intending to do the other.*

If you're not very clear and disciplined as to which of these goals you are training, you may inadvertently reach for new heights in your performance when the plan was actually to perform at your established best. Your results will be inconsistent and riddled with errors.

Since you were under the impression that you were practicing the skill of performing at your best, you would attach these frequent errors to your best-performance process and lose confidence in that process. You don't give yourself the opportunity to build the confidence in your processes that you deserve and that you will need when *you* arrive at the competition.

If you recognize that you were actually pushing it when that wasn't your intent, you will understand the reason for the inconsistencies and errors. Become more disciplined about executing the plan. Your confidence in the system of performing at your best will become even stronger.

For best results, finish turning your best into your average before trying to make your best better. You must become so consistent that your best happens naturally. At that point you'll have built a strong foundation and are in the optimum position to launch from it and reach for a higher target.

In competition, your goal is to perform at your best. Is it crucial that you've spent a significant amount of time training the skill of performing at your best so that you are confident you can deliver that targeted performance when you need to.

Don't Fear Losing

In no way am I suggesting that we shouldn't be playing to win, fighting to win, and striving for perfection in everything we do. But as I see it, the realistic definition of perfection is doing the very best we are capable of doing. Since we are human, that may at times be short of absolute perfection.

It is not uncommon that the *fear of losing* has an even greater impact on one's performance than the *desire to win* does. Losing must be an absolutely terrible experience for us to fear it so.

My teams have trained hard and put all we had toward striving for victory and nothing short of it. But there were times we came up short. Losing was gut-wrenching. Instead of praise and admiration from our friends and colleagues, we received their sympathies: "Too bad," "You guys were great, really," "Ahh, you were so close." No matter how heartfelt and well intended they may have been, few things feel worse to a competitor than friends trying to provide comfort and sympathy to you after a defeat. I responded politely, but I didn't want to hear it.

I dreaded waking up the next morning, looking in the mirror and seeing the loser I had become. I held my head and covered my eyes. I slowly peeked out, expecting to see a smaller, weaker, slower, dumber, failed version of myself. Nope, there I was again, same as always. Maybe losing wasn't as demoralizing of an experience as I was expecting it to be.

No, losing stunk. My teammates and I had spent every cent we had and then borrowed more. We had lived in our vans in the desert and ate nothing but peanut butter and jelly. We had put 100 percent of ourselves into our training and improved tremendously. We had earned it. We thought that we deserved to win. We were good, damn good. We were sure we were the best. But we didn't do our best, and we lost.

The experience of losing was an essential part of the journey, one through which we learned lessons of vital importance.

A week after the meet, we debriefed every step of both our training and competition strategies. We learned a great deal and had a completely new understanding of what we needed to do differently in order to be better. With this information, we came up with an improved training plan that reenergized us.

In our defeat there was one lesson that was far, far more important than any others. *We learned to not fear losing.* We realized that our fear of losing, and becoming losers, had played a major role in preventing us from performing our best in competition. Those fears challenged our confidence and made us worry about how others would perceive us if we lost. This led us to question our training and kept us from relaxing and trusting our instincts to lead us as we had trained them to.

The fear of losing and becoming losers may very well have been the single biggest factor that kept us from winning.

The loss of the meet was the proof we needed that there was nothing to fear. Victory alone hadn't made us winners, and defeat did not define us as losers. Our true friends didn't feel any differently about us whether we won or lost. The people who loved us didn't love us any more or less one way or the other.

The truth is that we were unquestionably stronger, tougher, and better competitors when we returned to competition after the loss. The lesson we learned prepared us to enter competition fearlessly, without any caution. We arrived with nothing to lose and everything to gain. This approach gave us the confidence to always push for our best performance and to never settle for less.

We couldn't completely control whether we won or lost, so we didn't sweat it. What we did have complete control over was choosing to be fearless, choosing and demanding our personal best from ourselves, and expecting it from each other. Choosing to play to win.

It was an incredibly valuable lesson in "winning," and one that could only be learned by experiencing defeat.

9
Competitive Magic

IT IS ALL working for you. You know what your best is, and you are certain that you will deliver it. You and your team are confident in your abilities, but don't fear making mistakes. You keep your activity of choice in perspective and enjoy it for the fun and love of the game and the personal challenge it presents. You have learned to appreciate your teammates and yourself for who you are, not just for what you can do, and your respect for each other is strong enough to withstand any meet results. But you arrive at the competition and your heart is pounding, your brow sweating, and your fingers buzzing. You're still terrified!

Or are you? The physiological sensations we interpret as fear are also signs of an intensified state of readiness. *This high arousal increases our potential for strength, speed, and mental sharpness.* If properly utilized, becoming excited and tense in competition can be a very powerful tool and a great benefit to you. Don't be afraid of it.

It is natural when in "competition" to experience a higher state of arousal than normal. Heart pounding and fingers tingling are symptoms of being alert, energized, and ready for action. Don't interpret this as fear. It is only a game. There is nothing to be scared of. Don't allow yourself to go down that path.

It is not how you feel, but how you respond to these feelings, that will decide if you stay and fight or run in flight. And you can choose how you want to respond.

When you experience the physical symptoms of a high arousal level, stop, sit back, and take a few deep breaths. Confirm your goal and remind yourself of your training. Your goal is to do your best. You know exactly what your best is. You know how to deliver it and deserve to be confident that you will deliver it.

You've trained smart and proven it again and again in your training. You are not going to try to do any better than your best, and you will not accept any worse. Calm your mind down and allow your instincts to take over. It has worked in training, and it will work now.

These are confidence-building thoughts. Your goal is clear and you know you can achieve it. When you confirm your goals and think logically, the fear fades away and the sensations you are feeling tell you that your senses are on high alert and that you are ready. The sensations you once interpreted as fear are now the source of competitive magic.

Trusting our instincts to lead us to our best performance, in combination with this heightened arousal level, sets the stage for those moments when we do the unbelievable and actually perform beyond our best.

We don't usually "peak" at meets and reach a level of performance we have never achieved before by "trying" to do better. More often, we accomplish these amazing feats when our goal is clear, we have proven in training we can deliver it, and the circumstances of the moment demand that we deliver it.

It is a miniature version of what enables true heroes to perform miraculous tasks. What lifeguard, soldier, fireman, or policeman has ever saved a life without being terrified? What parent has rescued her child without her arousal level going through the roof? Their fears are far more intense than our competitive anxieties will ever be, and they performed far greater feats than we hope will ever be asked of us. If, when faced with fear or experiencing a high arousal level, they can perform these tasks, surely the rest of us are capable of performing at our best or better in an activity we've trained in.

Examples of Competitive Magic in Action

The 1995 World Skydiving Championships

At the 1995 world championships, the meet was very close between Arizona Airspeed and the French. We exited the aircraft on the fifth round with the first formation of the sequence intact. The "key person" signaled to break (release) the grips of the first formation, but not all of the team saw the break. There was total confusion as some of the team transitioned to the second formation while others were still building the first one. We were scrambling, complete chaos. Our first reaction was one of anger and panic, and our arousal level went off the charts.

Suddenly we froze. We took a breath, calmed down, and got control of our emotions. Without speaking a word, the decision was made to build the second formation. Our focus was intense and targeted only on the next point. We broke that formation and continued with the sequence faster than we had ever gone before.

We didn't "try" to go faster. Our anger had significantly raised our arousal to a level we had never experienced. But when we stopped and took a moment to calm down, we were able to control ourselves at this level of arousal. Our instincts took over, and we came back on fire. We recovered, accelerated, and maintained the fastest speed we'd ever achieved all the way to the finish line.

Had we allowed our fears and panic to get the better of us, we would have lost the jump and probably the meet. Instead, we did what was very possibly the fastest 4-way jump that had ever been done by any team up to that time.

We were flying so fast that the meet organizers thought we must have been using a performance-enhancing substance. It was really quite a compliment. They couldn't imagine that we were able to do this without some kind of extra chemical stimulation. (Oddly enough, and maybe because of this jump, in the following year, at the 1996 World Games, they began random drug testing to ensure the athletes were clean.)

We landed from the jump and didn't even know what to make of it ourselves. I remember asking my teammates, "What the hell was that? We've never gone that fast before." Later that day we had a long conversation trying to figure out what exactly happened that had brought about this level of performance. We determined that it was a combination of conditions and circumstances, most of which we had trained for.

1. We were a very well-trained team. We knew what our best was and what we had to do to perform at that level.
2. We had practiced pushing our best to new heights, and though that wasn't the plan for this jump, when the circumstances suddenly changed and demanded more from us, we weren't uncomfortable with the idea of going for it.
3. When our arousal level went through the roof, we knew to take a moment, calm down, and get it under control.
4. There was one thing which, after thinking it through, took us by surprise. We realized at that moment there was zero performance anxiety. We had just made a huge mistake that cost us 20 percent of our working time. We were pissed off, and since we had already screwed up, we weren't worried about it anymore. We had no concern for the final outcome, but we had total and complete concern for the immediate task at hand. Obviously this had freed us of something that had been holding us back, because we proceeded to outdo the best skydive we had ever done.

No matter how much we had discussed eliminating any performance anxiety in our training, it still was the one thing left that had held us back from performing at the very top of our potential. Without that fear, we were able to take our best to an entirely new level.

We went on to win the meet but didn't have another jump that was quite as good as that one was.

1997 World Skydiving Championships

At the 1997 world championships we had a similar experience. After seven rounds, we were in first place with a 6-point lead over France.

The eighth round was off to a good start, and we were several points into it. The key person broke the formation, but like in '95, everyone on the team didn't see the break. This time the result was far worse. The confusion that followed cost us 6 points. In one jump we had given away our entire lead. We went into the final round with only a 1-point lead, not nearly enough to be comfortable with.

One jump. The entire meet had come down to one jump. We were confident that we were the better team, but as we had just proven, anything can happen in one jump.

Fortunately, we had the experience from 1995 to reflect on.

Having won the 1994, 1995, and 1996 U.S. nationals as well as the world cup, World Games, and world championship, we were able to keep the "victory" itself in perspective. We were doing better handling the performance anxiety that I could have sworn we had trained not to have at all.

We were *always* playing to win. But we also knew that this victory alone did not define our value as human beings and competitors. The love and respect we had for each other and our team would not be changed by the results of this one meet. We weren't scared of losing.

That being said, *playing to win means hating to lose, refusing to lose.* The circumstances demanded we deliver our absolute best performance, and that was precisely what we were going to do.

When we lined up in the door to exit the plane on the final round, our determination was unquestionable, and previously unmatched. I knew that this was the feeling I had spent my entire life trying and wanting to experience. Finally, as I was waiting for "my cue," for the pilot to give the exit command, I felt a level of absolute fearless confidence I had never experienced before. I didn't care whether we won or lost. But I knew without a doubt that we were about to do a skydive that no team on earth was going to be able to come close to matching. I was so excited I couldn't wait to get out of the plane.

We paused prior to giving the exit count. Looking into each other's eyes, it was obvious that there was no fear, and no doubt. It was pure determination, pure certainty; we knew exactly what we were about to do and we had trained to do it.

It was easy to let go of any concern for the final results and focus only on the task at hand because this one jump would alone determine the outcome.

We knew our arousal level was too high and took one more deep breath to calm ourselves down so that our instincts could take over. We were *calm*. Our eyes were locked together, clearly *communicating* our feelings and intentions. We exited the plane and instantly established total *control*. We had chosen to be *confident* before even boarding the plane. That instinctive confidence took over, and we had one of the best jumps of our lives. We beat the French team by 3 points in one jump. The meet was over.

10
You Win the Competition Before It Starts

WE LANDED ON that final round of the 1997 world meet with an incredible feeling of success. But the feeling of satisfaction we felt after succeeding paled in comparison to the feeling of confident anticipation we felt prior to exiting the plane for that jump. Eagerly anticipating the coming challenge was far more powerful a feeling than looking back on it.

Prior to boarding the plane, we had already decided our future. It was our jump, and we would choose what to do with it. We knew exactly what our best was, and we had no doubt that we were going to do it. We had trained and prepared for this moment, and we were unquestionably determined to see it through.

From the time we boarded the plane until we were standing on the ramp ready to exit, our confidence and determination only became stronger. We didn't know if we would win, and we really didn't care. It didn't matter. We knew that we had to deliver our best. Standing in the door of the plane with this pure confidence and purpose was one of the most incredible experiences of my life. My heart was racing, but I was fearless.

I had never felt more like a winner than I did at that moment. And we hadn't won yet! The experience of the actual "victory" was nothing in comparison to feeling this absolute certainty during the moments leading up to it. That was truly "feeling the force."

This perspective, attitude, belief, and determination are the qualities that define what it means to be a winner. These are qualities you bring to the game. They aren't a result determined by the final outcome of the game.

It proved to me one more time that it wasn't about winning after all. It was about playing to win.

About the Author

DAN BRODSKY-CHENFELD HAS been a national skydiving competitor since 1983. Dan's extraordinary talent for bringing out the best in others has made him one of the most influential people in the history of skydiving and one of the most sought-after coaches in the world. Among his most recent successes is coaching the U.S. women's 4-way team Synchronicity (2004 and 2005) and the U.K. women's teams Airkix (2006) and Storm (2008) to victory at the world championships. As a competitor Dan has lead teams to multiple National Championship Gold Medal victories and World Championships. He lives in Temecula, California, with his wife and children. He runs Skydive Perris, one of the largest skydiving centers in the world, with his partners Pat and Melanie Conatser. Please visit his website at www.aboveallelsethebook.com.